Perspectives on Sport and Exercise Psychology, Vol. 1
Essential Processes for Attaining Peak Performance

D1716823

Perspectives on Sport and Exercise Psychology, Vol. 1

DIETER HACKFORT & GERSHON TENENBAUM (EDS.)

ESSENTIAL PROCESSES FOR ATTAINING PEAK PERFORMANCE

Editors of the Series
Perspectives on Sport and Exercise Psychology:
Dieter Hackfort & Gershon Tenenbaum

British Library Cataloguing in Publication Data
A catalogue record for this book is available from the British Library

Dieter Hackfort / Gershon Tenenbaum (Eds.)
Essential Processes for Attaining Peak Performance
Oxford: Meyer & Meyer Sport (UK) Ltd., 2006
ISBN 10: 1-84126-187-4
ISBN 13: 978-1-84126-187-4

© 2006 by Meyer & Meyer Sport (UK) Ltd.
Aachen, Adelaide, Auckland, Budapest, Graz, Johannesburg,
New York, Olten (CH), Oxford, Singapore, Toronto
Member of the World
Sports Publishers' Association (WSPA)
www.w-s-p-a.org
Printed and bound by: FINIDR, s. r. o., Český Těšín
ISBN 10: 1-84126-187-4
ISBN 13: 978-1-84126-187-4
E-Mail: verlag@m-m-sports.com
www.m-m-sports.com

CONTENTS

FOREWORD

The new series *Perspectives on Sport and Exercise Psychology* has been established to provide a sequence of books organized by renowned colleagues who are (a) leaders in a particular area of expertise and (b) invite researchers to contribute to an issue of fundamental relevance to the field. The first issue addresses a topic of fundamental relevance to the field of sport and exercise psychology: expert athletic performance. The contributions in this volume reflect state of the art and controversial discussions on the topic of athletic expertise. Chapters in this first volume utilize more space than is possible in scientific journals. Additionally, the composition of the volume is designed to expose the reader to different perspectives and to allow the reader to consider a variety of sub-domains within the topic of sport expertise. Thus, this volume contributes updated knowledge, a more holistic perspective on this body of knowledge, and a more comprehensive understanding of the topic of athletic expertise than is possible via journals or monographs authored by a single author. In this way the books in this *Series* complement other publication modes. Ultimately, the *Series* is a forum for researchers to discuss an issue of mutual interest, to exchange insights, and to acquire an updated overview of a body of knowledge on a significant topic in Sport and Exercise Psychology.

The first volume refers to a neo-traditional, fundamental, and significant issue in Sport Psychology: the essential processes for attaining peak performance. Recent progress in Developmental Psychology, Social Psychology, and Biological Psychology, as well as contributions from areas such as expertise, rationality and creativity, and perfectionism are also addressed in this initial volume. Leading experts in the field were asked to provide manuscripts based on their theoretical approach and the results of their research.

In the first volume of the *Series*, two chapters argue that it is necessary for sport psychology to develop (a) a comprehensive understanding which stems from a holistic perspective of athletic expertise, and (b) an integrated framework regarding athletic expertise. In chapter one Dieter Hackfort outlines an action theory perspective that focuses on an analysis of the action-situation of top athletes, and provides an empirical example based on this approach. The message from these empirical results is that a more differentiated view addressing the coordination and integration of one's career in sports and in academic or vocational life must consist of an appropriate definition of the action-situation. Later, in chapter eight, Michael Bar-Eli and colleagues provide an example of this by analyzing the famous Fosbury Flop. In their study various, and sometimes contradictory principles, are integrated in order for an optimal athletic outcome to emerge. Their conclusion is, in a sense, a paradoxical one: it is necessary and possible to integrate the principles of optimization and creativity, i.e., "creative optimization" and "optimized creativity."

Chapter two addresses the perpetual debate on the influences of nature and nurture with respect to expertise in athletics. The nature/nurture debate (chapter two) and the views on expertise (chapters four and five) are discussed in depth. In chapter two Michael Johnson and Gershon Tenenbaum argue that (a) the roles of nature and nurture in meeting or failing to achieve expertise in sport are multifaceted and multidimensional, and (b) a multidisciplinary approach is needed for an appropriate understanding of the roles of each factor as they relate to the development of expert sport performance. They demonstrate a straightforward approach of understanding expertise and clearly work through various rationales supporting a revision to the concept of "deliberate practice," when generalized to athletics. In spite of these criticisms, they also emphasize various useful and important aspects in the concept of deliberate practice that may be useful in capturing how expert athletes develop. Their arguments are related to the sport- (action-) specific differences, task-specific differences, and the complex interplay of action regulation systems, as explained by action theory (see chapter one). Of particular salience may be the interaction among cognitive processes, affective processes, and volitional motor behavior. Johnson and Tenenbaum point out the role of these and other potential factors that may lead to alterations to the theory of deliberate practice as it pertains to the sports domain.

In chapter three David Sacks, David Pargman and Gershon Tenenbaum delve into one aspect found in the previous chapter (two). They discuss a special aspect of the nature/nurture controversy by addressing it from a family systems perspective. This approach emphasizes focusing on the family system, rather than the individuals comprising it, as the system is the primary unit of interest for the study of expertise in sport. Based on this approach, systemic differences between an "Athletic Family" and "A Family with an Athlete" are described.

The issue of expertise is taken up again in chapter four. In this chapter Natalie Durand-Bush, Kim Thompson and John Salmela look specifically at coaching behavior. These authors introduce and discuss a coaching model that highlights the following factors: training, competition, organization, coaches' and athletes' personality tendencies, and context. This model can be easily linked with the concept of "action-situation" addressed in chapter one. Personal factors (e.g., coach's and athlete's affective and cognitive tendencies), the environment (e.g., context), and the task (e.g., training, competition, and organization) described by the action-situation discussion; all play vital roles as they appear to be antecedents for a specific group of actions (e.g., coaching behavior). Further elaboration on the relationship between the concepts of athletic expertise and deliberate practice, and the possible areas to investigate in order to overcome the shortcomings proposed in chapter two, may be useful in the area of sport psychology. This may be particularly important when developing coaching education programs. Coaching education programs must include information about training and competences based on exercise science, along with instructional and psycho-social competences, as well as skills for self-regulation and stress management in order to assist coaches in developing successful athletes. These topics are also emphasized in subsequent chapters (six and seven) of this volume.

The following chapter five by Joseph Baker and Jean Côté extends the issue of athletic expertise. These authors address the acquisition of expertise from a human development perspective by highlighting specific phases, and by exploring the relationship between deliberate practice, deliberate play, and other sport experiences. They argue against early specialization in sport as a method of developing peak performance. Their arguments are based on athletes' (a) perceptions of cost (e.g., drop out) - benefit (e.g., high performance) analyses, and (b) considerations of short term (e.g., enjoyment) and long term (e.g., motivation and willpower; chapter seven of this volume) effects. The debate about early specialization versus broader earlier experiences in sports as a foundation for the development of peak performance has a long tradition in sports and sport science. Recently, empirical evidence strongly supports the advantages of later specialization (see Guellich, Emrich & Prohl, 2004). This issue is closely connected with the debate on quality versus quantity as it relates to exercise and training (see chapter two). Some authors argue that quantity is less important than quality. This view must be challenged critically in the absence of task characteristics and practice objectives. When quality is viewed as a "relevant effort," it requires more specification (e.g., with regard to motivation, enjoyment, and cognition) as to the meaning of "relevance." For example, endurance training involves different elements than skill training or technique. Statements such as "relevant effort" must be differentiated in terms of the categories addressed by action theory; especially with respect to the task, e.g., skill acquisition and motor learning or endurance training.

Rod Dishman, in chapter six, and Anne-Marie Elbe and Jurgen Beckmann, in chapter seven, review a number of factors essential for, and closely connected with, elite sport achievement. Dishman refers to stress and provides an updated insight into the stress-exercise relationship. The influence of exercise on an individual's stress response and stress resistance is especially important, and hence thoroughly reported. As elite athletes frequently face numerous sources of stress, this is a relevant issue to this volume. Interestingly, exercise may improve one's ability to cope with stressful events, and it may improve idiosyncratic affective and cognitive methods of managing stressful situations like those often experienced in important competitions. The next chapter discusses the development of motivation and self-regulation. Elbe and Beckmann's illustrate their findings in this area relying on their own research conducted in the German elite schools of sports. Their chapter has much in common with the first chapter as the authors refer to the action theory concept of action control, and emphasize the significance of volition for attaining peak performance. Chapter seven, as well as chapter five, provides a common insight: for positive personality development, athletes need opportunities for social interactions. Sufficient leisure time is necessary to meet these goals.

The ninth and final chapter addresses the topic of perfectionism. Howard Hall introduces the concept of perfectionism and the empirical findings associated with its functional meaning. He discusses the role of perfectionism in sport by comparing two extreme views: perfectionism as a facilitative factor of world class performers at one end of the spectrum, and as a psychological impediment for athletic development at the other. It is possible that many coaches, as well as athletes, perceive perfectionism as a positive attribute. Empirical evidence reviewed in this chapter provides a compelling rationale to cast into doubt the idea that perfectionism optimally facilitates athletes' cognitions, affect, and behaviors as they relate to attaining expert athletic performance.

We hope that after reading the contributions in this book, not only will the authors be motivated to initiate further discussions on the topics found herein (e.g., deliberate practice, the development of expertise, perfectionism, and the optimal method to organize the developmental stages toward a career in elite sports), but also be motivated to refer to and utilize the various concepts and models provided here when considering their own approaches. Additionally, it is hoped that readers will add to the topics introduced in this text by contributing their own ideas and studies to further the scientific and applied understanding of expert athletic performance. Finally, we thank the authors and readers for their interest and participation in this project. We hope to enlarge and enrich our knowledge base and understanding of the essential processes for attaining peak performance in sport.

Dieter Hackfort
ASPIRE, Doha, Qatar

Gershon Tenenbaum
FSU, Tallahassee, USA

REFERENCE

Guellich, A., Emrich, E. & Prohl, R. (2004). Zeit verlieren um (Zeit) zu gewinnen "...auch im Leistungssport? - Empirische Explorationen in der Nachwuchsfoerderung" (To lose time in order to gain [time] "...also in high performance sport? - Empirical explorations in talent development"). In R. Prohl & H. Lange (Eds.), *Paedagogik des Leistungssports (Paedagogy of high performance sports)*, pp. 157-179. Schorndorf: Hofmann.

A Conceptual Framework and Fundamental Issues for Investigating The Development of Peak Performance in Sports

Dieter Hackfort

Contents

Summary

During the past decades numerous contributions from various disciplines have enlarged and improved the understanding of the processes required for attaining peak performance in sports. However, there continues (a) to be a need to recognize that an integrative approach is lacking (e.g., we miss a comprehensive conceptual framework), (b) a controversy regarding some fundamental issues, such as the concept of talent and its role in the developmental process, and (c) that some processes and interrelations that require further research are still neglected or even unnoticed, e.g., the stress induced by the interaction of simultaneous sports and academic or vocational training. These issues are discussed in this chapter.

The fundamental conceptual features regarding the action-theory approach are briefly outlined. Special emphasis is given to the concept of the action situation. This concept refers to three specific factors, i.e., the person, the environment, and the task. Investigations addressing the interrelationship among these factors strengthen future discussion and studies. Some currently neglected areas that may provide enormous insight into the precursors of and elements necessary for expert athletic performance include the person-environment interaction, and the roles of nature and nurture. Both of these topics are outlined from an action-theory perspective in order to clarify how an improved understanding of these factors enhances the understanding of sport expertise. Finally, this chapter uses a study that examined the relationship between the strain induced by simultaneously striving for peak athletic performance and being involved in academic pursuits or a vocational career. This research illustrates a more differentiated understanding of the action situation as it relates to athletes striving for peak performance.

The purpose of this chapter is to offer a conceptual framework designed to integrate a perspective on the processes essential for attaining peak performance in sports, and to demonstrate its theoretical usefulness as well as the need for additional empirical research on the factors essential for the development of elite athletes.

INTRODUCTION

For some time, athletes, coaches, and sport scientists believed that physical preconditions, physiological states, and the motor skills were the exclusive fundamentals required for peak performance in sports. They also believed that mental abilities (e.g., attention/attention control and concentration) as well as various psychological factors such as emotions, anxiety, stress resistance, staleness, motivation, will-power, self-confidence and self-efficacy, were necessary for attaining excellence. Because peak performance in competitive sports requires high levels of motor and mental abilities, brain and brawn must function jointly with optimal tuning in a particular situation and time. Overcoming the doubts worries, and fears of failure is an additional battle. For many athletes the most critical challenge is to learn the meaning of WIN (What is Important Now). Social science research into elite sports and peak performance provides evidence that in addition to biological factors, psychological and social factors are critical to the development and realization of high performance in various domains (see the contributions in this volume).

Recently emphases on social support, career planning, developmental trends, and management have been emphasized (see Hackfort, Duda & Lidor, in press). This is additional evidence that not only personal factors, but also environmental, and especially socio-ecological, factors are significant in understanding the pursuit of excellent athletic performance. What can be observed in sport science research in general, and in sport psychology in particular, are two differing orientations. In the first there is a tendency toward analysing detailed units, while the second reflects an inclination toward investigating a broader scope of elements, larger units, links, and interrelations that involve possible interactions among complex systems. Human beings are considered biopsychosocial units or systems; a term that indicates a multidisciplinary perspective. This perspective necessitates the use of an integrated framework and interdisciplinary research approaches. Secondly, psychological processes have functional meaning (the term "bio-psycho-social" reflects that there is a functional meaning of mediation and the mediating role of psychological processes in sport). Furthermore, biological, psychological, and social processes are interrelated. Therefore, there exists a need for a theoretical concept that bridges the gap between disciplinary approaches, e.g., the psycho-physiological and psycho-social functioning. Such a theoretical framework must consider a holistic perspective while also considering unique phenomena and basic processes. Holistic and elementarily oriented approaches need to converge, in order to be integrated. Biopsychology, psycho-physiology, psycho-somatic medicine, psycho-social, and psycho-ecological approaches are examples that link separate approaches. Future advancements in science, particularly in sport science and sport psychology, require the fostering of specializations without separation. Additionally, there is a need to consider the complexity of a system without neglecting its elements and fundamental processes (i.e., the "Gestalt"). One cannot understand a system without first understanding the elements and the underlying processes of that system. In turn, it is impossible to understand the functional meaning of single elements and processes without considering the links, interrelations, and the complex interplay within that system. Thus, in order to capture the essence of peak performance, it is assumed that both the system and its essential elements, the structure and the processes, the organization and the regulation (control) must be considered simultaneously.

In the past three decades in Germany, many psychologists and sport psychologists have worked toward a unified theoretical framework that integrates (a) the psychology of consciousness and (b) the psychology of stimulus-response in order to overcome the shortcomings inherent when separating central domains (i.e., a reductionist philosophy) of psychology, theoretical conceptualizations, and methodological approaches. Nowadays "Action Theory" (Handlungstheorie) is regarded as the most prominent concept in German sport psychology. The fundamental aspect of action theory is the "action" (Handlung), which involves behavioral, cognitive, and affective processes. "Acting" (Handeln) is a special class of human behaviour. It is defined as intentionally organized and purposive behavior in a special situation (Nitsch & Hackfort, 1984). In the following sections, the concept of the action situation is briefly introduced, and then additional fundamental action theory concepts are established in providing a framework for the investigation into, and the interpretation of research on, attaining peak performance in sports that emphasize psycho-social and psycho-pedagogical issues.

BASIC CONCEPTS FOR AN ACTION THEORY APPROACH TO INVESTIGATING THE ATTAINMENT OF PEAK PERFORMANCE

Human action is based on the dynamic interplay between a person and his or her environment with regard to a specific task. The basic relationship is person-environment as elaborated on by Kurt Lewin (1936). This relationship is fundamental for life in general, and for the behaviors of all living organisms. On a higher evolutionary level (especially with regard to the cognitive organization and cognitive processes), the person-environment relationship and interaction is organized and regulated to produce an intended outcome. Such intentions arise in the subject as soon as: (a) the existing interaction is no longer perceived as sufficient to meet the needs or goals of the subject, (b) a more rewarding relationship is subjectively perceived or anticipated elsewhere, or (c) a pleasant state is perceived to cease. Such subjective perceptions and evaluations are fundamental cognitive processes characteristic of human beings.

The cognitive processes underlying the creation of idiosyncratic intentions are essential for constructing an understanding of the person-environment relationship. These intentions constitute the definition of a task. Thus, a task is regarded as a concept specifying the interpretation of the person-environment relationship with respect to actions, which must be organized to stabilize or modify the person-environment relation. Actions are a special class of behavior defined as intentional, goal directed, organized and purposive (Nitsch & Hackfort, 1981, 1984) in situations. These situations are conceptualized as interpretations or definitions by the person (see Blumer, 1938; Mead, 1934) of his or her person-task-environment constellation (Hackfort, 1986). The action situation model is presented in Figure 1.

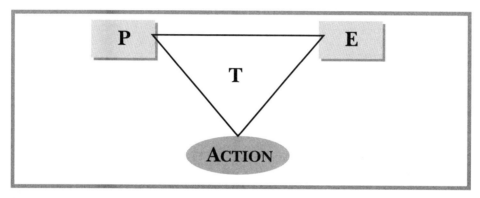

Figure 1 PET (Person, Environment, Task) - The action situation model.

The general intention underlying every action is to optimize the person-environment relationship (Nitsch, 2000), or one's situation, in order to maintain a favorable condition. This is done to improve one's level of adaptation or create a better person-environment fit. The criteria for "better" can be an emotional factor (e.g., more pleasant, comfortable), instrumental (less costly, or more beneficial), or an intellectual factor (e.g., a better understanding). With respect to the different systems (see Hackfort & Munzert, in press) such a fit may refer to one or numerous systems (see also Nitsch, 2000) as illustrated in Figure 2.

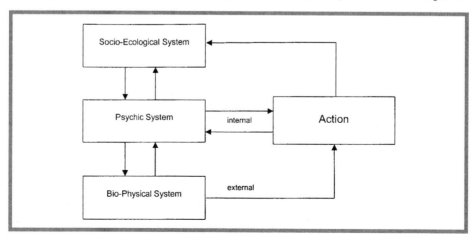

Figure 2 Systems related to actions.

As seen in Figure 2, actions have external and internal characteristics. The external characteristic is operationalized by movements and represents the behavioral part of an action. Essential for actions are psychic processes (an internal characteristic), which consist of cognitive and affective processes. With respect to these components and their functional meaning, an action-control system and a behavioral-control system are established (see Hackfort, Munzert, & Seiler, 2000). A model representing this concept is presented in Figure 3.

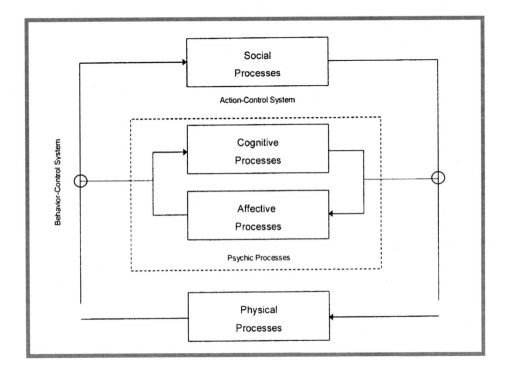

Figure 3 The action-control system.

To account for the attainment of peak performance, it is essential to refer to the processes regulated by the action-control system. Specifically, the interaction between physical and social processes is mediated by mental (psychic) processes. This concept is discussed in the nature-nurture debate (see Oerter & Montada, 2002). The interaction between these mental processes, i.e., cognitive and affective processes, is an essential component of the debate on appropriate practice design.

To further this discussion, I refer first to the analysis of the action situation, that is, the person-task-environment constellation. The specific task focused here is the attainment of peak performance. Additionally, this task is embedded in the development of an individual's sports career. Personal factors, environmental factors, and the interactions of these factors are considered with a special emphasis on these tasks (see Figure 4).

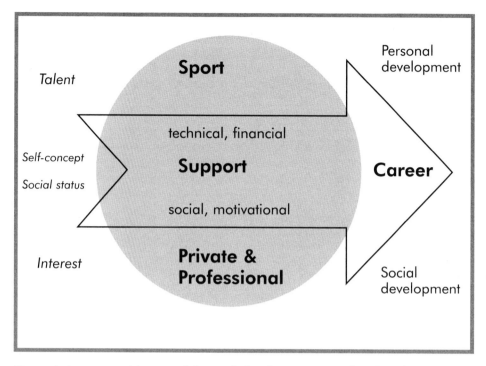

Figure 4 A conceptual framework for analyzing the attainment of peak performance.

This is an established framework for empirical investigations in elite sports (e.g., Hackfort & Birkner, 2004). Selected results from previous research will now be provided and some topics discussed in other contributions in this book will also be highlighted.

APPLICATION OF ACTION-THEORY CONCEPTS TO ESSENTIAL PROCESSES FOR THE ATTAINMENT OF PEAK PERFORMANCE

PERSON-ENVIRONMENT, NATURE-NURTURE

The biological and social scientists join in the nature-nurture discussion with a conceptualization that the brain is a remarkably elastic entity that allows for enormously flexible mental processes. This is the basis for information processing and mental development. Additionally, these processes define one's ease of or difficulty in making changes. Thus, nature is also not fixed or inflexible. The neurological network and its development are strongly dependent on exercise and training (Hollmann, 1998; Hollmann & Fischer, 1994), a movement-perception-emotion dynamism, that is on acting.

The development of talent requires, as do developmental processes in general (see Hackfort, 2003), that "development" be considered a dynamic concept and that "talent" also be considered dynamic. Not only does the environment influence the person and the unfolding of his or her personal characteristics, but the person also influences the environment and the organization of that environment, e.g., ecological conditions by actions. Furthermore, feedback processes must be considered in the dynamic interplay of person and environment. From an action theory perspective, the developmental process and progress (in terms of ontogenesis as well as phylogenesis) dictates the degree to which he or she is able to organize and control his or her actions and the action situations[1]. Due to the meaning of these dynamical interactive processes in development, various forms of social support become important.

For an advanced discussion on the impact of nature and nurture on talent development, one must pay attention to (a) the updated knowledge about basic functional relationships, and (b) the empirical findings with regard to the concept of talent. It is important to consider that in current developmental psychology population-based genetic statistical studies need careful interpretation. The variance of a group does not represent a variance of a single person's characteristics. Rost (2002) argues that heritage is a concept based on population-oriented statistics in empirical research, which refers to population-based variance. A single measurement, however, lacks variance. Furthermore, genes do not directly cause anything. The activity of these molecules influences the synthesis of proteins in a cell.

Hence, the complex interplay of effects, feedback processes, and direct and indirect influences on and within the system must be considered. Within the framework of such a systemic approach, environmental factors affect the biological metabolism, and via these processes there is an effect on the genetical processes which, in turn, influence the developmental process. In his important contribution on "Heredity, environment, and the question of 'how,'" Anastasi (1958) emphasized the necessity of functional analyses. A conceptual framework that overcomes the difficulty of linking processes in different subsystems is needed to bridge the gap between physiological, biological, and psychological conceptualizations. One must also consider the meta-theoretical challenge of different categories (see Ryle, 1949) used when elaborating on theoretical concepts from different disciplinary perspectives or theoretical standpoints (e.g., the use of "mind", "mental", "psyche" on the one hand and "body", "physical" on the other).

At present, the concept of talent is regarded very critically in psychology, and attracts less attention in empirical psychological research than in pedagogy or pedagogical psychology (Rost, 2002). The concept of talent is closely associated with research on intelligence. The hierarchical models of intelligence are mostly accepted in empirically-based psychology (Carroll, 1993). It is a common understanding that "high talent," in terms of an intellectual capacity, can be described by using a test that provides a quantitative operationalization of the general intelligence factor "g" indicating that an individual's score locates him or her two standard deviations above the mean of the referential population. Despite efforts to differentiate the concept of intelligence by (a) determining styles of thinking (e.g., convergent and divergent; Guilford, 1964), (b) social factors like one's ability to lead, and (c) psychomotor aspects (Marland, 1971), such models still lack empirical proof as do

---

1 In this context "more" does not necessarily mean "better." A quantitative perspective is related to one's qualitative perspective, but does not determine it. Environmentalists, particularly, have strong doubts about a positive influence of people on the environment that is beneficial in the long term. The issue of "sport and environment" needs special consideration, and is still not sufficiently established in sport-related developmental psychology.

recent endeavors to postulate multiple intelligences (e.g., Gardner, 2000). It seems logical to assume that different intelligences and various talents exist from everyday experience, but there is not sufficient empirical proof for this assumption to date.

Considering talent as a disposition, one can question how general or specific, and how complex is this disposition. One may also ask whether socialization processes can alter such a disposition. The more specific the task, the less influential is heritage. Socialization becomes more important as the task becomes more complex. The more specific and complex a sport is (with special respect to sensori-motor control) the less influential are an individual's genes. If the mere physical preconditions are decisive for the successful practice of a sport (e.g., height in basketball) the influence of nature and genetics is higher.

A DYNAMIC, ACTION-BASED UNDERSTANDING OF TALENT

The traditional understanding of talent refers to an inherited personal disposition for high performance potential. At the beginning of the 20th century talent was neither regarded in terms of only an intellectual or cognitive potential, nor was it regarded as isolated from volition, motivation, and emotion (Meumann, 1913; Stern, 1916). These conceptualizations referred to coordinated personal factors, which comprise talent. Talent is not a unified construct or a uni-dimensional trait. The essential components comprising talent are interest, motivation, and persistence. These are interrelated in dynamic action processes. In addition, it has to be considered that in the developmental process, the potential for learning is marked as domain specificity. Evidence demonstrates that, in general, ability level slightly above average is in principal sufficient to achieve high performance (Hany, 2000). Studying subjects with high intelligence or a talent (Ericsson et al., 1993: Trost & Sieglein, 1992) point out the following conclusions:

*   Interest and motivation are decisive. Successful people are different from others; it has less to do with the intellectual abilities ("talent" in a simplistic understanding) than with motivation and interest.

*   Will-power, persistence, and care are decisive in the process of practice (acting). This was proven by comparative studies on internationally successful female violinists, violin teachers, and hobby violinists.

A general theory of expertise does not exist. In principal, we assume an optimal organization of the action space or action field when conceptualizing expertise. Additionally, a single action situation is needed for the advancement of talents, that is, an optimal fit of the person-environment-task constellation. This "optimal" constellation has to be defined in detail with respect to the specific requirements of the domain. An essential aspect is emphasized in recent sport psychology research: the coordination between personal and social resources (Hackfort, 2001; Hackfort & Birkner, 2004). Figure 5 provides an overview of this coordination founded on the concept of action situation.

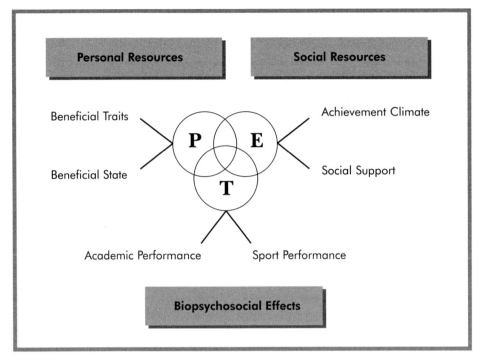

Figure 5 The essential resources and elements of the action situation for talents.

As various elements of this framework are discussed in further chapters of this volume, the influence of the relationship among vocational education and training, the attainment of peak performance in sports, and the process of career development is offered next.

ADVANCEMENT OF ELITE ATHLETES BY VOCATIONAL EDUCATION

BACKGROUND OF STUDY

For more than 25 years, a special program for sports and for the professional promotion of young elite athletes has been conducted in the Federal Boarder Guard of Germany. The program is sponsored by the Ministry of The Interior of Germany. This program is carried out centrally in a specific boarding school in Bad Endorf (a tiny town in the southern part of Germany, in Bavaria). The unique feature of this model is the arrangement of sports and vocational training via an integrated schedule for a period of four months each year, while the rest of the year is completely free for sports training. After four years, the athletes' complete their vocational training, however, they may stay in the Federal Boarder Guard as full-time athletes until the end of their sport careers if they so choose. Subsequently, at the end of their sports career the athletes have the opportunity to stay with the boarder guard for full time employment.

As part of an initiative for quality management, a study examining the organizational structure, the processes, and the outcome of the model over the last 25 years was conducted[2]. The study consisted of a four-stage analysis:

(1) The professional status of athletes after the transition into their post-sports career.

(2) The athletes' sports and professional career development.

(3) The external and internal conditions of the model, especially with respect to each athlete's individual experiences with the dual stressors of sports and vocational training.

(4) The athlete's contentment with the coordination of the dual stressors, and the transition phase into professional life.

METHOD

Qualitative measurements (i.e., semi-structured interviews) and quantitative measurements (i.e., questionnaires) were utilized in this study. Within the scope of the quantitative analyses, 100 former athletes from the school (i.e., 40% of the participants who went through this model in the last 25 years) responded to the initial questionnaire. In addition, 22 former athletes were interviewed. To ensure representativeness with regard to relevant factors of the athletes' population, the interviewees were selected following a stratified randomized plan considering age, sex, sport, and professional status after the end of their sports careers.

RESULTS

The core outcome of this study identified the *different forms* of combined mentally and physically stressful experiences. Theoretically, the identification of these mental factors refers to the more precise distinction between external stressors and internal stress-experiences (Lazarus & Launier, 1978). Evidence did not support the common sense assumption that a combination of mentally and a physically external stress (i.e., a dual stressors) is causally determining *"double-stress"* in every athlete. This may only be the case for those athletes who did not facilitatively access the required mental (e.g., coping mechanisms) or social (e.g., social support) resources, or who possibly relied on inadequate training. Athletes who believed that to become a champion always required maximizing the time spent on training experienced more "double-stress" in times of obligatory educational phases than did athletes who possessed a more advanced understanding of training (e.g., knowing about the dangers of overtraining and the benefits of reducing training at times). Support was revealed for the concept that athletes with a more differentiated understanding of training, or athletes with access to appropriate mental and social resources, may experience a combined mental and physical stress either in a *compensating* or even synergistic way, or they might realize transfer effects. *Compensating effects* may arise in various ways. A reciprocal *equalization* may be experienced when the mental stress equalizes a one-sided training lifestyle that lacks mental demands, or when the training *compensates* for a monotonous and boring class. A *compensating variation* may be experienced when mental or educational demands

---

2 The study was sponsored by the Federal Institute for Sport Science in Germany, VF 0408/09/07/2001-2003, and realized in cooperation with Dr. Hans-Albert Birkner (see Hackfort & Birkner, 2004).

prevent the development of training-boredom. *Distraction* effects may occur in times of failure in sports as academic success may distract athletes from their unsatisfying sports performances. The *transfer effects* described by the interviewed athletes referred to (a) the transfer between the sports and the professional domain (and vice versa), and (b) the transfer from the dual stress situation at the Bad Endorf School into other spheres of life. Numerous transfer effects that related to skills (e.g., improved time-management, concentration, social skills), abilities (e.g., improved self-assertion and autonomy), or even to traits (e.g., increased stress and frustration tolerance) were expressed by the athletes. Furthermore, some of the athletes denied any existing relationship between their sport and vocational training domains. Concretely, they looked at the vocational training as secondary to sports or they were convinced that the two domains should be strictly separated if someone wants to be successful in sports.

In so far as obstructive effects of dual stressors, as well as the beneficial effects of transfer and compensation, are reported in other studies (Jones & Hardy, 1990; Mayocchi & Hanrahan, 2000). This, however, is clearly not the case for the identified synergistic effects. Synergistic effects go beyond simple compensation effects as they do not only compensate for unfavorable deficits in other domains. "Synergistic" means that there is a certain combination of processes and effects that jointly contribute to future outcomes. From the interviews it was learned that the athletes felt that they can achieve higher performance in both sports and academic domains. Synergistic effects stem from the fact that adequate physical activity intensity results in numerous neural activation processes that positively impact learning and memory-tasks (Hollmann, de Meirleir, Fischer, & Holzgraefe, 1993).

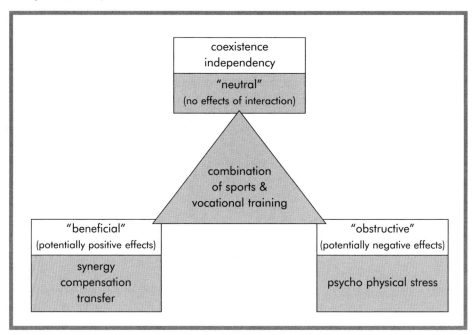

Figure 6 Modes of individual experiences - a combination of mental and physical strain.

The (artificial) reduction of time resources for sports training due to additional educational/vocational training may have positive impacts on sports performance. We concluded that (a) the potential danger of overtraining and burn-out may be reduced in young athletes, (b) the effectiveness of training sessions may somewhat increase by elevating effort and concentration, and (c) higher training-efficiency and the prevention of overtraining may result in a higher overall sport performance. In this study we found that several of the athletes had their greatest successes immediately after the four-month phase of integrated sports and vocational training, which can be taken as a prove for the above mentioned relation.

In addition to these effects congruent with the differentiated understanding outlined above, some further effects on motivation were revealed, which contribute to the elaboration of the concept. After class the athletes reported increased positive anticipation and improved motivation for sport training and competition. This effect was likely a result of the relative decrease in physical activity or sport participation. Additionally, an educational success can help young athletes overcome critical phases in their sports career, especially when experiencing failures and frustration. In this case, educational success for young athletes may be a critical reason for keeping up with the sport activity because their need for social acknowledgement and proof of competence does not rely solely on their sport performance. Such motivational effects may be of special importance with regard to coping with performance crises and drop-out-prevention. The motivational effects may also serve as mediators for other synergistic effects. The different synergistic effects, combining physical and mental stressors are illustrated in Figure 7.

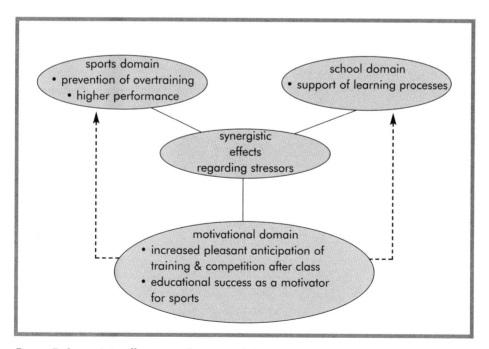

Figure 7 Synergistic effects - combination of stressors.

CONSEQUENCES

These findings bring into question the traditional paradigms regarding the development of elite sports in at least two ways. First, the findings question actual training-paradigms used by coaches and athletes who strongly believe in the predominant effect of quantity and intensity. It is highly doubtful that high quantities are necessary to reach a high performance level in a number of endurance sports, but it may be useful to periodically shift the focus of training from quantity to quality, or at least to increase the quality. Changes in the focus of training to quality may result in a shift to greater efficiency in training sessions as espoused in deliberate practice methods (Ericsson et al., 1993). Such a change in training focus may be of special importance for young athletes in order to prevent potential physical and motivational overtraining. Coaches and athletes must consider potential synergistic, and from their point of view even paradoxical, effects resulting from reductions in training quantity and increases in professional demands.

Referring to vocational training as a factor in a loss of athletic training time is likely to reinforce the development of "two-fold-stress," and thus inhibit the development of synergistic effects. Hence, the importance of *different* and more deliberate training methods is required to enhance skill-level.

The results of this research study do not support the "complete focus on sport" beliefs of some coaches. The findings refute the appropriateness of some coaches striving to protect their athletes from any non-sports related demands with the objective of maximizing sports performance. By focusing only on sports, athletes are likely missing the chance to engage synergistic effects that lead to maximizing their (a) sport performance and (b) motivation to have a long career in high performance sports. Furthermore, a positive impact of additional vocational training on the intellectual status of the athlete must be considered. The findings suggest that a focus solely on sports, or solely on vocational training, at one time may not lead to optimal sport or professional performance.

A narrow focus may sometimes enhance the development of under-achievement either in the professional or sport domains. Instead of continuing to rely on the former paradigm, the proven effects of improved sport performance by adding intellectual demands such as vocational training should be taken into consideration, at least with young athletes. In the future, the basic conditions, specific demands, and resources leading to synergistic effects in situations of dual sports and vocational stressors should be identified precisely with respect to the specific circumstances and be provided to the athletes if possible.

In general, the results of the study may change the direction of research and recommendations for the advancement of elite athletes. Therefore the question is no more if nor simply how to integrate vocational training into the life of an athlete without losing his or her sports performance. The question is how to integrate vocational training into the life of an athlete so that the two domains can complement each other. This will likely lead to engaging the synergistic effects of increased sports and academic or professional performance.

FINAL REMARKS

There is a lack of research on the effect and effeciency of programs to foster talents and to develop athletes' special potentials. In sport science, such investigations are needed. Hany (2000) pointed out that there is a high probability of obtaining good learning results where children with talent and motivation come together and work in cooperation with motivated and competent teachers. In this case, optimal preconditions for learning are given, but the influence of the special program remains unproven. In order to confirm the unique effect of a certain program, it is necessary to prove that it is more appropriate than other programs, which have been delivered to the (same) population, such as talented kids. Such investigations must refer to the interaction of the task (program), the environment (teacher etc.), and the person (talent) pointed out by the action-theory approach. Classical experimental designs with a pure knowledge orientation obviously have to be complemented to ensure progress on this issue and the limitations of empirical studies have to be overcome by an action research approach.

In the context of achievement motivation (see Elbe & Beckmann in this volume) it is assumed that an appropriate success orientation is based on the component "hope for success," and is associated with a realistic aspiration level and goal setting. Thus, an unrealistic level of aspiration (e.g., very low or very high aspiration levels) are symptoms for "fear of failure" (Heckhausen, 1980), or a tendency to avoid failure (Fuchs, 1963). These conclusions are supported by evidence from various studies, and they are already used for practical recommendations in sports (e.g., Wessling-Lünnemann, 1984).

However, the findings consist of group-based statistics rather than single-case studies. Such results are of minor meaning for elite sports and top athletes as there are only a few who are considered elite by definition, in so far as the general consequences of those studies are not necessarily usable for special cases or special individuals as highly talented children or top athletes. Contrary to these assumptions, various reports from top athletes (interview based) point to extreme high levels of aspiration, extraordinary goals, and visions like wanting to become "number one" in the sport, a world champion, and an olympian gold medalist. Those people believe that it is possible to achieve something which looks like an illusion in the eyes of others; they are convinced they are able to achieve something which seems to be an utopia for average people. This orientation and aspiration level is combined with effort, enthusiasm, and a consequence, which determines the daily lifestyle and regimen in nearly every aspect (e.g., nutrition, training, sleep, regeneration etc.). Following an interview with Steffi Graf, one of the most prominent female tennis players in the 20th century, in which she reported about the first meeting with her first professional coach Boris Breskvar in her later career, the journalist concluded: obviously it has to be this rare combination of talent and obsession, which produces the world star Steffi Graf. From a scientific point of view, it is interesting to note that such potential was combined with a special attitude, ability, and motivation, which have to fit and be further developed by the coach, the family, and the program (scope of tasks). To extend the person-environment concept and the concept of person-environment fit from an action-theory perspective, it is essential to organize a person-task-environment fit for the attainment of peak performance.

REFERENCES

Anastasi, A. (1958). Heredity, environment, and the question "how"? *Psychological Review*, 65, 197-208.

Beckmann, J., Szymanski, B. & Elbe, A.-M. (2004). Erziehen Verbundsysteme zur Unselbständigkeit? Entwicklung von Sporttalenten an einer Eliteschule des Sports (Do relational systems in sports educate toward dependency? Development of talents in sports in an elite school of sports). *Sportwissenschaft, 34*, 65-80.

Blumer, H. (1938). Social psychology. In E. P. Schmidt (Ed.), Man and society (pp. 144-198). New York: Prentice Hall.

Carroll, J. B. (1993). *Human cognitive abilities*. Cambridge: Cambridge University Press.

Ericsson, K. A., Krampe, R. T., & Tesch-Römer, C. (1993). The role of deliberate practice in the acqusition of expert performance. *Psychological Review, 100*, 363-406.

French, J. R. P., Rodgers, W. & Cobb, S. (1974). Adjustment as person-environment fit. In G. V. Coelho, D. A. Hamburg & J. E. Adams (Eds.), *Coping and adaptation* (pp. 316-333). New York: Basic Books.

Fuchs, R. (1963): Funktionsanalyse der Motivation (Functional analysis of motivation). *Zeitschrift für experimentelle und angewandte Psychologie, 10*, 626-645.

Gardner, H. (2000). Intelligence reframed: Multiple intelligences for the 21st century. New York: Basic Books.

Guilford, J. P. (1964). *Persönlichkeit. Logik, Methodik und Ergebnisse ihrer quantitativen Erforschung (Personality. Logic, method and results of quantitative research)*. Weinheim Beltz.

Hackfort, D. (1986). *Theorie und Analyse sportbezogener Ängstlichkeit (Theory and analysis of sport-related trait anxiety)*. Schorndorf: Hofmann.

Hackfort, D. (2001). Karriere im Sport - psychosoziale Aspekte eines Karrieremanagements unter besonderer Berücksichtigung von Eliteschulen des Sports (Career in sports - Psychosocial aspects of career management with special respect to elite schools of sport). In A. Güllich (Ed.), *Perspektiven der Nachwuchsförderung (Perspectives for the advancement of talents)* (pp. 153-165). Frankfurt/M.: DSB/BL.

Hackfort, D. (2003). *Studientext Entwicklungspsychologie 1 (Textbook Developmental Psychology 1)*. Göttingen: Vandenhoeck & Ruprecht.

Hackfort, D. & Birkner, H.-A. (2004). *Förderung von Hochleistungssportlern durch Berufsausbildung (Advancement of elite athletes by vocational education)*. Koeln: Sport & Buch Strauß.

Hackfort, D., Duda, J. & Lidor, R. (Eds.). (in press). *Handbook of research in applied sport and exercise psychology - international perspectives*. Morgantown, WV: FIT.

Hackfort, D. & Munzert, J. (2005, in press). Mental simulation. In D. Hackfort, J. Duda & R. Lidor (Eds.), *Handbook of research in applied sport and exercise psychology - international perspectives*. Morgantown, WV: FIT.

Hackfort, D., Munzert, J., & Seiler, R. (2000). *Handeln im Sport als handlungspsychologisches Modell (Acting in sports as an action-psychology model)*. Heidelberg: Asanger.

Hany, E. (2000). Muss man unterschiedlich hoch begabte Kinder unterschiedlich fördern (Is it necessary to foster children differently high in talent differently?) In H. Wagner (Ed.), *Begabung und Leistung in der Schule (Talent and performance in school)* (pp. 71-96). Bad Honnef: Bock.

Heckhausen, H. (1980). *Motivation und Handeln (Motivation and action).* Berlin: Springer

Hollmann, W. (1998). Interview (interview). *BISp Informationen, 2,* 7-9.

Hollmann, W., de Meirleir, K., Fischer, H. G. & Holzgraefe, M. (1993). ‹ber neuere Aspekte von Gehirn, Muskelarbeit, Sport und Psyche (On new aspects of brain, muscular work, sport, and psyche). *Deutsche Zeitschrift für Sportmedizin, 44,* 478-490.

Hollmann, W. & Fischer, H.G. (1994). Gehirn, muskuläre Arbeit und Psyche (Brain, muscular work, and psyche). *Spektrum der Wissenschaft, 8,* 25-27.

Jones, J. G. & Hardy, L. (Ed.) (1990). *Stress and performance in sport.* New York: Wiley & Sons.

Lazarus, R. S. & Launier, R. (1978). Stress-related transactions between person and environment. In L. A. Pervin & M. Lewis (Eds.). *Perspectives in interactional psychology* (pp. 287-327). New York: Plenum.

Lewin, K. (1969). *Grundzüge der topologischen Psychologie (Fundamentals in topological psychology).* Bern: Huber

Marland, S. P. jr. (1971). *Education of the gifted and talented (Vol. 1, 2).* Washington D. C.: Report to Congress.

Mayocchi, L. & Hanrahan, S. J. (2000). Transferable skills for career change. In D. Lavallee & P Wylleman (Eds.), *Career transitions in sport. International perspectives* (pp. 95-110). Morgantown, WV: Fitness Information Technology.

Mead, G.H. (1934). *Mind, self, and society.* Chicago: University of Chicago Press.

Meumann, E. (1913). *Intelligenz und Wille (Intelligence and volition).* Leipzig: Barth.

Nitsch, J. R. (2000). Handlungstheoretische Grundlagen der Sportpsychologie (Action theory fundamentals for sport psychology). In H. Gabler, J. R. Nitsch & R. Singer (Eds.), *Einführung in die Sportpsychologie, Teil 1 (Introduction to sport psychology, Part 1, pp. 43-164).* Schorndorf: Hofmann.

Nitsch, J. R. & Hackfort, D. (1981). Stress in Schule und Hochschule - eine handlungspsychologische Funktionsanalyse (Stress in school and university - an action psychology functional analysis). In J. R. Nitsch (Ed.), *Stress* (pp. 263-311). Bern: Huber.

Nitsch, J. R. & Hackfort, D. (1984). Basisregulation interpersonalen Handelns im Sport (Tuning of interpersonal acting in sports). In E. Hahn & H. Rieder (Hrsg.), *Sensumotorisches Lernen und Sportspielforschung (Sensori-motor learning and research in sports games; pp. 148-166).* Köln: bps.

Oerter, R. & Montada, L. (Eds.). (2002). *Entwicklungspschologie (Developmental psychology. 5th ed.).* Weinheim: Beltz.

Rost, D. H. (2002). Notwendige Klarstellungen (Necessary clarifications). *Report Psychologie, 27* (10), 624-634.

Ryle, G. (1949). *The concept of mind.* New York: Bames & Noble.

Stern, W. (1916). Psychologische Begabungsforschung und Begabungsdiagnose (Psychological research on talent and talent diagnosis). In P. Petersen (Ed.), *Der Aufstieg der Begabten (The promotion of the gifted; pp. 105-112).* Leipzig: Barth.

Wessling-Lünnemann, G. (1984). Sensibilisierung für motivationsförderndes Lehrerverhalten im Sportunterricht (Sensitization for teacher behavior to enhance motivation in sport classes). In D. Hackfort (Ed.), *Handeln im Sportunterricht (Acting in sport classes; pp. 224-261).* Köln: bps.

THE ROLES OF NATURE AND NURTURE IN EXPERTISE IN SPORT

MICHAEL B. JOHNSON AND GERSHON TENENBAUM

CONTENTS

SUMMARY

The dilemma regarding whether or not innate talent is a salient component of sport performance has been of interest for many decades. Howe, Davidson, and Sloboda (1998) rely on the position that if innate talent exists then this talent would be detectable at an early age, yet the literature supports the notion that some form of "talent" exists. However, Howe et al. continue to espouse the following requirement regarding talent: "These early indications of talent provide a basis for predicting who is likely to excel" (pp. 399-400). Their tenant is that if early, predictive detection of talent is lacking, then talent must not exist, and therefore, only training, motivation, and self-confidence (all detectable) can explain expert performance. Others disagree. Rose stated that people inherit dispositions, not destinies. However, it appears that until a direct connection can be verified between genetic predispositions and sport performance, the debate will continue.

This issue is addressed later in this chapter while specific aspects addressing the essential components of expert performance in the sport domain are discussed in the following sections.

An athlete's achievement level in sport involves a number of factors. An athlete's environment (e.g., his or her family, peers, and training) as well as the individual's cognitions, perceptions, self-efficacy, and affect can all impact his or her achievement level in sport. Not only is it possible for each of these factors to play a salient role in this endeavor, but interactions among these factors are likely to operate in a systemic fashion and thereby aide or inhibit one in reaching various performance levels in sport. Knowledge of an athlete's personal and family history, ways he or she perceives/constructs the world, as well as understanding his or her current states, will likely enhance an understanding of why a particular level of expertise was or is attained.

Scientific literature supports the noticeable impact of one's family and upbringing, his or her historic and current practice regimens, and the individual's genetic makeup, cognitions, perceptions, self-efficacy, and affect have on athletic performance. These factors can primarily be found on two continua: controllability and level of achievement. Each of these factors is measurable, and the measurement tools continue to improve. However, future research must entertain the possibility that athletes function within a system. The "Butterfly Effect" avers that a change in one factor, regardless of its size, can have far reaching impacts in other areas that may, or may not be anticipated. An area of investigation that extends current research paths exploring the lives of experts may include both qualitative and quantitative methods in order to compare experts and non-experts, while controlling for as many variables as possible (e.g., domain, coach, and gender). Such research may further enlighten the path toward understanding more fully the development of expertise in athletics.

INTRODUCTION

It is often common for observers of athletic events to state that a successful participant is "talented." This declaration is almost exclusively used to describe someone who consistently performs highly difficult acts correctly, or simple tasks exceedingly quick. The development of this capability is of great interest to a number of people in many domains. However, before a discussion of exceptional athletic capabilities can be examined, the term "talent" requires investigation. Once this is accomplished we can link the required parameters for the development of expertise in sport, which is conceptualized resulting from two global factors: nurture (i.e., environment, practice, etc.) and nature (i.e., genes, neural networks, etc.).

Among researchers and scientists, the questions surrounding the definition of "talent," and what leads to highly skilled athletic performances, have stirred an intense debate. Sport performers, coaches, spectators, sponsors, and psychologists all have an interest in athletic talent, expertise, and the development of expertise. Any discussion regarding talent and expertise requires a definition of these terms. Unfortunately, the scientific literature offers little in terms of a universally agreed upon definition (Durand-Bush & Salmela, 2001). One definition of "talent" offered by Howe, Davidson, and Sloboda (1998) states that talent must include the following five factors: (a) it originates genetically, (b) it may not be fully apparent at an early age, (c) early indications of talent provide a basis for predicting eventual expertise, (d) only a few have it, and (e) it is relatively domain specific. Howe et al. do not support the notion of talent but they do espouse the perspective that athletes develop expertise as a result of environmental factors such as intense training rather than some notion of innate "talent." When asked to respond to Howe et al., a number of researchers replied that excluding innate abilities from the equation involving expertise development is probably inaccurate (Bates, 1998; Csikszentmihalyi, 1998; Detterman, Gabriel, & Ruthsatz, 1998; Feldman & Katzir, 1998; Gagne, 1998; Heller & Ziegler, 1998; Plomin, 1998; Rowe, 1998; Rutter, 1998; Schneider, 1998; Sternberg, 1998; Trehub & Schellenberg, 1998; Winner, 1998; Zohar, 1998), while others were more agreeable (Charness, 1998; Eisenberger, 1998; Ericsson, 1998a; Irvine, 1998; Lehman, 1998; Simonton, 1998; Starkes & Helsen, 1998; Tesch-Romer, 1998; Weisberg, 1998). Working from this definition of talent it becomes more apparent that motor and physical skills, genetic factors, cognitive capabilities, perceptual abilities, self-efficacy beliefs, affective experiences, coping strategies, and the quality and amount of practice may each play a role in an athlete's performance level. The extent of these factors' roles in the development of expert athletic performance is of vital interest in the nature versus nurture debate (Bloom, 1985; Tenenbaum, 1999).

It is also important to differentiate between those who perform expertly and those who are experts in a field. Research has shown that experienced psychotherapists do not attain higher levels of successful patient treatment than do novice therapists (Dawes, 1994), and expert stock-market analysts and bankers cannot forecast market prices more reliably than university instructors and students (Stael von Holstein, 1972). Therefore, expert performers are further defined as people who can consistently demonstrate a very high performance level relative to the general population in a particular domain (Ericsson, 1998a, 1998b; Ericsson, Krampe, & Tesch-Romer, 1993). As this definition pertains to sport, an expert athlete is one who performs at the highest level over an extended period of time.

Literature regarding variables that account for, or contribute to expertise in sport include research into knowledge (French & Thomas, 1987; McPherson & Thomas, 1989; Starkes, 1987; J. R. Thomas & Thomas, 1998), perceptual ability (Abernethy, 1990, 1992), biological and physiological characteristics (J. R. Thomas & Thomas, 1998; K. T. Thomas, 1994), psychological characteristics (J. R. Thomas & Thomas, 1998), maturation (Baxter-Jones, Helms, Maffull, Baines-Preece, & Preece, 1995; Boucher & Mutimer, 1994; Brewer, Balsom, Davis, & Ekblom, 1992), self-efficacy beliefs (Bandura, 1977, 1986, 1990, 1997; Feltz & Lirgg, 2001), and practice (Ericsson & Charness, 1994; Starkes, Deakin, Allard, Hodges, & Hayes, 1996; Starkes & Helsen, 1998; K. T. Thomas, 1994). The degree to which each of these factors impact the development of expert performance has led to much discussion. Researchers tend to support the specific line maintained by their empirical results. However, a possibility exists that their views may be complimentary, rather than conflicting.

The debate about the role of nature and nurture in the context of sport expertise and its development has existed for many years. Some researchers postulate that "nature," i.e., an athlete's physical gifts, innate ability, or "talent" (as it will be referred to throughout this chapter), plays a prominent role in obtaining exceptional success in sport, in addition to other performance domains (Eysenck, 1995; Simonton, 1994; Sternberg, 1996; Winner, 1996a, 1996b). Others advocate the "nurture" perspective, i.e., performers become highly successful as a result of environmental factors such as intense training (Ericsson et al., 1993; Howe et al., 1998) or familial influences (Stevenson, 1990). It is reasonable to surmise that the development and attainment of athletic expertise may well rely on a favorable natural predisposition and optimal nurturance for a particular domain. To argue that expertise is due to the predominance of either of these to the exclusion of the other may be flawed because it is likely that expertise in sport involves more than possessing an exceptional amount of knowledge in a particular athletic domain. Concurrently, it is likely that a lack of understanding in a specific sport context would exclude an athlete from becoming an expert in that domain. Figure 1 (Tenenbaum, 1999) shows a model illustrating the relationships between nature and nurture in the development of expertise in sport.

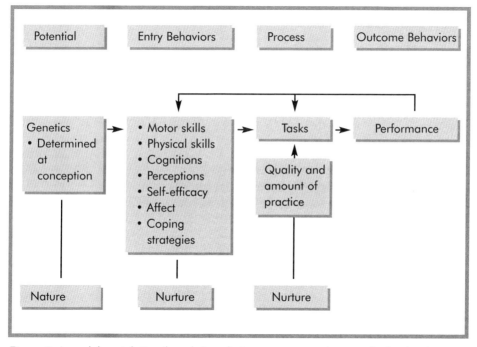

Figure 1 A model postulating the relations between nature and nurture in the development of expertise in sport. (adapted from Tenenbaum, 1999, p. 114)

An individual's genetic endowment is impacted by certain entry factors (e.g., motor and physical skills, cognitions, perceptions, self-efficacy, affect, and coping strategies) that influence the quality and amount of practice an individual may facilitatively engage in. This engagement level then influences the individual's performance, or achievement level. Performance, in turn, affects the athlete's alterable entry behaviors, completing a feedback loop that is unique for each individual, but similar among people. The literature on expertise in sport supports this integrated view and illuminates various reasons underlying the development of expertise in sport.

Expert athletic performance involves a complex interaction among entry and environmental factors, including feedback systems that enable performance interpretation, which affect entry behaviors and inputs experienced by the athlete. Just as other types of systems, human systems constantly adapt to the environment so as to preserve their niche, or to expand it. Systems theory suggests that all behavior in the case of expert performance must be understood through the adaptive mechanisms utilized before trying to change or improve that behavior. Scientific evidence provides support for each of these factors alone and for interactions among some.

A CONCEPTUAL OVERVIEW

Few researchers offer models that illustrate the involvement of specific factors in the development of expertise in sport. This review of the expertise development in sport literature begins with the research that supports the environmental view, and then the literature supporting the talent view. This is followed by a summary of the literature addressing the essential factors of expert performance in sport. The three most prominent pieces of research in the field are Bloom's (1985) stages of talent development, Côté's (1999) stages of sport participation, and Ericsson et al.'s (1993) notion of deliberate practice.

NATURE VS. NURTURE VIEW ON THE DEVELOPMENT OF EXPERTISE IN SPORT

THE ENVIRONMENTAL VIEW

Bloom (1985), Kalinowski (1985) and Monsaas (1985) interviewed 120 athletes, musicians, artists, and scientists who achieved imminent success in their chosen field. The athletes in this group included 21 sprint freestyle swimmers who represented the United States of America in at least one of the 1968, 1972, or 1976 Olympic Games (Kalinowski, 1985), and 18 tennis players who were born and raised in the USA and ranked in the top 10 in the world sometime between 1968 and 1979 (Monsaas, 1985). Bloom's work resulted in the identification of three stages of talent development: (a) The early years (initiation), (b) the middle years (development), and (c) the late years (perfection).

In Bloom's (1985) model the early years were dominated by fun and playful activities. In these years the athlete often participated in more than one sport activity, was excited about just participating, and relied heavily on the adults (e.g., parents and coaches) in his or her life for guidance and support. In this first stage, the future elite athlete was rarely, if ever, identified as destined for expertise in his or her field. This suggests a possibility that if adults in the life of the athlete emphasize the importance of winning and performance, or other "non-playful" goals, to an athlete in this stage, they are probably limiting the child's chances for eventual high-level performance in that particular sport domain (Coakley, 1992; Margenau, 1990; Roberts, Treasure, & Hall, 1994). In the middle years it was revealed that sport became much more serious to the athlete and his or her self-identity changed. Participants felt of themselves as "swimmers" or "tennis players," rather than as people who swam or played tennis, while other activities either decreased in importance or were abandoned altogether. The athlete became more achievement oriented during this stage and relied on his or her parents for moral and financial support. In the late years, the athlete became almost obsessed with the chosen sport as it dominated his or her life. Motivation to attain the highest achievement levels in his or her sport became almost solely intrinsic. Coaches were highly respected task masters, while the parents' role decreased tremendously because the athlete assumed total responsibility for his or her own improvement.

In his study, Côté (1999) interviewed four athletes who were 18 years of age. All were national level athletes for their age in their sport. Côté also interviewed 11 of the athletes' family members. Of specific interest was how the family dynamic influenced the development of expertise in sport. Based on his findings, Côté proposed three distinct stages of sport participation: (a) sampling, (b) specializing, and (c) investment stages.

In the sampling years, parents encouraged their children to participate in multiple sports with the goal of enjoyment, not achievement. Coaches and parents were interested in offering the young athlete "fun" opportunities, motor skill development, motivation, constructive values, a positive self-image, and enjoyable sporting experiences. Côté called this "deliberate play." Additionally, parents of three of the four athletes felt that their child had special talents in sport. This finding supported Dweck's (1986) contention that parents' beliefs may reinforce their children's beliefs, and perhaps self-efficacy, which is a determinant of progress and success.

In Côté's second stage, the specializing years, each athlete limited participation to one, or perhaps two sports while increasing his or her commitment level. Social support from significant others (e.g., coaches, siblings, parents) supported the athlete's intrinsic enjoyment, and his or her ever increasing success influenced the decision to become more dedicated to the chosen sport. Practice became more structured and focused, while fun and excitement were retained. Parents increased their involvement in their child's sport during this stage, and increased their time and financial commitments to their child's efforts. Notably, this additional commitment on the parents' part seemed to be undertaken to offset any obligations the athlete might have had over and above those to school or sport. Additionally, older siblings often were perceived as role models, particularly in exhibiting a positive work ethic.

During the third stage, the investment years, elite level performance was pursued. These years were much more intense than the previous specialization stage. Deliberate practice replaced deliberate play at this point. Parents continued to show great interest in their child's efforts by providing emotional and financial support. Extraordinary efforts in the area of the athlete's career often came at a price for other family members, but it is interesting to note that even though the parents were aware of their child rearing discrepancies they justified these with the belief that the potential accomplishments of the high achieving child were worth the tradeoff.

In another recent study, Durand-Bush (2000) found support for Côté's model, while offering an additional fourth stage: maintenance. This stage occurred after Côté's investment stage, and was found in athletes who had achieved Olympic and World Championship gold medals. In this most advanced stage, the athlete felt a greater amount of external pressure resulting from being the best in his or her sport. Côté's (1999) model also contains a fourth stage, however, he calls it "the recreational years." In the recreational years, children who cannot, or who decide not to, invest what is necessary to reach elite levels of sport, enter a period where they practice one to several sports in order to experience enjoyment, personal growth, stay fit, and preserve an overall healthy life.

DELIBERATE PRACTICE

Based on extensive work, Ericsson et al. (1993) introduced the concept of deliberate practice as a means to achieve expert performance. Ericsson et al. found that high levels of performance were reached in a gradual manner following many years of domain specific activities.

Deliberate practice refers to those training activities that specifically address improvement of an individual's performance, and it requires specific parameters. There must be: (a) a well defined task with appropriate difficulty level, (b) high effort, and (c) opportunities for repetition and error correction. Additionally, deliberate practice is typically designed by an expert coach to optimize the athlete's training regimen (Ericsson et al., 1993). In other words, deliberate practice is any highly structured goal directed activity aimed exclusively at improving performance, and it is not necessarily inherently motivating or enjoyable. Therefore, it is important to note that, according to this concept, regular activity does not typically lead to improvement beyond some initial, short-term performance improvement. Support for this contention in sport contexts is found in studies with soccer players (Helsen, Starkes, & Hodges, 1998), wrestlers (Starkes et al., 1996), and middle-distance runners (Young, 1998). Limitations to the amount of deliberate practice one can engage in include (a) resource constraints (e.g., adequate time, energy, coaches, and facilities), (b) motivational constraints (i.e., the fact that deliberate practice is not inherently enjoyable, and therefore the athlete must be motivated by the potential of future improved performance), and (c) effort constraints, also known as learned industriousness (Eisenberger, 1998). Additionally, the highest level of achievement in vigorous sport was typically in athletes' mid- to late-twenties (Ericsson, 1990; Schulz & Curnow, 1988). This illustrates that continued development often extends beyond the point of physical maturity, implying that situational experience is required for athletes to improve their performance. This view is that any healthy individual who engages in a sufficient number of hours of deliberate practice in a given field will become an expert in that field, and that his or her performances can be reproduced and verified. Ericsson (1998b) noted that any scientific progress in understanding expertise depends on the ability of observers and scientists to distinguish verifiable observations of specific behaviors from inferences about the mediation of general capacities. Ericsson (1998b) tempered the stand regarding reproducibility by stating:

> The probability of making a major innovation is so small that it is rare that the same individual will make more than a single one during their entire life. Thus, making a major innovation is not a reproducible superior performance for even the most eminent and accomplished scientists and artists. (p. 80)

Ericsson's views imply that nurture is everything, or at least very near it, in the pursuit of developing outstanding performance. However, this does not mean that the theory of deliberate practice espouses that practicing for a prerequisite number of hours is sufficient to reach an elite performance level. Even when two individuals are exposed to the same opportunities to develop expertise, they do not necessarily reach similar levels of achievement. Ericsson et al. (1993) found that experience alone was not a good predictor of performance level. Only when people face failures of their entrenched procedures do they actively engage in learning and modification of their skills (Ericsson, 1998b). The importance of concentration for deliberate practice to occur is an important concept due to its differentiation from mindless drilling and playful engagement. Drills and play may, if anything, strengthen the athlete's current cognitive and motor structures regarding performance, but would do little or nothing to change or improve his or her performance (Ericsson, 1998b).

A shortcoming of the theory of deliberate practice itself lies in the three limitations to the amount of deliberate practice. Since all human beings are different to some degree (e.g., height, gender, bone structure, and eyesight), there are inherent differences between people that may require them to engage in different amounts of deliberate practice in order to achieve expert performance. It has been shown that endurance sports lead to physiological enlargement of the heart and to an increase in the heart wall's thickness, depending on the kind of endurance sport and on the intensity and extent of training (Pelliccia, 1996). However, the adaptation of the heart may be modified by several factors including anthropometric parameters, gender, and genetic traits (Pelliccia, 1996). Deliberate practice alone does not permit a person shorter than two meters in height to play center on an NBA basketball team, nor will the most optimal application of deliberate practice allow a female to run the 100m faster than the male Olympic Games champion in that event. Additionally, Gualdi-Russo and Graziani (1993) showed that different somatotypes correlate with performance level in some sport domains, with an increase in the mesomorphic component for those involved in sports such as ballgames and martial arts, and with a strong endomorphic component for athletes such as swimmers. Since people are different, they possess different predispositions. It is proposed that people's environments can influence their eventual performance level to a great degree, but not dictate it as genetic predispositions may greatly influence one's potential in a particular domain.

DELIBERATE PRACTICE IN SPORT CONTEXTS

As this theory stated earlier, the amount of deliberate practice an individual engages in mediates the development of exceptional skill levels and physiological characteristics in elite performers (Ericsson et al., 1993; Hodges & Starkes, 1996; Krampe & Ericsson, 1996). Additionally, Ericsson and Lehman (1996) contended that basic physiological adaptations permit extended intense practice thereby suggesting an additional factor involved in the deliberate practice model than is currently considered.

Deliberate practice requires innovative, engaging, and/or diverting activities that allow the athlete to continually refine his or her performance using knowledge of results and feedback. As such, elite performers who compete in different sport domains are extremely rare and perhaps non-existent, although Christine Witty (USA Olympian in cycling and speed skating) is an example of one such athlete. Additionally, there are no immediate external rewards for deliberate practice as there are in other activities such as paid work. The amount of time an individual can commit to deliberate practice is limited (Ericsson et al., 1993). Optimal performance via deliberate practice in sport contexts requires extensive physical effort and mental concentration (i.e., quantity and quality), which is offset by periods of recovery. This is due to the highly taxing nature of deliberate practice in both physical and psychological dimensions. Therefore, the athlete must achieve a balance between bouts of deliberate practice and rest or recovery, which can be passive or active. This leads to the likely conclusion that an activity (e.g., rest) that is highly relevant to expert performance may be low in effort and concentration.

In their original research into deliberate practice, Ericsson et al. (1993) investigated violinists' (N = 30) perceptions of practice in three areas: (a) relevance to improving performance, (b) inherent pleasure of the activity, and (c) the effort required to perform the activity. Three different performance level violinists, all with more than 10 years of experience, were included in their analysis. No difference was revealed among any of the groups in terms of their perceptions of practice. All groups felt that practicing alone, taking lessons, and performing by oneself were the three most relevant training exercises. Furthermore, the violinists expressed their perception that these activities required substantial effort. In another study analyzing the backgrounds of two expert athletes, Thomas and Thomas (1999) interviewed two elementary school physical education teachers. Each teacher had instructed a student in prior years who was now an expert athlete. Both teachers stressed that the former students worked hard (practice), knew what to do (knowledge), and demonstrated positive attitudes and coordinated skill execution. The teachers stressed that the quantity of practice each student engaged in was less important than the quality (i.e., relevant effort) of that practice. In a related manner, research into soccer expertise (Helsen, Hodges, Van Winckel, & Starkes, 2000) showed a positive linear relationship between accumulated individual plus team practice, and skill level (Deakin & Cobley, 2003), and Helsen et al. (2000) showed that elite ice skaters spent their on-ice time much more efficiently than did novices.

Originally, Ericsson et al. (1993) believed that the qualities of deliberate practice were generalizable across contexts. Sport specific investigations into the deliberate practice theory, e.g., wrestling (Hodges & Starkes, 1996), and field hockey and soccer (Helsen et al., 1998), found that those practice activities judged most relevant to performance level were also perceived as relatively more enjoyable than other components of practice. Helsen et al. surmised that enjoying a sport, including effortful practice, is a prominent factor contributing to athletes' long-term dedication to their sport. Additionally, in an effort to differentiate between physical and mental effort, Helsen et al. and Hodges and Starkes examined concentration. These researchers showed that the concentration required to participate in a sport was highly correlated with relevance, but separate from physical effort. Additionally, they found no difference among international, national, and provincial caliber athletes in their perceptions of practice according to the dimensions of relevance, effort, concentration, and enjoyment.

The "sport-modified version of deliberate practice" (Helsen et al., 1998; Hodges & Starkes, 1996) agrees with the deliberate practice theory in every point except one - practice activities that are relevant and effortful are enjoyable. Ericsson (1996) proposed that this is due to the social nature of sport practice. However, recent research did not fully support this contention. A study including a group of Canadian middle distance runners of three different performance levels (Young & Salmela, 2002) did not find any activities that conformed to the original definition of deliberate practice. Additionally, an investigation into explanations for the enjoyment of effortful competitive swimming did not uphold the social factors line of reasoning as social factors were ranked fourth in importance out of eight alternatives by the athletes, well behind the factors of challenge and mastery (Watanabe, 2000). Furthermore, running and swimming often can be solitary sports providing little social interaction during effortful bouts.

Expert and novice athletes in the martial arts (karate) were assessed relative to the sport applicability of Ericsson et al.'s (1993) theory of deliberate practice (Hodge & Deakin, 1998). Hodge and Deakin found positive relationships between the relevance of a practice task and the effort put forth by the athlete, as well as the enjoyment of that task by the athlete. These findings are in contrast to the original deliberate practice tenant that holds: for practice to effectively aid sport performance it is not necessarily inherently unenjoyable. These findings direct the search for alternative reasons to support the sport-modified version of deliberate practice and that alterations based on context should be made to the deliberate practice model if it is to be used in the sport domain.

Support for the sport-modified version of deliberate practice includes research that found support for divergent pleasurable and unpleasurable states resulting in changes to athletes' body chemistry (Dishman, 1982, 2005; Hatfield, 1991). Additionally, biochemical influences associated with highly exertive exercise are implicated with positive mood shifts (Dishman, 1982, 2005; Markoff, Ryan, & Young, 1982; Sacks, 1981), and opponent-process theory supports an increase in exercise-induced affect during workouts of high exertion (Solomon, 1977). Additionally, since the primary goal of practice is to improve performance, any practice activity that elicits feelings or emotions similar to those desired in competition are interpreted as enjoyable (Hanin, 1980; Kerr, 1989).

   Deliberate practice in sport is also championed as a way to improve elite athletes' strength and power in sports contexts to a level exceeding that of novices (Ericsson, 2003). However, true or not, this may be a moot point. It is highly possible that athletes who produce less power are superior performers relative to others due to efficiencies of their movements, e.g., running economy and swimming technique. A more salient point of deliberate practice in sport may relate to the impact of a practice routine on the effectiveness (as opposed to the brute power) of movement an athlete brings to his or her domain.

The theory of deliberate practice also puts forth that an essential characteristic of expertise is that it must include sustained high-level performance. Unstable performance is supposed to demonstrate fluctuations in underlying control processes that negatively impact performance level. Abernethy, Farrow, and Berry (2003), however, point out that the converse is not necessarily true, i.e., "consistent high-level performance by experts does not necessarily imply stability in the type of control processing being used nor does it imply stability in the processes that mediate expert performance" (p.353). The theory of deliberate practice counters with support from Newell and Rosenbloom (1981) who illustrated that the time taken to roll a cigar improves by 62% from the 10th to the 1,010th cigar, while improvement from the 2,000,010th to the 2,001,010th cigar is only 0.01%. However, in many sport domains the salient issue is that the time to complete a task improves while there is an alteration in the type of control processing used to attain that achievement level.

Other theories emphasize the important role of "natural" factors in expert performance. Theories of evolutionary adaptation (Darwin, 1859/1964) support the premise that living organisms change and adapt to the environment, or they cease to exist. Organisms that get too far ahead, or fall too far behind the requirements needed to survive in the current environment fail to survive. Additionally, organisms adapt physiologically and psychologically at differing rates based on unique environmental factors. As such, it is reasonable to hypothesize that different people differ in their inherited psychological and physiological characteristics based on their ancestral transformations. Therefore, one can surmise that idiosyncratic, genetic predisposed adaptations to deliberate practice play a role in the level of athletic performance achieved via a dynamic interaction between the person and the environment (i.e., nature and nurture).

The views of three primary proponents of the environmental development of expertise hypothesis (Bloom, Coté, and Ericsson) can be integrated with others who support the "nature" views. The role of genetics, cognitions, perceptions, self-efficacy, and affective factors each find unique empirical support. Each of these brings important insight to the nature vs. nurture debate to varying degrees. An individual discussion of each construct is presented in the following sections.

Genetic Factors

The literature on genetics supports both concepts of innate talent and environmental influences on expertise in sport. The following subsections review the genetic research in the areas of twins and adoptions, behavioral, cognitive, physical, physiological, maturational, and gene-environment interactions and correlations as they relate to the development of expertise in sport.

Twin and adoption studies

Research looking into twins and adoptions can be a rich source of investigating the genetic influences on expertise in sport, as well as other domains. If a person's genetic factors affect a particular trait, then monozygotic twins, who share 100% of their genetic material, should be more similar to each other than dizygotic twins, who, like ordinary siblings with the same parents, share on average only 50% of their genetic material. Adoption studies, on the other hand, involve determining the degree to which adopted individuals resemble both their biological relatives (an indication of genetic influences) as well as their adoptive families (an indication of environmental influences). A limitation of adoption studies is that adoptive homes are likely to under represent those who are living at the extremes of poverty. Therefore, the importance of environmental influences may be underestimated.

Due to the strengths of twin and adoption studies this subsections' review of genetics will frequently refer to the literature regarding twin and adoption studies as they relate to the development of athletic expertise.

BEHAVIOR GENETICS

Behavioral geneticists have not found explicit and irrefutable evidence of environmental influences on sport performance. This appears inconsistent with the literature in developmental psychology, which reflects a strong association between rearing circumstances and psychological outcome (McGue & Bouchard, 1998). This conundrum may be due to environmental measures that reflect the influence of genetic factors (Plomin, Owen, & McGuffin, 1994). However, the heritable nature of environmental exposure may implicate the gene-environment correlational processes, and the mechanisms by which genes and the environment jointly influence human potentials (McGue & Bouchard, 1998). Additionally, parents with two or more children have been found to treat their children differently (Dunn, Stocker, & Plomin, 1990). There is support for the position that poor child rearing tactics are often genetically mediated, e.g., an alcoholic parent with a genetic predisposition for alcoholism is likely to rear a child in an environment conducive to the child developing alcoholism (Ge, Conger, Cadoret, Neiderhiser, & Yates, 1996; Lytton, 1990; Pike, McGuire, Hetherington, Reiss, & Plomin, 1996).

Studies indicate that most behavioral characteristics are heritable (McGue & Bouchard, 1998) even though there are a limited number of confirmed linkages or gene associations for behavioral traits. There are, however, some promising leads. Twin and adoption studies that investigated the personality traits of extraversion, agreeableness, conscientiousness, neuroticism, and openness, reported a strong genetic heritability and low environmental effects on these traits (T. J. Bouchard, 1994; Loehlin, 1992). Additionally, heritability for social attitudes (Eaves & Eysenck, 1974), radicalism and tough-mindedness (Scarr & Weinberg, 1981), and religious interests, attitudes and values (Waller, Kojetin, Bouchard, Lykken, & Tellegen, 1990) were found to be genetically, not environmentally, determined. While studying the genetic determinants of sports participation and resting metabolic rate in a group of twins and their parents, Beunen and Thomis (1999) found that if one of the parents or co-twins was active in sport, then it was more likely that the other child would also be active in sport.

In the Minnesota Twin Family Study, Hur, McGue, and Iacono (1996) reported that heritability estimates for leisure activities varied from 6% for religious activities to 57% for intellectual activities, and concluded that interests and engagement in aptitude-based leisure time activities are affected by genetically influenced individual talents and abilities. McGue and Bouchard's review of behavioral genetic research indicates that environmental factors are important, but contrary to the expectations of many behavioral scientists, salient environmental factors appear to be those that are not shared by relatives who are raised together. Shared environmental factors include characteristics such as family income, parental child-rearing strategies, and level of intellectual stimulation within the home. Non-shared environmental dynamics include examples such as accidents, peer affiliations, and differential parental treatment not shared by reared together relatives. People's temperament, which is mostly inherited, affects the social interactions they engage in, and it is these interpersonal interactions that carry risks for psychopathology (Rutter, 2000). This does not imply that genetics alone determine outcomes. Environmental factors may have an impact on behaviors that shape or select personal experiences. However, an adverse experience likely occurs due to genetically influenced, individual behaviors regarding social experiences that are sought out by the individual. Therefore, it is highly possible that a person's behavior may not be genetically dictated, but be genetically mediated. In other words, research supports the possibility that there exists an indirect genetically predetermined disposition to seek out certain behaviorally congruent environments. It is these behaviors that can play an integral role in a person's development level in sport.

COGNITIVE CHARACTERISTICS

Hereditability of cognitive abilities is a multifaceted construct, and may have an ambiguous impact on the development of expertise in sport. The heritability of general cognitive abilities (e.g., IQ) appears to be substantial while specific mental abilities appear to be somewhat less heritable (McGue & Bouchard, 1998; Pederson, Plomin, Nesselroade, & McClearn, 1992). Additionally, shared environmental influences on cognitive abilities is low (Teasdale & Owen, 1984). Studies with twins who were reared apart showed a substantial correlation of IQs among monozygotic twins that could not be accounted for by contact between the twins, or by the placement of the twins in adoptive homes with similar environments (T. J. Bouchard, 1997; Pederson et al., 1992).

Since there is support in the literature for a lack of inherited specific mental abilities, and since many sports require a deep and broad knowledge base in their domain as a prerequisite of expertise, then it stands to reason that the effects of inherited cognitive ability on specific expertise in sport is likely to be limited.

PHYSICAL CHARACTERISTICS

In addition to behavioral characteristics, genetic factors also determine, to a large extent, various physical characteristics (Bates, 1998; Plomin, 1998; Rowe, 1998; Zohar, 1998), which can play a large role in an athlete's performance level. Other research shows that many human anatomical and physiological characteristics adapt to intense practice, as do perceptual, motor, and cognitive competencies (Azar, 1996 January; Keele & Ivry, 1987; Schlaug, Jancke, Huang, & Steinmetz, 1995; Takeuchi & Hulse, 1993). Landauer and Whiting (1983) studied the impact of stressful physical practices in a number of societies. Results showed that those societies with the highest stress levels had males who averaged two inches more in height, and females who reached menarche approximately two years earlier (i.e., 11 years as compared to 13). Apparently, changes within people can occur in order to adapt to the environment. However, it has also been posited that some biological factors can facilitate, while others limit, performance in particular sports (Malina, 1994, 1996; Spurgeon & Giese, 1980; Spurgeon, Spurgeon, & Giese, 1984), e.g., a 6 foot tall 16 year old girl would probably not be a world class gymnast, and a cyclist with 65% fast-twitch muscle fibers could have difficulty finishing the Tour de France cycling race.

PHYSIOLOGICAL MAKEUP

Human skeletal muscle fiber composition could be construed as being advantageous to successful performance in selected athletic events (e.g., sprinters benefit from having a greater proportion of fast twitch muscle fibers than slow twitch muscle fibers). In terms of genetic heritability of certain muscle fiber types, the present evidence is equivocal as to whether habitual participation in a given type of physical activity is responsible for a higher percentage of a given fiber type (Gollnick & Matoba, 1984). Human genetic variation in gene products and in the non-coding of DNA is quite extensive (C. Bouchard, 1988). While this variation does not influence the primary structure of the proteins, it may have considerable impact on gene expression. Bouchard argues that it is not currently possible to conclude with confidence that the significance of modest racial differences in genetic variation account for racial differences in performance. However, as of the year 2000 Caucasian peoples of Eurasian ancestry hold 46 of the top 50 all-time performances in the hammer throw and Kenyans from the Nandi district (an elevated area in the western part of the country) produce world class distance runners at a rate of almost 23 times the global per capita norm (Entine, 2001). Clearly, slight differences in genetics may play a significant role in an athlete's predisposition to potential expertise in a particular discipline.

Twin and parent-child correlations for resting metabolic rate indicate a moderate genetic effect. Hagberg, Moore, and Ferrell (2001) showed that angiotensin-converting enzyme genotype, a genetic marker found in mitochondrial DNA, affects VO2 max, and therefore endurance performance capacity. Studies by C. Bouchard et al. (1986) and Prud'Homme, Bouchard, Leblanc, Landry, and Fountaine (1984) found support for the genotype-dependency of VO2max aerobic power. Twenty-nine pairs of monozygotic twins and 19 pairs of dizygotic twins, all males ages 18-31 years, performed an ergometer test. Findings did support the heritability of peak aerobic power, even after adjusting for anthropometric characteristics, such as life-style factors, anaerobic energy generation, and mechanical efficiency. However, the mechanisms influencing this genotype are currently unclear.

In another study, Gyagay et al. (1998) found that 64 Australian national rowers had an excess of the angiotensin-converting enzyme compared with a normal population, suggesting that the form DNA presents in human beings may be associated with a person's potential for athletic excellence. Additionally, 32 male twins, eight monozygotic and eight dizygotic pairs, with similar perinatal and environmental backgrounds were studied for their running economy (Rodas et al., 1998). No significant differences were observed between the twin groups with respect to running economy at any speed, or in their VO2 max relative to body mass. However, a genetic component for markers of anaerobic metabolism was present. In a related study, it was found that mechanical efficiency had no significant genetic component for a bicycle ergometer test to exhaustion (Fagard, Bielen, & Amery, 1991).

Physiological factors play a role in athletic expertise. There is substantial support for the trainability and heritability of a number of physiological factors. Therefore, it is highly likely that a person's performance potential in a particular sport domain is influenced by genetics (i.e., nature) to some degree.

MATURATION

Late sexual maturation of gymnasts and early maturation of swimmers suggests some form of sports-specific selection in young male athletes aged 8-19 years (Baxter-Jones et al., 1995). Training did not appear to affect the young athletes' growth and development, rather their continued success in sport appeared to be related to inherited traits. Additionally, some research supports an interaction between practice at certain developmental stages and biological factors. For example, studies investigating performers in baseball (Thompson, Barnsley, & Stebelsky, 1991), hockey (Barnsley & Thompson, 1988; Boucher & Mutimer, 1994), soccer (Dudink, 1994), and tennis (Dudink, 1994) found that a higher proportion of elite performers were born in the months of the year which translated into these athletes being chronologically older than their peers when they participated in age grouped competition at younger ages. This suggests that enhanced self-efficacy may be impacted by an athlete's age relative to his or her peers. Additionally, research findings suggest that what coaches perceive to be early talent may be explained by physical precocity associated with a relative age advantage (Helsen et al., 2000) thereby supporting a mediating effect of the environment (i.e., coaches' perceptions) on maturation. A person may be more inclined to participate in an activity (i.e., sport) with more intensity (physically and mentally) if he or she is receiving positive feedback and encouragement from an adult who the athlete perceives to have a significant impact on his or her life.

GENE-ENVIRONMENT INTERACTIONS AND CORRELATIONS (rGE)

Research in the area of genetics has also targeted the possibility of gene-environment interactions, i.e., genetically influenced individual differences in the sensitivity one has to specific environmental factors (Eaves, 1984; Mather & Jinks, 1982), and gene-environment correlations (rGE), which refer to the effects genes have on a person's likelihood of being exposed to particular environmental circumstances (Rutter & Silberg, 2002). Support for rGE is suggested by the evidence that, through their behavior, people to some extent shape and select their environments (Rutter, Dunn, Plomin, Simonoff, & Pickels, 1997), and this process can be either predominately active or passive (Rutter & Silberg, 2002). In other words individuals have a genetically influenced tendency to seek, create, or otherwise end up in particular kinds of environments. These two concepts may be important issues in the role of genetic and environmental influences on an individual's performance level in sport.

There is also evidence that physiological adaptations to intense practice lead to improvements in maximal oxygen consumption (VO2 max) (Benson, 1998; Cullinane, Sady, & Vadeboncouer, 1986; Dressendorfer, Wade, & Scaff, 1985; Houmard, Kirwan, & Flynn, 1989; Leitch, Clancy, & Flenley, 1975; Niemela, Palatsi, Ikaheimo, Takkunen, & Vuori, 1984; Patterson, Shephard, & Cunningham, 1979; Schulman, Fleg, & Goldberg, 1996; Spina, 1999; Spina, Ogawa, & Martin, 1992), and lactate threshold (Acavedo & Goldfarb, 1989; Costill, Thomason, & Roberts, 1973; Farrell, Wilmore, Coyle, Billing, & Costill, 1979; Keith, Jacobs, & McLellan, 1992; Lucia, Hoyos, Perez, & Chicharro, 2000; MacDougall, 1977; McCullagh, Poole, Halestrap, O'Brien, & Bonen, 1996; McDermott & Bonen, 1993; Sjodin, Jacobs, & Svedenhag, 1982; Tanaka et al., 1986; Weltman, 1989;

Weston, Karamizrak, Smith, Noakes, & Myburgh, 1999) in aerobic sporting contexts. Other research showed that neural adaptations are context-specific to the athlete's movement (Thorstensson & Karlsson, 1976), the speed of that movement (Seger, Arvidsson, & Thorstensson, 1998), and can cross over from one limb to the other (Moritani & DeVries, 1979). Motor recruitment patterns may be important in determining how efficiently an athlete moves (Conley & Krahenbuhl, 1980), and how explosive strength and power training added to existing practice regimens can elicit positive physiological adaptations (Paavolainen, Hakkinen, Hamalainen, Nummela, & Rusko, 1999), which may be due to neural adaptations (Hakkinen & Komi, 1985; Hakkinen, Komi, & Alen, 1985; Sale, 1991).

It has been shown that trained athletes are mechanically more efficient than untrained individuals (Morgan, Bransford, & Costill, 1995), and that economy in sports such as running may be related to the volume practiced by the athlete (Conley, Krahenbuhl, & Burkett, 1984; A. Jones, 1998; Pate, Macera, & Bailey, 1995). Additionally, Balson, Seger, Sjodin, and Ekblom (1992) showed that different recovery intervals affect athletes' ability to recruit motor units. Furthermore, athletes with similar VO2 max require different oxygen consumption at similar power output levels (Horowitz, Sidossis, & Coyle, 1994), and a lower VO2 max in some elite level runners can be compensated for with exceptional running economy (Londeree, 1986; Morgan et al., 1995). Therefore, there is a large variability in the amount of oxygen consumed by highly trained runners (Conley & Krahenbuhl, 1980; Morgan et al., 1995). Additionally, it was shown that running economy is made up of several factors including an athlete's anthropometrics, physiology, biomechanics, and technical factors (Bailey & Pate, 1991). This information leads to the likely conclusion that nature and nurture work together to influence the probability of expert athletic performance.

Previous research also showed that there is a minimal difference between sedentary and elite athletes in terms of the physiological adaptation effects of training, but there is a significant difference in what elite athletes focus on in order to elicit expertise. Elite runners, for example, having probably reached their potential VO2 max, and only being able to elicit small increases in their lactate threshold, can continue to make noticeable improvements in their running economy (Balson et al., 1992; Conley et al., 1984; Horowitz et al., 1994; A. Jones, 1998; Londeree, 1986; Morgan et al., 1995; Pate et al., 1995). Although continued research in this area will provide valuable insight, it appears that the efficiency of an athlete's technique may be a key to expert performance. Therefore, those who can adapt most efficiently to environmental conditions will achieve the highest levels of performance. Nevertheless, variables exist that are outside an athlete's control, i.e., genetics (Dennis & Noakes, 1999). Therefore, intelligent and purposeful training (i.e., deliberate practice) may only be capable of permitting an athlete to reach his or her performance potential, not expand it.

In addition to factors that have a direct influence on the level of expertise an athlete develops, there exists the very real possibility that a synergistic relationship exists between one's innate potential and his or her environment. The following section discusses the potential of the existence of such a relationship.

NATURE AND NURTURE INTERACTION

The interaction between "nature" factors and "nurture" factors may be a vital issue. In fastball sports, it is commonly acknowledged that a large portion of expertise develops during childhood (Ripoll & Benguigui, 1999). Therefore, expertise in some contexts may be dependent upon an interaction between the athlete's physical development and his or her environment. Maturational and experiential factors that result in expertise in childhood may be the result of early behavioral adaptations. However, early development seems to be specifically associated with natural settings, since this development only appears in the laboratory under conditions that closely match those found in sport domains. These developments lead to the possible conclusion that changes associated with perceptual, cognitive, and motor functions are related to both the structural maturation of the brain, and to the emergence of organizational patterns nurtured by the athlete's interaction with his or her environment (Nougier & Rossi, 1999). However, few studies have examined this possible interaction (Enns & Richards, 1997; Nougier, Azemar, Stein, & Ripoll, 1992).

Considering that an athlete is only a part of a very complex system involving environmental, physiological, and psychological subsystems, it may be the case that no single factor can explain a majority of either the development of, or the end result of reaching expert performance levels in sport. Therefore it appears highly likely that an enhanced environment (e.g., training or familial support) will improve an athlete's performance. However, the likelihood that an enhanced environment alone will result in a truly expert performance is not likely unless most, if not all, of the "nature" factors are present. Training may be able to only permit an athlete to attain his or her predetermined potential.

REFERENCES

Abernethy, B. (1990). Anticipation in squash: Differences in advance cue utilization between expert and novice players. *Journal of Sport Sciences, 8,* 17-34.

Abernethy, B. (1992). Visual search strategies and decision-making in sport. *International Journal of Sport Psychology, 22,* 189-210.

Abernethy, B., Farrow, D. & Berry, J. (2003). Constraints and issues in the development of a general theory of expert perceptual-motor performance. In J. L. Starkes & K. A. Ericsson (Eds.), *Expert performance in sports: Advances in research on sport expertise* (pp. 349-370). Champaign, IL: Human Kinetics.

Acavedo, E. & Goldfarb, A. (1989). Increased training intensity effects on plasma lactate, ventilatory threshold, and endurance. *Med Sci Sports Exercise, 21,* 563-568.

Azar, B. (1996). Why is it that practice makes perfect? Monitor: *American Psychological Association, 18.*

Bailey, S. & Pate, R. (1991). Feasibility of improving running economy. *Sports Medicine, 12,* 228-236.

Balson, P., Seger, J., Sjodin, B. & Ekblom, B. (1992). Maximal intensity intermittent exercise: effect of recovery duration. *International Journal of Sports Medicine, 13(7),* 528-533.

Bandura, A. (1977). Self-efficacy: Toward a unifying theory of behavioral change. *Psychological Review, 84,* 191-215.

Bandura, A. (1986). *Social foundation of thought and action: A social cognitive theory.* Englewood Cliffs, NJ: Prentice-Hall.

Bandura, A. (1990). Perceived self-efficacy in the exercise of personal agency. *Journal of Applied Sport Psychology, 2,* 128-163.

Bandura, A. (1997). *Self-efficacy: The exercise of control.* New York: Freeman.

Barnsley, R. H. & Thompson, A. H. (1988). Birthdate and success in minor hockey: The key to the NHL. *Canadian Journal of Behavioral Science, 20,* 167-176.

Bar-Or, O. (1975). Predicting athletic performance. *Physician and Sports Medicine, 3,* 81-85.

Bates, P. B. (1998). Testing the limits of the ontogentic sources of talent and excellence. *Behavioral and Brain Sciences, 21,* 407-408.

Baxter-Jones, A., Helms, P., Maffull, N., Baines-Preece, J. & Preece, M. (1995). Growth and development of male gymnasts, swimmers, soccer and tennis players: A longitudinal study. *Annals of Human Biology, 22,* 381-394.

Benson, R. (1998). Running. In E. R. Burke (Ed.), *Precision heart rate training* (pp. 68-69). Champaign, IL: Human Kinetics.

Beunen, G. & Thomis, M. (1999). Genetic determinants of sports participation and daily physical activity. *International Journal of Obese Related Metabolic Disorders, 23* (Supplement 3), S55-S63.

Bloom, B. S. (1985). *Developing talent in young people.* New York: Ballentine.

Bouchard, C. (1988). Genetic basis of racial differences. *Canadian Journal of Sports Science, 13(2),* 104-108.

Bouchard, C., Lesage, R., Lortie, G., Simoneau, J. A., P., H., Boulay, M., et al. (1986). Aerobic performance in brothers, dizogotic and monozygotic twins. *Medicine and Science in Sports and Exercise, 18(6),* 639-646.

Bouchard, T. J. (1994). *Genes, environment and personality. Science, 264,* 1700-1701.

Bouchard, T. J. (1997). IQ similarity in twins reared apart: Findings and response to critics. In R. J. Sternberg & E. L. Grigorenko (Eds.), *Intelligence: Heredity and environment* (pp. 126-160). New York: Cambridge University Press.

Boucher, J. & Mutimer, B. (1994). The relative age phenomenon in sport: A replication and extension with ice-hockey players. *Research Quarterly for Exercise and Sport, 65,* 371-381.

Brewer, J., Balsom, P., Davis, J. & Ekblom, B. (1992). The influence of birth date and physical development on the selection of a male junior international soccer squad. *Journal of Sport Sciences, 10,* 561-562.

Charness, N. (1998). Explaining exceptional performance: Constituent abilities and touchstone phenomena. *Behavioral and Brain Sciences, 21,* 410-411.

Coakley, J. (1992). Burnout among adolescent athletes: A personal failure or social problem. *Sociology of Sport Journal, 9,* 271-285.

Conley, D. & Krahenbuhl, G. (1980). Running economy and distance running performance of highly trained athletes. *Med Sci Sports Exercise, 12,* 357-360.

Conley, D., Krahenbuhl, G. & Burkett, L. (1984). Following Steve Scott: Physiological changes accompanying training. *Physician and Sports Medicine, 12,* 103-106.

Costill, D., Thomason, H. & Roberts, E. (1973). Fractional utilization of the aerobic capacity during distance running. *Med Sci Sports Exercise, 5,* 248-252.

Côté, J. (1999). The influence of the family in the development of talent in sport. *The Sport Psychologist, 13,* 395-417.

Csikszentmihalyi, M. (1998). Fruitless polarities. *Behavioral and Brain Sciences, 21,* 411.

Cullinane, E. L., Sady, S. T. & Vadeboncouer, L. (1986). Cardiac size and VO_2max do not decrease after short-term exercise cessation. *Med Sci Sports Exercise, 18,* 420-424.

Darwin, C. (1859/1964). *On the origin of species.* Cambridge, MA: Harvard University Press.

Dawes, R. M. (1994). *House of cards: Psychology and psychotherapy built on myth.* New York: Free Press.

Deakin, J. M. & Cobley, S. (2003). An examination of the practice environments in figure skating and volleyball: A search for deliberate practice. In J. L. Starkes & K. A. Ericsson (Eds.), *Recent advances in research on sport expertise.* Champaign, IL: Human Kinetics.

Dennis, S. & Noakes, T. (1999). Advantages of a smaller bodymass in humans when distance running in warm, humid conditions. *European Journal of Applied Physiology, 79,* 280-284.

Detterman, D. K., Gabriel, L. T., & Ruthsatz, J. M. (1998). Absurd environmentalism. *Behavioral and Brain Sciences, 21,* 411-412.

Dishman, R. K. (1982). Compliance/adherence in health related exercise. *Health Psychology, 1(3),* 237-267.

Dishman, R. K. (2006). Does cardiorespiratory fitness moderate stress responses and recovery? In D. Hackfort & G. Tenenbaum (Eds.), *Essential Processes in Attaining Peak Performance* (pp. 110-136). Oxford: Meyer & Meyer.

Dressendorfer, R., Wade, C. & Scaff, J. (1985). Increased morning heart rate in runners: a sign of overtraining? *The Physician and Sportsmedicine, 13(8),* 77-86.

Dudink, A. (1994). Birth date and sporting success. *Nature, 368,* 592.

Dunn, J. F., Stocker, C. & Plomin, R. (1990). Nonshared experiences within the family: Correlates of behavioral problems in adult twins. *Developmental Psychopathology, 2,* 113-126.

Durand-Bush, N. (2000). *The development and maintenance of expert performance: Perceptions of Olympic and world champions.* Unpublished doctoral dissertation, University of Ottawa, Canada.

Durand-Bush, N. & Salmela, J. H. (2001). The development of talent in sport. In R. N. Singer, H. A. Hausenblas & C. M. Janelle (Eds.), *Handbook of sport psychology* (2nd ed., pp. 269-289). New York: Wiley.

Dweck, C. S. (1986). Motivational processes affecting learning. *American Psychologist, 41,* 1040-1048.

Eaves, L. J. (1984). The resolution of genotype x environment interaction in segregation analysis of nuclear families. *Genetic Epidemiology, 1,* 215-228.

Eaves, L. J. & Eysenck, H. J. (1974). Genetics and the development of social attitudes. *Nature, 249,* 288-289.

Eisenberger, R. (1998). Achievement: The importance of industriousness. *Behavioral and Brain Sciences, 21,* 412-413.

Enns, J. & Richards, J. (1997). Visual attentional orienting in developing hockey players. *Journal of Experimental Child Psychology, 64,* 255-275.

Entine, J. (2001, December). The race to the swift - if the swift have the right ancestry. *Peak Performance, 12,* 1-6.

Ericsson, K. A. (1990). Peak performance and age: An examination of peak performance in sports. In P. B. Baltes & M. M. Baltes (Eds.), *Successful aging: Perspectives from the behavioral sciences* (pp. 164-195). Cambridge: Cambridge University Press.

Ericsson, K. A. (1996). The acquisition of expert performance: An introduction to some of the issues. In K. A. Ericsson (Ed.), *The road to excellence: The acquisition of expert performance in the arts and sciences, sports, and games* (pp. 1-50). Mahwah, NJ: Lawrence Erlbaum Associates.

Ericsson, K. A. (1998a). Basic capacities can be modified or circumvented by deliberate practice: A rejection of talent accounts of expert performance. *Behavioral and Brain Sciences, 21,* 413-414.

Ericsson, K. A. (1998b). The scientific study of expert levels of performance: General implications for optimal learning and creativity. *High Ability Studies, 9(1),* 75-100.

Ericsson, K. A. (2003). The development of elite performance and deliberate practice: An update from the perspective of the expert-performance approach. In J. L. Starkes & K. A. Ericsson (Eds.), *Recent advances in research on sport expertise.* Champaign, IL: Human Kinetics.

Ericsson, K. A. & Charness, N. (1994). The relative age phenomenon in sport: A replication and extension with ice-hockey players. *American Psychologist, 49, 725-747.*

Ericsson, K. A., Krampe, R. T. & Tesch-Romer, C. (1993). The role of deliberate practice in the acquisition of expert performance. *Psychological Review, 100,* 363-406.

Ericsson, K. A. & Lehman, A. C. (1996). Expert and exceptional performance: Evidence of maximal adaptation to task constraints. *Annual Review of Psychology, 47,* 273-305.

Eysenck, H. J. (1995). *Genius: The natural history of creativity.* Cambridge, UK: Cambridge University Press.

Fagard, R., Bielen, E. & Amery, A. (1991). Heritability of aerobic power and anaerobic energy generation during exercise. *Journal of Applied Physiology, 70(1),* 357-362.

Farrell, P., Wilmore, J., Coyle, E., Billing, J. & Costill, D. (1979). Plasma lactate accumulation and distance running performance. *Med Sci Sports Exercise, 11,* 338-344.

Feldman, D. H. & Katzir, T. (1998). Natural talents: An argument for the extremes. *Behavioral and Brain Sciences, 21,* 414.

Feltz, D. L. & Lirgg, C. D. (2001). Self-efficacy beliefs of athletes, teams, and coaches. In R. N. Singer, H. A. Hausenblas & C. M. Janelle (Eds.), *Handbook of sport psychology* (Vol. 2, pp. 340-361). New York: Wiley and Sons.

French, K. E. & Thomas, J. (1987). The relation of knowledge development to children's basketball performance. *Journal of Sport & Exercise Psychology, 9,* 15-32.

Gagne, F. (1998). A biased survey and interpretation of the nature-nurture literature. *Behavioral and Brain Sciences, 21,* 415-416.

Ge, X., Conger, R. D., Cadoret, R. J., Neiderhiser, J. M. & Yates, W. (1996). The developmental interface between nature and nurture: A mutual influence model of child antisocial behavior and parent behaviors. *Developmental Psychology, 32,* 574-589.

Geron, E. (1978). *Psychological assessment of sport giftedness.* Paper presented at the International symposium on psychological assessment in sport, Netanya, Israel.

Gimbel, B. (1976). Possibilities and problems in sports talent detection research. *Leistungssport, 6,* 159-167.

Gollnick, P. D. & Matoba, H. (1984). The muscle fiber composition of skeletal muscle as a predictor of athletic success: An overview. *The American Journal of Sports Medicine, 12(3),* 212-217.

Gualdi-Russo, E., & Graziani, I. (1993). Anthropometric somatotype of Italian sport participants. *The Journal of Sports Medicine and Physical Fitness, 33(3),* 282-291.

Gyagay, G., Yu, B., Boston, T., Hahn, A., Celermajer, D. S. & Trent, R. J. (1998). Elite endurance athletes and the ACE I allele - the role of genes in athletic performance. *Human Genetics, 103(1),* 48-50.

Hagberg, J. M., Moore, G. E. & Ferrell, R. E. (2001). Specific genetic markers of endurance performance and VO_2max. *Exercise and Sport Science Review, 29(1),* 15-19.

Hakkinen, K. & Komi, P. (1985). Effects of explosive type strength training on electromyographic and force production characteristics of leg extensor muscles during concentric and various stretch-shortening cycle exercises. *Scandinavian Journal of Sport Science, 7,* 65-76.

Hakkinen, K., Komi, P. & Alen, M. (1985). Effects of explosive type strength training on isometric force and relaxation time, electromyographic and muscle fibre characteristics of leg extensor muscles. *Acta Physiologica Scandinavica, 125,* 587-600.

Hanin, Y. (1980). A study of anxiety in sports. In W. F. Straub (Ed.), *Sport psychology: An analysis of athlete behavior* (pp. 236-249). Ithaca, NY: Mouvement.

Harre, D. (1982). *Trainingslehre.* Berlin, Germany: Sportverlag.

Hatfield, B. (1991). Exercise and mental health: The mechanisms of exercise-induced psychological states. In L. Diamant (Ed.), *Psychology of sports, exercise, and fitness.* New York: Hemisphere.

Havlicek, I., Komadel, L., Komarik, E. & Simkova, N. (1982). *Principles of the selection of youth talented in sport.* Paper presented at the International Conference on the Selection and Preparation of Sport Talent, Bratislava, Czechoslovakia.

Heller, K. A. & Ziegler, A. (1998). Experience is no improvement over talent. *Behavioral and Brain Sciences, 21,* 417-418.

Helsen, W., Hodges, N. J., Van Winckel, J. & Starkes, J. L. (2000). The roles of talent, physical precocity, and practice in the development of soccer expertise. *Journal of Sport Sciences, 18(9),* 727-736.

Helsen, W., Starkes, J. L. & Hodges, N. J. (1998). Team sports and the theory of deliberate practice. *Journal of Sport & Exercise Psychology, 20,* 13-25.

Hodge, T. & Deakin, J. M. (1998). Deliberate practice and expertise in the marial arts: The role of context in motor recall. *Journal of Sport & Exercise Psychology, 20(3),* 260-279.

Hodges, N. J. & Starkes, J. L. (1996). Wrestling with the nature of expertise: A sport specific test of Ericsson, Krampe, and Tesch-Romer's (1993) theory of deliberate practice. *International Journal of Sport Psychology, 27,* 400-424.

Horowitz, J., Sidossis, L. & Coyle, E. (1994). High efficiency of type I muscle fibers improves performance. *International Journal of Sports Medicine, 15,* 152-157.

Houmard, J. A., Kirwan, J. P. & Flynn, M. G. (1989). Effect of reduced training on submaximal and maximal running responses. *International Journal of Sports Medicine, 10,* 30-33.

Howe, M. J. A., Davidson, J. W. & Sloboda, J. A. (1998). Innate talents: Reality or myth? *Behavioral and Brain Sciences, 21,* 399-442.

Hur, Y., McGue, M. & Iancono, W. G. (1996). Genetic and shared environmental influences on leisure-time interests in male adolescents. *Personality Individual Differences, 21(5),* 791-801.

Irvine, S. H. (1998). Innate talents: A psychological tautology. *Behavioral and Brain Sciences, 21,* 419.

Jones, A. (1998). A 5-year physiological case study of an Olympic runner. *British Journal of Sport Medicine, 32,* 39-43.

Jones, M. B., & Watson, G. G. (1977). *Psychological factors in the prediction of athletic performance.* Paper presented at the International Symposium on Psychological Assessment in Sport, Netanya, Israel.

Kalinowski, A. G. (1985). The development of Olympic swimmers. In B. S. Bloom (Ed.), *Developing talent in young people* (pp. 139-192). New York: Ballentine.

Keele, S. W., & Ivry, R. I. (1987). Modular analysis of timing in motor skill. In G. E. Bower (Ed.), *The psychology of learning and motivation* (pp. 183-228). New York: Academic Press.

Keith, S., Jacobs, I. & McLellan, T. (1992). Adaptations to training at the individual anaerobic threshold. *European Journal of Applied Physiology, 65,* 316-323.

Kerr, J. H. (1989). Anxiety, arousal, and sport performance. In D. Hackfort & C. Spielberger (Eds.), *Anxiety in sports: An international perspective* (pp. 137-151). New York: Hemisphere.

Krampe, R. T. & Ericsson, K. A. (1996). Maintaining excellence: Deliberate practice and elite performance in young and older pianists. *Journal of Experimental Psychology: General, 124(4),* 331-359.

Landauer, & Whiting. (1983). In V. Guidano & G. Liotti (Eds.), Cognitive processes and emotional disorders. New York: Guilford Press.

Lehman, A. C. (1998). Historical increases in expert performance suggest large possibilities for improvement of performance without implicating innate capacities. *Behavioral and Brain Sciences, 21,* 419-420.

Leitch, A. G., Clancy, L. & Flenley, D. C. (1975). Maximal oxygen uptake, lung volume and ventilatory response to carbon dioxide and hypoxia in a pair of identical twin athletes. *Clinical Science and Molecular Medicine, 48(3),* 235-238.

Loehlin, J. C. (1992). *Genes and environment in personality development.* Newbury Park, CA: Sage.

Londeree, B. (1986). The use of laboratory test results with long distance runners. *Sports Medicine, 3,* 201-213.

Lucia, A., Hoyos, J., Perez, M. & Chicharro, J. (2000). Heart rate and performance parameters in elite cyclists: a longitudinal study. *Med Sci Sports Exercise, 32,* 1777-1782.

Lytton, H. (1990). Child and parent effects in boys' conduct disorder: A reinterpretation. *Developmental Psychology, 26,* 683-697.

MacDougall, J. (1977). The anaerobic threshold: its significance for the endurance athlete. *Canadian Journal of Sports Science, 2,* 137-140.

Malina, R. M. (1994). The young athlete: Biological growth and maturation in a biocultural context. *Exercise and Sport Science Review, 22,* 389-433.

Malina, R. M. (1996). The young athlete: Biological growth and maturation in a biocultural context. In F. L. Smoll & R. E. Smith (Eds.), *Children and youth sport* (pp. 161-186). Dubuque, IA: Brown & Benchmark.

Margenau, E. (1990). *Sports without pressure.* New York: Gardner Press.

Markoff, R. A., Ryan, P., & Young, T. (1982). Endorphins and mood changes in long-distance running. *Medicine and Science in Sports and Exercise, 14,* 11-15.

Mather, K., & Jinks, J. L. (1982). *Biometrical genetics: The study of continuous variation.* London: Chapman & Hall.

McCullagh, K., Poole, R., Halestrap, A., O'Brien, M. & Bonen, A. (1996). Role of the lactate transporter (MCT-1) in skeletal muscles. *American Journal of Physiology, 271* (Endocrinology and Metabolism 34), E143-150.

McDermott, J. & Bonen, A. (1993). Endurance training increases skeletal muscle lactate transport. *Acta Physiologica Scandinavica, 147(3),* 323-327.

McGue, M. & Bouchard, T. J. (1998). Genetic and environmental influences on human behavioral differences. *Annual Review of Neuroscience, 21,* 1-24.

McPherson, S. L. & Thomas, J. (1989). Relation of knowledge and precision in boys' tennis: Age and expertise. *Journal of Experimental Child Psychology, 48,* 190-211.

Monsaas, J. A. (1985). Learning to be a world-class tennis player. In B. S. Bloom (Ed.), *Developing talent in young people* (pp. 211-269). New York: Ballentine.

Montpetit, R. & Cazorla, G. (1982). La detection du talent en natation. *La Revue de l'Entraineur, 5,* 26-37.

Morgan, D., Bransford, D., & Costill, D. (1995). Variation in the aerobic demand of running among trained and untrained subjects. *Med Sci Sports Exercise, 27,* 404-409.

Moritani, T. & DeVries, H. (1979). Neural factors vs. hypertrophy in time course of muscle strength gain. *American Journal of Physiology & Medical Rehabilitation, 58,* 115-130.

Newell, A., & Rosenbloom, P. S. (1981). Mechanisms of skill acquisition and the law of practice. In J. R. Anderson (Ed.), *Cognitive skills and their acquisition* (pp. 1-55). Nillsdale, N J: Erlbaum.

Niemela, K., Palatsi, I., Ikaheimo, M., Takkunen, J. & Vuori, J. (1984). Evidence of impaired left ventricular performance after an uninterrupted competitive 24-hour run. *Circulation, 70,* 350-356.

Nougier, V., Azemar, G., Stein, J. F. & Ripoll, H. (1992). Covert orienting to central visual cues and sport practice relations in the development of visual attention. *Journal of Experimental Child Psychology, 54,* 347-362.

Nougier, V., & Rossi, B. (1999). The development of expertise in the orienting of attention. *International Journal of Sport Psychology, 30,* 246-260.

Paavolainen, L., Hakkinen, K., Hamalainen, I., Nummela, A. & Rusko, H. (1999). Explosive strength training improves 5-km running time by improving running economy and muscle power. *Journal of Applied Physiology, 86(5)*, 1527-1533.

Pate, R., Macera, C. & Bailey, S. (1995). Physiological, anthropometric, and training correlates of running economy. *Med Sci Sports Exercise, 24,* 1128-1133.

Patterson, D., Shephard, R. & Cunningham, D. (1979). Effects of physical training upon cardiovascular function following myocardial infarction. *Journal of Applied Physiology, 47(482-489).*

Pederson, N. L., Plomin, R., Nesselroade, J. R. & McClearn, G. E. (1992). A quantitative genetic analysis of cognitive abilities during the second half of the life span. *Psychological Science, 3,* 346-353.

Pelliccia, A. (1996). Determinants of morphologic cardiac adaptation in elite athletes: The role of athletic training and constitutional factors. *International Journal of Sports Medicine, 17(3),* S157-S163.

Pike, A., McGuire, S., Hetherington, E. M., Reiss, D. & Plomin, R. (1996). Family environment and adolescent depressive symptoms and antisocial behavior: A multivariate genetic analysis. *Developmental Psychology, 32,* 590-603.

Plomin, R. (1998). Genetic influence and cognitive abilities. *Behavioral and Brain Sciences, 21,* 420-421.

Plomin, R., Owen, M. J. & McGuffin, P. (1994). The genetic basis of complex human behaviors. *Science, 264,* 1733-1739.

Prud'Homme, D., Bouchard, C., Leblanc, C., Landry, F & Fontaine, E. (1984). Sensitivity of maximal aerobic power to training is genotype-dependent. *Medicine and Science in Sports and Exercise, 16(5),* 489-193.

Ripoll, H., & Benguigui, N. (1999). Evergence of expertise in ball sports during child development. *International Journal of Sport Psychology, 30,* 235-245.

Roberts, G. C., Treasure, D. C. & Hall, H. K. (1994). Parental goal orientations and beliefs about the competitive sport experience of their child. *Journal of Applied Social Psychology, 24,* 634-645.

Rodas, G., Calvo, M., Estruch, A., Garrido, E., Ercilla, G., Arcas, A., et al. (1998). Heritability of running economy: A study made on twin brothers. *European Journal of Applied Physiology, 77(6),* 511-516.

Rose, R. J. (1995). Genes and human behavior. *Annual Review of Psychology, 46,* 625-654.

Rowe, D. C. (1998). Talent scouts, not practice scouts: Talents are real. *Behavioral and Brain Sciences, 21,* 421-422.

Rutter, M. (1998). What can we learn from highly developed special skills? *Behavioral and Brain Sciences, 21,* 422-423.

Rutter, M. (2000). Psychosocial influences: Critiques, findings, and research needs. *Developmental Psychopathology, 12,* 375-405.

Rutter, M., Dunn, J. F, Plomin, R., Simonoff, E. & Pickels, A. (1997). Integrating nature and nurture: Implications of person-environment correlations and interactions for developmental psychology. *Developmental Psychopathology, 9,* 335-364.

Rutter, M., & Silberg, J. (2002). Gene-environment interplay in relation to emotional and behavioral disturbance. *Annual Review of Psychology, 53,* 463-490.

Sacks, M. H. (1981). Running - A psychosocial phenomenon. In L. Diamant (Ed.), *Psychology of Sports, Exercise, and Fitness* (pp. 237-248). New York: Hemisphere.

Sale, D. (1991). Neural adaptation to strength training. In P. Komi (Ed.), *Strength and power in sports. The encyclopedia of sports medicine* (pp. 249-265). Oxford, UK: Blackwell.

Scarr, S. & Weinberg, R. A. (1981). The transmission of authoritarianism in families: Genetic resemblance in social-political attitudes. In S. Scarr (Ed.), *Race, social class, and individual differences.* Hillsdale, NJ: Erlbaum.

Schlaug, G., Jancke, L., Huang, Y. & Steinmetz, H. (1995). In vivo evidence of structural brain asymmetry in musicians. *Science, 267,* 699-701.

Schneider, W. (1998). Innate talent or deliberate practice as determinants of exceptional performance: Are we asking the right questions? *Behavioral and Brain Sciences, 21,* 423-424.

Schulman, S. P., Fleg, J. L. & Goldberg, A. P. (1996). Continuum of cardiovascular performance across a broad range of fitness levels in healthy older men. *Circulation, 94,* 359-367.

Schulz, R. & Curnow, C. (1988). Peak performance and age among superathletes: Track and field, swimming, baseball, tennis, and golf. *Journal of Gerontology: Psychological Sciences, 43,* 113-120.

Seger, J., Arvidsson, B. & Thorstensson, A. (1998). Specific effects of eccentric and concentric training on muscle strength and morphology in humans. *European Journal of Applied Physiology, 79,* 49-57.

Simonton, D. K. (1994). *Greatness: Who makes history and why.* New York: The Guilford Press.

Simonton, D. K. (1998). Defining and finding talent: Data and a multiplicative model? *Behavioral and Brain Sciences, 21,* 424-425.

Sjodin, B., Jacobs, I. & Svedenhag, J. (1982). Changes in onset of blood lactate accumulation (OBLA) and muscle enzymes after training at OBLA. *European Journal of Applied Physiology, 29,* 45-57.

Solomon, R. L. (1977). An opponent process theory of motivation: The affective dynamics of drug addiction. In J. D. Maser & M. E. P. Seligman (Eds.), *Psychopathology: Experimental models* (pp. 66-103). San Francisco: W. H. Freeman.

Spina, R. (1999). Cardiovascular adaptations to endurance exercise training in older men and women. *Exercise and Sport Science Review, 27,* 317-332.

Spina, R., Ogawa, T., & Martin, T. (1992). Exercise training prevents decline in stroke volume during exercise in young healthy subjects. *Journal of Applied Physiology, 72,* 2458-2462.

Spurgeon, J. H. & Giese, W. K. (1980). Physique of world-class female basketball players. *Scandinavian Journal of Sport Science, 2,* 63-69.

Spurgeon, J. H., Spurgeon, N. L. & Giese, W. K. (1984). Physique of world-class female swimmers. *Scandinavian Journal of Sport Science, 1,* 11-14.

Stael von Holstein, C. A. S. (1972). Probabilistic forecasting: An experiment related to the stock market. *Organizational Behavior and Human Performance, 8,* 139-158.

Starkes, J. L. (1987). Skill in field hockey: The nature of the cognitive advantage. *Journal of Sport & Exercise Psychology, 9,* 146-160.

Starkes, J. L., Deakin, J. M., Allard, F., Hodges, N. J. & Hayes, A. (1996). Deliberate practice in sport: What is it anyway? In K. A. Ericsson (Ed.), *The road to excellence: The acquisition of expert performance in the arts and science, sports and games* (pp. 81-106). Mahwah, NJ: Erlbaum.

Starkes, J. L., & Helsen, W. (1998). Practice, practice, practice: Is that all it takes? *Behavioral and Brain Sciences, 21*, 425-426.

Sternberg, R. J. (1996). Costs of expertise. In K. A. Ericsson (Ed.), *The road to excellence: The acquisition of expert performance in the arts and sciences, sports, and games.* Mahwah, NJ: Erlbaum.

Sternberg, R. J. (1998). If the key's not there, the light won't help. Behavioral and Brain *Sciences, 21*, 425-426.

Stevenson, C. L. (1990). The early careers of international athletes. *Sociology of Sport Journal, 22*, 591-601.

Takeuchi, A. H. & Hulse, S. H. (1993). Absolute pitch. *Psychological Bulletin, 113*, 345-361.

Tanaka, K., Watanabe, H., Konishi, Y., Mitsuzono, R., Sumida, S., Tanaka, S., et al. (1986). Longitudinal associations between anaerobic threshold and distance running performance. *European Journal of Applied Physiology, 55(3)*, 248-252.

Teasdale, T. W. & Owen, D. R. (1984). Heritability and familial environment in intelligence and educational level - a sibling study. *Nature, 309*, 620-622.

Tenenbaum, G. (1999). The development of expertise in sport: Nature and nurture. *International Journal of Sport Psychology, 30*, 113-116.

Tesch-Romer, C. (1998). Attributed talent is a powerful myth. *Behavioral and Brain Sciences, 21*, 427.

Thomas, J. R. & Thomas, K. T. (1998). Senior women of lower and higher golf handicaps: How psychological and physiological characteristics influence performance. *In Science and golf III.* Champaign, IL: Human Kinetics.

Thomas, K. T. (1994). The development of expertise: From Leeds to legend. *Quest, 46*, 199-210.

Thomas, K. T. & Thomas, J. (1999). What squirrels in the trees predicts about expert athletes. *International Journal of Sport Psychology, 30*, 221-234.

Thompson, A. H., Barnsley, R. H. & Stebelsky, G. (1991). Born to play ball: The relative age effect and major league baseball. *Sociology of Sport Journal, 8*, 146-151.

Thorstensson, A. & Karlsson, J. (1976). Effect of strength training on EMG of human skeletal muscle. *Acta Physiologica Scandinavica, 98*, 232-236.

Trehub, S. E. & Schellenberg, E. G. (1998). Cultural determinism is no better than biological determinism. *Behavioral and Brain Sciences, 21*, 427-428.

Waller, N. G., Kojetin, B. A., Bouchard, T. J., Lykken, D. T. & Tellegen, A. (1990). Genetic and environmental influences on religious interests, attitudes, and values: A study of twins reared apart and together. *Psychological Science, 1*, 1-5.

Watanabe, G. (2000). *Explanatory perspectives of enjoyment during effortful practice for competitive swimmers of varying levels of expertise.* Unpublished master thesis, School of Human Kinetics, University of Ottawa.

Weisberg, R. W. (1998). Creativity and practice. *Behavioral and Brain Sciences, 21*, 429-430.

Weltman, A. (1989). The lactate threshold and endurance performance. *Advances in Sports Medicine & Fitness, 2*, 91-116.

Weston, A., Karamizrak, O., Smith, A., Noakes, T. & Myburgh, K. (1999). African runners exhibit greater fatigue resistance, lower lactate accumulation, and higher oxidative enzyme activity. *Journal of Applied Physiology, 86(3)*, 915-923.

Winner, E. (1996a). *Gifted children: Myths and realities.* New York: Basic Books.

Winner, E. (1996b). The rage to master: The decisive role of talent in the visual arts. In K. A. Ericsson (Ed.), *The road to excellence* (pp. 271-302). Mahwah, NJ: Erlbaum.

Winner, E. (1998). Talent: Don't confuse necessity with sufficiency, or science with policy. *Behavioral and Brain Sciences, 21,* 430-431.

Young, B. W. (1998). *Deliberate practice and skill acquisition in Canadian middle distance running.* Unpublished master's thesis, University of Ottawa, Canada.

Young, B. W. & Salmela, J. H. (2002). Perceptions of training and deliberate practice of middle distance runners. *International Journal of Sport Psychology, 33,* 167-181.

Zohar, A. H. (1998). Individual differences in some special abilities are genetically influenced. *Behavioral and Brain Sciences, 21,* 431-432.

THE ROLE OF THE FAMILY IN ATHLETIC PERFORMANCE: NATURAL AND ENVIRONMENTAL INFLUENCES

DAVID N. SACKS, DAVID PARGMAN AND GERSHON TENENBAUM

CONTENTS

SUMMARY

It is clear that one's family plays a major role in the unique personality, talents, and other characteristics that one develops. The question is the extent to which the family's contribution reflects genetic dispositions passed from parents to children, environmental influences stemming from the dynamics inherent in the family system, or an interaction of both.

The genetic and environmental aspects of a sport-involved family's influence on an athlete have not been well delineated. Thus, this chapter begins with a brief overview of the evidence for genetic and environmental familial influences on non sport-related psychological characteristics, including mental health and intelligence. The potential for applying principles derived from these areas to the study of family influences in sport are discussed. We then address findings and implications for family influences on the development of talent and expertise, with particular attention to the role of the family in sport-related outcomes. Areas discussed include parental correlates of athlete anxiety and enjoyment, the intensity of family involvement, and the interaction between family health and level of involvement. The chapter concludes by briefly addressing issues emerging when one employs a systemic approach to view family influences in sport. These topics include challenges in measuring family dynamics and treating the family system, rather than the individual, as the unit of inquiry.

INTRODUCTION

Any discussion of genetic (natural) and environmental (nurtured) factors on individual differences must, by necessity, include consideration of the individual's family of origin. It is clear that one's family plays a major role in the unique personality, talents, and other characteristics that one develops. The question is the extent to which the family's contribution reflects genetic dispositions passed from parents to children, environmental influences stemming from the dynamics inherent in the family system, or an interaction of both.

This chapter begins with a brief overview of the evidence for genetic and environmental familial influences on selected psychological characteristics. It then addresses findings and implications for family influences on the development of talent and expertise, with particular attention to the role of the family in sport-related outcomes. The chapter concludes with several additional considerations, from a family systems perspective, regarding the family's influence on an individual's sport experience.

FAMILY INFLUENCES ON PSYCHOLOGICAL OUTCOMES

While the purpose of this chapter is to explicate family influences on athletic performance, by first devoting some attention to its impact on broader psychological variables, the family's effect on sport-related outcomes may be viewed in this broader context. Thus, this section addresses family genetic and environmental influences on the development of mental health and substance-related disorders, as well as intelligence and other abilities.

INFLUENCES ON PSYCHOLOGICAL DISORDERS

It is quite well established that a number of psychological disorders do run in families (Zuckerman, 1999). The extent to which this trend is due to the family environment, as opposed to genetics, is unclear. However, several adoption and twin studies support the notion that genetics do play a causal role in the development of substance-related disorders. (see, for example, Goodwin et al., 1974; McGue, 1993; Pickens et al., 1991). The methodology in these studies typically involves sampling children, some of whom were adopted and others of whom were raised by their biological parents, but all of whom were born to parents with certain substance-related disorders. Results indicate that even when children are adopted at birth, wherein an addicted father contributes only his genes, the risk for substance-related disorders in his children increases significantly (Zuckerman, 1999).

It may seem unusual to begin a discussion of family influences on athletic performance with a brief discourse on psychological disorders. There are several reasons for doing so. First, a number of studies have elucidated the genetic and environmental influences of families on the emergence of psychological disorders (especially substance-related disorders) in their children. A second reason for exploring disorders comes from recognizing trends in the findings, which demonstrate that while both genetics and family environments have an influence, neither has a deterministic effect on individual outcomes. That is, neither heritable traits nor a particular home environment ensure that a child will develop a disorder. While not yet tested empirically, it is reasonable to assume that this principle holds true for sport-related outcomes as well. Finally, the evidence indicates that a child who inherits a disposition to develop substance-related disorders, and who also lives in a home with one or more adults with such disorders, has the highest risk of developing a substance-related disorder himself. One may infer a parallel principle in sport, in which a child endowed with superior genes, and who also is raised in a family that values sport, has the highest probability of developing talent.

Of course, one might question the appropriateness of borrowing principles discovered via the study of psychological disorders, which individuals and society generally attempt to *avoid*, and summarily applying these findings to athletic performance, which many individuals and families strive to *enhance*. Clearly, forming hypotheses related to these principles and testing them with studies that sample from among various sport populations is an appropriate direction for future research. A more contiguous area of inquiry yielding similar principles involves natural and environmental influences of the family on intelligence and other abilities.

INFLUENCES ON INTELLIGENCE AND OTHER ABILITIES

Controversy has existed for some time regarding the heritability of certain aptitudes, with an emphasis on intelligence (Hernstein & Murray, 1994; Neisser et al., 1996). While debate remains, the preponderance of the evidence suggests that much of the variability in intelligence test scores is accounted for by variance in genetic factors. Estimates regarding the influence of genes for children are on the order of 45% explained variance. However, this influence appears to increase with age, with estimates as high as 75% variance accounted for by late adolescence, and from 68% to 78% for adults (Neisser et al., 1996). Conversely, environmental influences tend to decrease with age, accounting for only 35% of the variability in childhood IQ scores, and decreasing to almost zero by adolescence. Some research has suggested that these trends hold true for a number of other abilities and individual outcomes as well (see Plomin, DeFries, McClearn, & McGuffin, 2001).

These findings may at first seem counterintuitive, as one might expect genetic influences to decrease over time, as individuals experience more and more varied environmental influences during adolescence and adulthood. In fact, the results have surprised the behavioral geneticists conducting this line of research (Gottfredson, 2002). However, when one considers that genetic and environmental factors *interact* with one another to influence individual differences, these findings appear quite logical.

Consider two children: one born with an inherited potential to develop a high IQ, the other born with lower levels of such genetic fabric. If both children are exposed for an extended period of time to a learning environment with incomplete instruction (i.e., their teachers do not cover all of the material in great detail), these students will not derive equal benefit from their similar experiences. The research suggests that the child born to parents with higher IQs will derive the greater benefit from this environment. Thus, the genetic factors have greater explanatory power than does the environment, as individuals with certain genotypes benefit more from the same experience than do other individuals (Gottfredson, 2002).

It should be noted that meaningful differences do exist between athletic and traditional educational environments, and the unique effects of genetic and environmental factors may differ somewhat in sport-related contexts. The vast majority of all children attend some type of educational setting, while a much smaller proportion experience sport environments. Thus, while most individuals do have the opportunity to benefit from gene-environment interactive effects on intelligence, only a portion of those with the genetic potential actually have occasion to exercise these capabilities through sport experiences. The research shows that families, especially parents, have a meaningful level of influence both on their children's entry into sport and exercise environments (Jambor, 1999; Kimiecik, Horn, & Shurin, 1996), as well as their decision to persevere in their athletic experiences (Coakley, 1992).

This caution notwithstanding, the gene-environment interaction principles described above can be related to sport. Consider two young athletes who begin a training program with vastly different inherited potentials. Given the same training conditions, they are unlikely to benefit equally. Given identical levels of motivation and previous exposure, the athlete who brings to the environment the greater genetic potential will see a greater increase in performance than will his less genetically gifted counterpart, and these differences will increase over time. That is, with increased exposure to the same environment, the genetic factors will become increasingly influential.

It should also be noted that an ostensibly similar environment may be perceived quite differently by different athletes. Thus, while comparable training and social conditions may indeed have strong influences on each individual, these effects could be largely idiosyncratic, and they could go undetected by studies employing traditional methods designed to quantify proportions of explained variance.

While here again we are looking to research in other areas to infer the extent to which natural and environmental influences sport-related outcomes, there is also evidence that genetic factors do influence a variety of life outcomes, including education level, occupation, and income (Plomin, Lichtenstein, Pederson, McClearn, & Nesselroade, 1990). Notwithstanding arguments that genetic influences are minimal on certain outcomes (Ericsson & Charness, 1994), it is reasonable to expect that similar patterns will emerge in sport-related research, especially if one considers increasingly influential theories that regard athletic skills, such as kinesthetic abilities, as a type of intelligence (Gardner, 1983).

Especially relevant to the issue of family influences on individual outcomes is the distinction that behavioral geneticists draw between shared and nonshared environments. Shared environment refers to characteristics within a family that are shared by siblings, while the nonshared environment includes any experiences that occur outside of the family system and are unique for each individual. Findings demonstrate that nonshared, rather than shared experiences, have a much greater influence on the development of individual differences in abilities (Neisser et al., 1996; Plomin, DeFries, McClearn, & McGuffin, 2001). It is therefore tempting to assume that the environment created by a family plays only a minor role in determining outcomes. Such a conclusion is flawed for two reasons. The first concerns the obvious role that families have in steering children towards or away from unique experiences outside of the home, such as sport participation or other activities. In other words, the shared (family) environment experienced by siblings not only provides an immediate influence on their abilities, but also has a secondary effect via the nonshared environments towards which each sibling is guided.

A second reason to avoid concluding that the family-dictated experience provides a weak influence on individual outcomes requires some understanding of the dynamic, systemic nature of families. As a system, a family is comprised of several interacting units or family members. These individuals comprise the shared environment, yet the perceived nature of that environment differs, depending upon the individual family member's position within the system (Becvar & Becvar, 1996). Indeed, one strategy used to assess family system dysfunction is to examine the congruence of members' perceptions of the environment (Sawin & Harrigan, 1995). No two individuals view the system in the same way, and what is ostensibly a single, shared environment has differential effects on specific family members. Clearly, the family environment may not have identical effects on all siblings.

This should not imply that the family has little influence on individual outcomes. These effects are largely idiosyncratic, however, and cannot be expected to account for large proportions of variability in quantitative measures employed in traditional methodologies. To clarify, if the predictor variable (shared environment), as measured, has restricted variability, while the dependent variable (outcome) is unique for each sibling, statistical measures of association will necessarily yield findings of limited explained variance.

FAMILY INFLUENCES ON SPORT-RELATED OUTCOMES

Having briefly explored several issues with implications for family influences on general psychological outcomes, the literature regarding familial effects on sport behavior can be viewed within this broader context. Much of the work in this area has concerned parental influences on child and adolescent athletes.

SOCIALIZATION INTO SPORT AND PHYSICAL ACTIVITY

A youth's entry into sport, like most other activities, involves a socialization process. Some research has shown that parents provide the strongest influence on the sport socialization process (Jambor, 1999). Others indicate that, while parents may not provide the primary social influence on youth sport participation for all ages, they continue to play an important role in a child's decision to participate across developmental stages (Eccles & Harold, 1991; Lewko & Ewing, 1980; Lewko & Greendorfer, 1988). Lewko and Greendorfer argued that parental influence, while especially salient during pre-adolescent entry into sport, may not be as strong as peer and school influences during adolescence. Nevertheless, their review of the literature on socialization into youth sport reveals that family influences remain a factor, if not the predominant factor, in socializing a child into sport. The above-referenced studies, which address a variety of sports and both genders, indicate that parents who value sport experiences are more likely to encourage their children to participate in organized sport activities.

Parental influences have been shown to predict children's levels of non-sport physical activity as well. Children whose parents value physical activity are more likely than their peers to engage in regular exercise (Anderson & Wold, 1992; Brustad, 1993, 1996a; Kimiecik, Horn, & Shurin, 1996). A child's entry into sport or other forms of physical activity is clearly more than a haphazard occurrence. Rather, it is a reflection of underlying family values.

With the notable exception of Kimiecik et al. (1996), who conducted in-home interviews with families to supplement their use of self-report measures, most of the research in these areas has relied on correlating parental preferences with children's levels of physical activity and sport involvement. Thus, direct observations from these linear strategies allow one to conclude only that parental beliefs predict children's behavior. It is quite possible, however, as Kimiecik et al. discuss, that other meaningful differences exist between the family systems of physically active youths and the families of their more sedentary peers.

PARENTAL CORRELATES OF SPORT-RELATED VARIABLES

A sizeable body of literature addresses the association between family characteristics and sport-related outcomes. The bulk of this research addresses the relationship between certain qualities or perceptions of sportsparents and the anxiety, enjoyment, attrition rates, and talent of youth sport participants. A review of this literature reveals that despite the apparent tendency on the part of many parents to focus on their children's win-loss records (Ferguson, 1999; Greenburg & Bernstein, 2000), most sport psychologists and youth coaches have been concerned with family influences on outcomes other than performance (Gould, 1996; Vanden Auweele & Rzewnicki, 2000).

In pursuing questions regarding the role of the family in sports, researchers have studied the amount of enjoyment experienced by young athletes perhaps more than any other variable. Studies have repeatedly indicated that children enter and continue to participate in sport primarily because they find it fun (Martens, 1978; Smoll & Smith, 1996). Thus, the question of which parental tendencies correlate with children's enjoyment or intrinsic motivation in sports becomes highly relevant. Findings here consistently reveal that children of parents who provide support without pressure, value effort and competition over winning, and encourage process rather than outcome goals are more likely to enjoy participating in sports (Babkes & Weiss, 1999; Brustad, 1996; Hardy, 1993; Martens, 1978; McPherson & Brown, 1988; Power & Woolger, 1994; Smoll, 2001).

Not surprisingly, findings show the converse is true regarding anxiety among young athletes. Parents who pressure their youngsters to win and communicate, either overtly or covertly, that the outcome is more important than the process appear to promote high levels of sport-related anxiety in their children (Brustad, 1996b; Margenau, 1990; White, 1998). For these children, sports cease to be fun. In many cases, the sport-related outcomes become more important to the parent than to the child (Coakley, 1992; Margenau, 1990). The result is an increase in attrition rates as these children, who no longer enjoy playing sports, decide to drop out (Martens, 1978).

THE NATURE AND INTENSITY OF FAMILY INVOLVEMENT

One means of addressing the effectiveness of family members in promoting an enhanced sport experience is to determine whether parents are under or over-involved with their children's sport participation. Experts in this area advise that parents provide the greatest benefit when they adopt a moderate level of involvement (Byrne, 1993; Hellstedt, 1990). Several scenarios of the possible interactions among athlete, family, and sport environment are depicted in Figures 1-3.

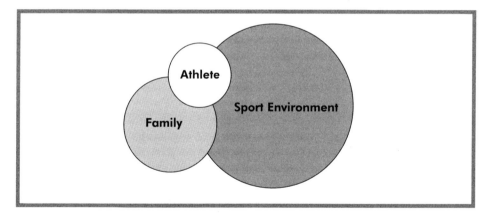

Figure 1 A family with a moderate level of involvement in the child's sport participation.

Figure 1 represents a family that is moderately involved with the child's sport environment. As the overlapping circles indicate, some of the family's activities revolve around the sport, but the major portion of the family system's identity is independent of this environment. In addition, the athlete's identity includes membership in the family and sport environment, as well as outside activities. In this scenario of moderate involvement, a parent is presumed to provide encouragement and support for the young athlete without inducing undue pressure to win or overemphasizing the importance of the child's sport participation (Byrne, 1993; Hellstedt, 1990).

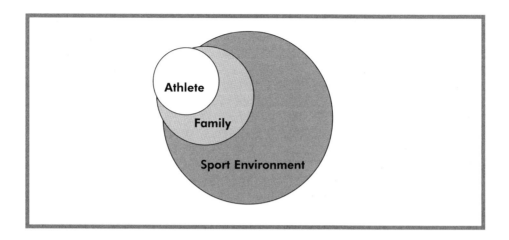

Figure 2 A depiction of a family that is over-involved with the child's sport participation.

The family depicted in Figure 2 is over-involved in the child's sport. Nearly all of the family's activities are enmeshed with the sport environment. For the athlete, this means that being a part of the family requires participation in the sport. Thus, the child may perceive that in order to develop her own identity, she must seek non-sport activities, which may also involve the risk of disappointing her parents. Such a situation may cause the child to drop out of sport (Coakley, 1992).

Figure 3 portrays a family that is under-involved with the child, as well as with his sport. In this scenario, the athlete is likely to experience a lack of connectedness with his family, and participating in sport may allow him to enter an environment wherein he can become an integral component of a system. Thus, sport allows him to fulfill a need for belongingness that is not met via his family of origin (Maslow, 1968).

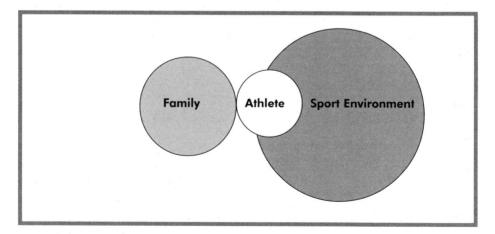

Figure 3 A depiction of a family that is under-involved with both the athlete and the sport environment.

Obvious problems exist with parents who are over-involved or under-involved with their children's sports. Therefore, the published sport-related literature suggests that a moderate level of involvement is ideal (Byrne, 1993; Hellstedt, 1990). The implication here is that once the intensity of the family's involvement with the sport is assessed, parents can be counseled to increase or decrease their involvement accordingly. While such a notion is relatively straightforward and appealing, it assumes that the intensity of parental involvement is a sport specific phenomenon, rather than a reflection of family system dynamics. Thus, while a coach or sport psychologist might wish to caution parents to tone down their intense involvement with a young athlete's sport participation, such advice may only scratch the surface of an ongoing parenting style. As indicated in Figures 1-3, the relationship between athlete and family, which is represented roughly by the proportion of the overlapping circular areas, is assumed to supercede and influence the child's participation in sport.

Support for this perspective is found in several lines of evidence. First, when describing their work with young athletes and their families, practitioners reveal that, oftentimes, the presenting sport-related problem is merely an indicator of an underlying family issue (Burnett, 2000; Hellstedt, 1995, 2000; Stainback & LaMarche, 1998). Second, as Stein, Raedke, and Glenn (1999) have demonstrated, more critical than the *amount* of parental involvement on sport-related variables, such as anxiety and enjoyment, is the child's perception regarding the *appropriateness* of involvement levels. The child's perception of parental behaviors may, indeed, more adequately reveal the nature of the interaction among family members, as some children perceive moderate levels of involvement as "too much," while others view relatively high levels as "too little." In addition, the limited published research on children coached by their parents (who are thus, by definition, heavily involved with the children's sports) shows that these athletes experience levels of motivation and competitive anxiety similar to that of their peers (Barber, Sukhi, & White, 1999). Finally, qualitative studies examining the family's role in the development of expertise reveal that certain family patterns, common across a variety of sport and non-sport domains, exist prior to the eventual expert's experience with the chosen activity (Bloom, 1985; Côté, 1999; Durand-Bush & Salmela, 2002; Stevenson, 1990). These patterns include parental involvement in their children's activities that may be considered quite intense. Findings from this line of research are discussed next.

FAMILY INFLUENCES ON THE DEVELOPMENT OF TALENT

Research concerning the influence of the family on the development of talent has been conducted primarily by identifying highly successful athletes and employing qualitative methods to examine their families (Bloom, 1985; Côté, 1999; Sloane, 1985; Stevenson, 1990). These studies have generally taken the form of interviews with parents, siblings, and the athletes themselves to encourage retrospection regarding the nature of the family dynamics throughout the athlete's development into an expert.

Certainly, each family is unique, and families of expert performers are no exception. Nevertheless, certain patterns appear to characterize families of expert performers in a variety of individual (Côté, 1999; Sloane, 1985) and team sports (Côté, 1999; Stevenson,

1990), as well as other, non-sport performance domains (Bloom, 1985; Csikszentmihalyi, Rathunde, & Whalen, 1993). Such families tend to be child-centered, which is to imply that they place the interests of the children at the forefront of family concerns. Interviews demonstrate that while these parents generally avoid dictating which activities their children must pursue, they do encourage industriousness and expect the children to commit themselves fully once they have selected an activity (Bloom, 1985; Sloane, 1985). Thus, these parents convey high expectations without undermining the children's sense of self-determination (Deci & Ryan, 1985). These expectations are stable across both athletic and academic pursuits and are communicated equitably to all children in the family.

These families valued the discovery of one's abilities, and the children explored a variety of activities (Côté, 1999; Côté & Hay, 2002). In the cases studied, once the future experts began to experience meaningful success in their chosen domains, their families made a variety of adjustments and sacrifices in order to help the children further develop their talents. The families began to reorganize around the talented children's pursuits. In some cases, adjustments were extreme, including instances in which one or both parents relocated homes with the child in order to be closer to elite training and coaching opportunities (Sloane, 1985).

For virtually all of the family systems studied, a gradual process of change occurred as the children developed into expert performers (Bloom, 1985; Côté, 1999; Côté & Hay, 2002; Stevenson, 1990). Bloom characterized this process as consisting of the early, middle, and later years. More recently, Côté and Hay (2002) described the development of talent in terms of the sampling years (when the child samples a variety of sport and non-sport activities), the specializing years (when the child demonstrates aptitude in a specific domain and elects to pursue it exclusively), and the investment years (when the child and family commit to the pursuit of elite status). This gradual process in the development of athletic expertise has been supported by recently published studies of world and Olympic champions (Durand-Busch & Salmela, 2002; Gould, Diffenbach, & Moffet, 2002)

It bears noting here that the family dynamics involved in this developmental process contrast sharply with images presented by the mass media portraying sportsparents who decide that their children, still at a young age, are destined for elite levels of play (Ferguson, 1999; Greenburg & Bernstein, 2000). This disparity suggests that a great number of parents, by emphasizing the importance of performance and winning to their young athletes at too early an age, are undermining their children's chances for success in the sport environment (Coakley, 1992; Roberts, Treasure, & Hall, 1994).

INTERACTIONS BETWEEN FAMILY HEALTH AND INVOLVEMENT LEVEL

Given the tremendous amount of time and effort an individual must commit in order to achieve expertise in a performance domain (Ericsson & Charness, 1994), it is not surprising that the families of expert performers tend to contribute intensively to this process. For most sport activities, a child does not possess the resources, monetary or otherwise, which are generally required to achieve elite status. Certainly, exceptions exist, especially in particular sports that do not entail a great deal of cost, and exceptional individuals with little or no family support may still achieve success (Such a scenario is reflected in Figure 3.). Notwithstanding such possibilities, studies on talent development suggest that a total family commitment is required to take advantage of the ideal coaching, training, and competitive opportunities available. Thus, the families of experts appear to be heavily involved, perhaps even over-involved, with their children's athletic pursuits (Bloom, 1985; Côté, 1999; Sloane, 1985; Stevenson, 1990). Such intensity of family involvement appears a reasonable, if not necessary, component in the development of talent, yet it contradicts the suggestions of sport psychology practitioners and researchers who encourage moderate levels of parental involvement (Byrne, 1993; Hellstedt, 1990).

Several explanations may resolve this apparent contradiction. The first has to do with the improper use of the term involvement (and the associated terms of moderate, over, and under-involvement), which has been utilized to describe a rather complex series of interactions among parents, children, and the sport environment. Parents who pressure their children to win or who interfere with a coach's responsibilities may be characterized as "over-involved." Likewise, a parent who conveys little concern for the child's experiences appears "under-involved." Such usage of these terms, however, implies that parental involvement is a uni-dimensional, linear variable that is present in low to high amounts. It may be more appropriate to consider involvement as a multi-dimensional construct that includes "desirable" and "undesirable" interactions among family members and the sport environment. Thus, the parent who behaves inappropriately at a child's sporting event might appear to be over-involved, but a more accurate description would characterize this family member as being involved in an undesirable manner. The deciding factor, therefore, is not how heavily the parent is involved, but whether this involvement reflects strong family relationships (Stein et al., 1999; Wylleman, 2000).

Conceptualizing parent or family involvement in such a fashion enables the reasonable assumption that the families of elite athletes studied were intensively involved with the children's sport participation, but that this involvement reflected healthy interactions among the family members. In support of this view, Wylleman (2000) cited several studies suggesting that the quality of relationships between young athletes and their parents plays a decisive role in whether the children reach elite levels.

Another possible explanation for the lack of congruence between recommended levels of involvement and the intense levels found among families of elite athletes acknowledges that such extreme levels do, indeed, have the potential to produce harmful consequences. Sport participation entails coping with challenges, and competing successfully at an elite level requires the ability to tolerate large amounts of stress. It is reasonable to assume that the same holds true for families of athletes. When a child excels in sport and rises to a higher level of competition, the family, in order to encourage further improvement, may also become more intensively involved. As this pattern continues, family members may develop strengthened relationships, but the family system also undergoes a great deal of stress, which is potentially harmful to its functioning.

The notion that dysfunction is the result of an interaction between stress and pre-existing vulnerabilities enjoys wide acceptance in the study of individual psychopathology

(Zuckerman, 1999). This concept may also apply to families of athletes. Perhaps only the healthiest family systems are capable of maintaining their functioning in the face of the extreme stressors associated with participation in elite sport. From this perspective, suggestions for families to adopt a moderate level of involvement are aimed at minimizing the stressors, but do not address the health of the family unit. An additional approach would entail addressing a family's diathesis (i.e., its susceptibility to dysfunction). This could be accomplished through family therapy, as any vulnerabilities may become exacerbated in the process of raising an elite athlete. Indeed, even the families of highly successful athletes appear to suffer some consequences from their sport involvement. As several of these families have adapted to the demands of the talented children's respective sports, some siblings have reported feelings of emotional neglect and unfair treatment (Côté, 1999; Sloane, 1985). In addition, the elite performers themselves are not immune to the damaging effects of parental pressures to excel (Stevenson, 1990). Among the families of elite young athletes who have been examined, however, these problems appear limited to a manageable level. It may be the case that rich and varied experience gained through intensive sport involvement produces enhanced family relationships. It is also possible the families studied had previously established strengths that may have allowed them to withstand the stressors that cause many children to drop out of sport altogether (Coakley, 1992; Martens, 1978).

It is notable that the interactive influence of family health and involvement levels on sport-related outcomes parallels the gene-environment interactions discussed earlier in this chapter. Whereas behavioral geneticists have found that *individuals* with different genotypes derive unequal benefits from similar environments, the hypothesis offered here is that *family systems* with varying levels of dysfunction are affected differently through their sustained experiences in sport. As noted earlier, published studies comparing the family dynamics of highly successful athletes to those who had achieved less success or had dropped out of sport are not readily available. Nonetheless, one might expect that, just as genetic factors demonstrate increasing influence on various psychological outcomes as individuals age, family system health becomes increasingly influential with sustained, intensive sport involvement. Supporting this notion, a recent study (Sacks, 2003) found that only four of 88 elite, university level athletes perceived mild levels of family dysfunction. A probable explanation for this finding is that few unhealthy families manage to tolerate the intensive and sustained exposure to sport environments that is require for athletes to reach an elite level.

ADDITIONAL CONSIDERATIONS FROM A FAMILY SYSTEMS PERSPECTIVE

CHALLENGES IN MEASURING FAMILY DYNAMICS

Terms such as family health and dysfunction have been used to refer to the manner in which the various members comprising a family interact with one another. A major challenge facing researchers and practitioners who wish to address family dynamics is assessing family functioning in a valid manner. Measuring this construct is especially problematic because it is defined in various ways by different parties (Halvorsen, 1991;

Sawin & Harrigan, 1995). According to Halvorsen, "Some professionals define family functioning in terms of structure, others in terms of the family's interactional nature, others in terms of transactional processes, and still others in terms of the psychological characteristics of family members" (p. 50). Notwithstanding this impediment, a number of systems-based, self-report instruments have been validated for the purpose of measuring family functioning and are currently in use by mental health practitioners working with families (Grotevant & Carlson, 1989; Halvorsen, 1991; Sawin & Harrigan, 1995). These instruments can be quite useful for measuring specific aspects of family dynamics in order to compare a family to a norming sample.

There are, however, drawbacks involved in using quantitative measures to assess a family system. As Deacon and Piercy (2001) note, these instruments actually assess an individual family member's perceptions of the family, rather than measuring the actual functioning of the system. While perceptions of family functioning can be useful in themselves, and while discrepancies among various members' perceptions can be used to infer the presence of dysfunction, it should be recognized that a self-report instrument has limitations in this regard.

Several writers (Deacon & Piercy, 2001; Sawin & Harrigan, 1995) also point out that quantitative instruments tend to reduce holistic systems to specific variables measured on a linear continuum and, in the process, fail to capture important nuances within a family. These authors suggest that qualitative forms of assessment provide a useful complement to quantitative measures. Some of the qualitative techniques employed by family therapists and researchers include observational methods, genograms, family networks, eco-maps, art assessments, want-ads, family sculptures, and reenactments of an important event or typical day, to name a few (Deacon & Piercy, 2001; Sciara, 2001; Widmer & La Farga, 2000).

These and other qualitative methods of assessing families have their limitations as well. Only a trained therapist is qualified to conduct and interpret most of these techniques. Often, a good deal of trust must be established between a family member and therapist before these assessments can occur, as engaging in activities that reveal private family matters is, in itself, part of a therapeutic process. Thus, to conduct this type of research, one must be sensitive to the welfare of participants, as well as to one's own qualifications to gather these types of data. Certainly, conducting studies on family influences in sport presents several challenges, but it also holds the potential for meaningful findings.

THE SYSTEM AS THE UNIT OF INTEREST

Throughout this chapter, reference has been made to family influences on the individual. By necessity, this requires one to view a family, and the individuals who comprise it, as separate entities. Certainly, individuals do exist within a family. A systemic perspective, however, entails viewing the family as a holistic unit. As Bertalanffy (1968) writes:

> It is necessary to study not only parts and processes in isolation, but also to solve the decisive problems found in the organization and order unifying them, resulting from dynamic interaction of parts, and making the behavior of parts different when studied in isolation or within the whole. (p. 31)

In short, a systems approach views phenomena and entities as organizations of separate parts, all of which continually interact within their coherent system. For obvious reasons, such an approach favors studying the whole as well as its parts.

A truly systemic approach to the matter would construe the major issue not so much one of how family members influence an athlete's sport experience, but rather how well equipped is the family itself for success in sport. Of course, a specific athletic member of the family actually trains and competes in a sport. However, this individual may be viewed as the family system's point of entry into the sport environment. While the athlete is a visible representative, the entire family system is involved with the sport experience. The fact that this involvement varies considerably reflects relative strengths and weaknesses, as well as developmental processes (Hellstedt, 1995), in the athletic family system.

The notion that a single individual draws the majority of attention, even while the general dynamics of the family are of primary concern, is commonly understood by family systems theorists (Becvar & Becvar, 1996; Papero, 1990). Family therapists recognize that specific family members are usually identified as the "targeted" or "identified patient" for practical reasons, though systemic treatment modalities address the functioning of the entire family unit. Such a perspective represents one potentially useful approach for practitioners who work with athletic families.

AN "ATHLETIC FAMILY" VERSUS "A FAMILY WITH AN ATHLETE"

The systemic approach offered above proposes that the family itself be considered the unit of interest. Thus, associated research methods and intervention techniques would address the "athletic family," as opposed to a "family with an athlete." As employed here, these terms are adapted from a common practice among family counselors and therapists to distinguish, for example, an "alcoholic family" from a "family with an alcoholic." In the former, the family adapts to the alcoholic member, and the remaining members interact in such a way (e.g., by taking on added responsibilities) to allow the system to maintain its unhealthy method of operation. In the latter, the health of the family as a whole emerges as the greater concern, which tends to encourage the identified patient to change, or at least to operate independently as an alcoholic.

In the present analogy, a family with an athlete could be any family with a member who happens to participate in sport. The fact that an individual engages in this particular activity does not necessarily alter the goals or dynamics of the family system. For this type of system, the family may nurture the sportsperson and retain a certain level of influence on this activity, but the athlete acts more or less as an independent agent.

An athletic family, by contrast, may be characterized as a system that is arranged according to one or more members' athletic endeavors. For a family characterized as this type, sport-related goals serve as the system's organizing principles. That is, athletics becomes the family's identity, and the interactions among members of the system are geared towards these goals. Here, the concept of family influence is subsumed by a reality in which the athlete is the center of the system, and her goals become the system's goals. Indeed, as reported earlier, it is not unusual for an entire family to alter its lifestyle and relocate in order to take advantage of elite training and coaching opportunities (Sloane, 1985).

It may be tempting to propose that an athletic family provides increased facilitative effects on sport-related outcomes, compared to a family with an athlete, though this is not necessarily the case. It is fair, however, to assume that for an athletic family, the stakes are higher in the sport environment. With the potential for increased stress levels for the athlete, a high degree of family health becomes especially valuable for these systems.

In this chapter, we have attempted to delineate the genetic and environmental aspects of a sport-involved family's influence on an athlete. As this is an issue about which much is not known, we have drawn not only upon sport-based literature, but also upon non-sport lines of research and attempted to apply them to the sport domain. At present, the extent to which these various approaches and theories, which are prevalent in the study of psychopathology, intelligence, and family systems, will prove useful in athletic settings is unclear. Certainly, an athlete's family is a salient source of influence, and clarifying the nature of this influence represents both a challenging and worthwhile endeavor.

REFERENCES

Anderson, N. & Wold, B. (1992). Parental and peer influences on leisure-time physical activity in young adolescents. *Research Quarterly for Exercise and Sport, 63,* 341-348.

Babkes, M. L. & Weiss, M. R. (1999). Parental influence on children's cognitive and affective responses to competitive soccer participation. *Pediatric Exercise Science, 11,* 44-62.

Becvar, D. S. & Becvar, R. J. (1996). *Family therapy: A systemic integration* (3rd ed.). Boston: Allyn & Bacon.

Bertalanffy, L. V. (1968). *General system theory: Foundations, development, applications.* New York: George Braziller.

Bloom, B. S. (1985). Generalizations about talent development. In B. S. Bloom (Ed.), *Developing talent in young people* (pp.507-549). New York: Ballantine Books.

Brustad, R. J. (1993). Who will go out and play? Parental and psychological influences on children's attraction to physical activity. *Pediatric Exercise Science, 5,* 210-223.

Brustad, R. J. (1996a). Attraction to physical activity in urban schoolchildren: parental socialization and peer influences. *Research Quarterly for Exercise and Sport, 67,* 316-323.

Brustad, R. J. (1996b). Parental and peer influenceon children's psychological development through sport. In F. L. Smoll & R. E. Smith (Eds.), *Children and youth in sport: A biopsychosocial perspective* (pp. 112-124). Dubuque, IA: Brown & Benchmark.

Burnett, D. J. (2000, October). *The role of parents in youth sports.* Workshop presented at the annual meeting of the Association for the Advancement of Applied Sport Psychology, Nashville, TN.

Byrne, T. (1993). Sport: It's a family affair. In M. Lee (Ed.), *Coaching children in sport* (pp. 39-47). London: E & FN Spon.

Coakley, J. (1992). Burnout among adolescent athletes: A personal failure or social problem. *Sociology of Sport Journal, 9,* 271-285

Côté, J. (1999). The influence of the family in the development of talent in sport. *The Sport Psychologist, 13,* 395-417.

Côté, J. & Hay, J. (2002). Children's involvement in sport: A developmental perspective. In J. M. Silva & D. Stevens (Eds.), *Psychological Foundations of Sport* (2nd ed, pp. 484-502). Boston: Merrill.

Csikszentmihalyi, M., Rathunde, K. & Whalen, S. (1993). *Talented teenagers: The roots of success and failure.* New York: Cambridge University Press.

Deacon, S. A., & Piercy, F. P. (2001). Qualitative methods in family evaluation: Creative assessment techniques. *The American Journal of Family Therapy, 29,* 355-373.

Deci, E. L., & Ryan, R. M. (1985). *Intrinsic motivation and self-determination in human behavior.* New York: Plenum.

Durand-Bush, N. & Salmela, J. H. (2002). The development and maintenance of expert athletic performance: Perceptions of world and Olympic champions. *Journal of Applied Sport Psychology, 14,* 154-171.

Eccles, J. S. & Harold, R.D. (1991). Gender differences in sport involvement: Applying the Eccles' Expectancy-Value Model. *Journal of Applied Sport Psychology, 3,* 7-35.

Ericsson, A. K. & Charness, N. (1994). Expert performance: It's structure and acquisition. *American Psychologist, 49,* 725-747.

Ferguson, A. (1999, July 12). Inside the crazy culture of kids sports. Time, 154, 52-60.

Gardner, H. (1983). *Frames of mind: The theory of multiple intelligences.* New York: Basic Books.

Goodwin, D. W., Schulsinger, F. Molley, N., Hermnsen, L., Winoker, G. & Guze, S. B. (1974). Drinking problems in adopted and non-adopted sons of alcoholics. *Archives of General Psychiatry, 31,* 164-169.

Gotfredson, L. S. (2002). Gottfredson's theory of circumscription, compromise, and self-creation. In D. Brown (Ed.). Career Choice and Development (4th ed., pp. 85-148). San Francisco: Jossey-Bass.

Gould, D. (1996). Sport psychology: Future directions in youth sport research. In F. L. Smoll & R. E. Smith (Eds.), *Children and youth in sport: A biopsychosocial perspective* (pp. 405-422). Dubuque, IA: Brown & Benchmark.

Gould, D., Dieffenbach, K. & Moffett, A. (2002). Psychological characteristics and their development in Olympic champions. *Journal of Applied Sport Psychology, 14,* 172-204.

Greenburg, R. & Bernstein, R. (Executive Producers). (2000, October). *Real Sports with Bryant Gumbel* [Television broadcast]. New York: Home Box Office.

Grotevant, H. D. & Carlson, C. I. (1989) *Family assessment: A guide to methods and measures.* New York: Guilford Press.

Halvorsen, J. G. (1991). Self-report family assessment instruments: An evaluative review. *Family Practice Research Journal, 11,* 21-55.

Hardy, L. (1993). Sport: Counseling young athletes and how to avoid it. In M. Lee (Ed.), *Coaching children in sport* (pp. 179-190). London: E & FN Spon.

Hellstedt, J. C. (1990). Early adolescent perceptions of parental pressure in the sport environment. *Journal of Sport Behavior, 13,* 135-144.

Hellstedt, J. C. (1995). Invisible players: A family systems model. In S. M. Murphy (Ed.), *Sport psychology interventions* (pp. 117-147). Champaign, IL: Human Kinetics.

Hellstedt, J. C. (2000). Family systems-based treatment of the athlete family. In D. Begel & R. W. Burton (Eds.), *Sport psychiatry: Theory and practice* (pp. 206-228). New York: W. W. Norton & Company.

Herrnstein, R. J. & Murray, C. (1994). *The bell curve: Intelligence and class structure in American life.* New York: Free Press.

Jambor, E. (1999). Parents as children's socializing agents in youth soccer. *Journal of Sport Behavior, 22,* 350-359.

Kimiecik, J. C., Horn, T. S. & Shurin, C. S. (1996). Relationships among children's beliefs, perceptions of their parents' beliefs, and their moderate-to-vigorous physical activity. *Research Quarterly for Exercise and Sport, 67,* 324-336.

Lewko, J. H, & Ewing, M. E. (1980) Sex differences and parental influence in sport involvement of children. *Journal of Sport Psychology, 2,* 62-68.

Lewko, J. H. & Greendorfer, S. L. (1988). Family influences in sport socialization of children and adolescents. In F. Smoll, R. Magill, & Ash (Eds.), *Children in Sport* (3rd ed.) (pp. 287-300). Champaign, IL: Human Kinetics.

Margenau, E. (1990). *Sports without pressure.* New York: Gardner Press.

Martens, R. (Ed.). (1978) *Joy and sadness in children's sports.* Champaign, IL: Human Kinetics.

Maslow, A. (1968). *Toward a psychology of being* (2nd ed.). New York: Van Nostrand.

McGue, M. (1993). From proteins to cognitions: The behavioral genetics of alcoholism. In R. Plomin & G. E. McClearn (Eds.), *Nature, nurture, and psychology* (pp. 245-268). Washington, DC: American Psychological Association.

McPherson, B. D. & Brown, B. A. (1988). The structure, processes, and consequences of sport for children. In F. Smoll, R. Magill, & Ash (Eds.), *Children in Sport* (3ʳᵈ ed.) (pp. 265-286). Champaign, IL: Human Kinetics.

Neisser, U., Boodoo, G., Bouchard, T. J., Jr., Boykin, A. W., Brody, N., Ceci, S. J., et al. (1996). Intelligence: Knowns and unknowns. *American Psychologist, 51*, 77-101.

Papero, D. (1990). *Bowen family systems theory.* Boston, MA: Allyn & Bacon.

Pickens, R. W., Svikis, D. S., McGue, M., Lykken, D. T., Heston, L. L., & Clayton, P. J. (1991). Heterogeneity in the inheritance of alcoholism: A study of male and female twins. *Archives of Genral Psychiatry, 48*, 19-41.

Plomin, R., DeFries, J. C., McClearn, J. E. & McGuffin, P. (2001). *Behavioral Genetics* (3ʳᵈ ed.). New York: W.H. Freeman.

Plomin. R., Lichtenstein, P., Pederson, N. L., McClearn, G. E. & Nesselroade, J. R. (1990). Genetic influence on life events during the last half of the life span. *Psychology and Aging, 5* (1), 25-30.

Power, T. G., & Woolger, C. (1994). Parenting practices and age-group swimming: A correlational study. *Research Quarterly for Exercise and Sport, 65*, 59-66.

Roberts, G. C., Treasure, D. C. & Hall, H. K. (1994). Parental goal orientations and beliefs about the competitive sport experience of their child. *Journal of Applied Social Psychology, 24*, 634-645.

Sacks, D. N. (2003). Family influences and the athlete's sport experience: A systemic view. Unpublished doctoral dissertation, Florida State University.

Sawin, K. J. & Harrigan, M. P. (1995) *Measures of family functioning for research and practice* (P. Woog, Ed.). New York: Springer.

Sciarra, D. T. (2001). Assessment of diverse family systems. In L. A. Suzuki, J.G. Ponterotto, & P. J. Meller (Eds.), *Handbook of multicultural assessment: Clinical, psychological, and educational applications* (2ⁿᵈ ed.) (pp.135-168). Josey-Bass; San Francisco, CA.

Sloane, K. D. (1985). Home influences on talent development. In B. S. Bloom (Ed.), *Developing talent in young people* (pp. 439-476). New York: Ballantine Books.

Smoll, F. L. (2001). Coach-parent relationships in youth sports: Increasing Harmony and minimizing hassle. In J. M. Williams (Ed.). *Applied sport psychology: Personal growth to peak performance* (4ᵗʰ ed., pp. 150-161). Mountain View, CA: Mayfield.

Smoll, F. L., & Smith, R. E. (Eds.). (1996). *Children and youth in sport: A biopsychosocial perspective.* Dubuque, IA: Brown & Benchmark.

Stainback, R. D., & LaMarche, J. A. (1998). Family systems issues affecting athletic performance in youth. In K. F. Hays & E. M. Stern (Eds.), *Integrating exercise, sports, movement, and mind: Therapeutic Unity* (pp. 5-20). New York: Haworth Press.

Stein, G. L., Raedke, T. D., & Glenn, S. D. (1999). Children's perception of parent sport involvement: It's not how much, but to what degree that's important. *Journal of Sport Behavior, 22*, 591-601.

Stevenson, C. L. (1990). The early careers of international athletes. *Sociology of Sport Journal, 7*, 238-253.

Vanden Auweele, Y. & Rzewnicki, R. (2000). Putting relationship issues in sport in perspective. *International Journal of Sport Psychology, 31*, 573-577.

White, S. A. (1998). Adolescent Goal Profiles, Perceptions of the Parent-Initiated Motivational Climate, and Competitive Trait Anxiety. *The Sport Psychologist, 12,* 16-28.

Widmer, E. D., & La Farga, L-A. (2000). Family networks: A sociometric method to study relationships in families. *Field Methods, 12,* 108-128.

Wylleman, P. (2000). Interpersonal relationship in sport: Uncharted territory in sport psychology research. *International Journal of Sport Psychology, 31,* 555-572.

Zuckerman, M. (1999). *Vulnerability to psychopathology: A biosocial model.* Washington, DC: American Psychological Association.

EXPERT COACHES AND THE COACHING PROCESS

Natalie Durand-Bush, Kim A. Thompson, and John H. Salmela

Content

Summary

Research on expert coaching remains scarce in the literature, however, some key studies have shed light on the intricate and complex process of coaching at an expert level. Côté, Salmela, Trudel et al. (1995) postulated a coaching model that represents the knowledge and practice of multiple expert Canadian gymnastics coaches who are dedicated to the development of elite athletes. Since its inception, the model has been validated through research with expert coaches in several other sports. This chapter discusses the literature in terms of the components of the Coaching Model, that is, training, competition, organization, coach's and athlete's personal characteristics, and contextual factors.

Following the introduction of the Coaching Model, the important work completed by expert coaches to craft appropriate environments for the training of athletes at various developmental levels is discussed. Then, the role of expert coaches during competition is addressed. Organization is another important and often underestimated component of the coaching process. Results of studies highlighting some of the organizational tasks performed by expert coaches are presented. The personal characteristics of expert coaches and athletes have been empirically examined in some studies and are discussed in light of an optimal coaching process for the development of elite athletes. Finally, contextual factors such as culture and type of sport do play a role on the process of coaching. The findings of recent research examining the impact of such factors are reported.

INTRODUCTION - THE COACHING MODEL OF EXPERTISE

Research has shown that the development of expertise in sport and other performance domains is a dynamic, ongoing process that involves more than just the athletes or the performers themselves. Teachers and coaches appear to play different but significant roles throughout the life of these expert performers. According to researchers like B. S. Bloom (1985), Salmela (1996), Csikszentmihalyi, Rathunde, and Whalen (1993), and Partington (1995), coaches strive to create an environment in which athletes or performers can express themselves, extend their skills, and also take pleasure in what they do. Although the findings of B. S. Bloom, Csikszentmihalyi and colleagues, and Partington are insightful, they did not extensively focus on the context of sports.

In one seminal study, Côté, Salmela, Trudel, Baria, and Russell (1995) conducted in-depth interviews with 17 expert Canadian gymnastics coaches to examine the knowledge structures involved in producing Olympic level athletes. The inductive analysis of the data led them to postulate a model in which factors affecting the coaching process were categorized under three central components, that is, *training, competition,* and *organization*, as well as three peripheral components including *coach's personal characteristics, athlete's personal characteristics and level of development,* and *context* (see Figure 1). Côté et al.'s model is notable because it provides a comprehensive framework to explain the process of coaching and guide the actual practice of coaches in applied settings.

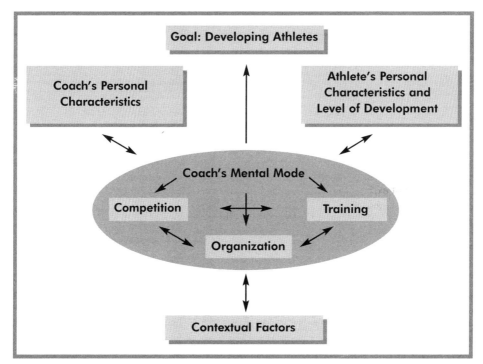

Figure 1 The Coaching Model: A grounded assessment of expert gymnastic coaches' knowledge. (Adapted, by permission, from Côté et al., 1995, *Journal of Sport and Exercise Psychology, 17,* 1-17).

One limitation of Côté, Salmela, and Trudel's (1995) study is that the Coaching Model was developed based on retrospective interview data elicited from gymnastics coaches only. However, since its inception, the model has been found to be applicable to the environment of team sports (G. A. Bloom, 1996; G. A. Bloom & Salmela, 2000) and combat sports (Moraes, 1998; Moraes & Salmela, 2001). Specifically, G. A. Bloom found that the Coaching Model represented the knowledge and work of expert coaches in field hockey, ice hockey, basketball, and volleyball. Interestingly though, these expert coaches reported spending more time completing organizational tasks and nurturing their relationships with their athletes than coaches of individual sports. This was mainly due to the complex nature of team sports involving not only several athletes but also opponents and referees or judges.

Recently, Gilbert and Trudel (2000) validated Côté et al.'s (1995) coaching model in a team sport context. They conducted a single-case study with an experienced university hockey coach using interviews and direct observations of the coach's actions over an entire season of play. Gilbert and Trudel corroborated all of the components found in the Coaching Model and also provided support for many of the categories identified within these components, despite significant contextual differences existing between the sports of hockey and gymnastics. These authors noted that their findings could not be generalized to the entire population of coaches because their study was based on a single case. They recommended that more research be conducted to continue the validation of Côté et al.'s coaching model in other sporting contexts.

The purpose of this chapter is to examine the process of coaching of expert coaches in light of the coaching model (Côté et al., 1995). Specifically, it addresses the following important aspects of the coaching process: (a) training, (b) competition, (c) organization, (d) coach and athlete personal characteristics, and (e) contextual factors.

TRAINING ATHLETES: CRAFTING AN APPROPRIATE ENVIRONMENT

The old slogan "Practice makes perfect," is still popular today for a reason. No one would deny that practice is a necessary mediating factor to achieve expertise in any domain. But just how much training does one need to engage in to reach the top? Is quality as important as quantity? Ericsson, Krampe, and Tesch-Römer (1993) believe that practice is the most significant factor in the development of high-level performance; but not just any kind of practice. Adopting an extreme environmental position, they proposed a theory of expertise predominantly based on what they termed "deliberate practice."

In their extensive review of the research on expert performance and their own studies with expert and amateur pianists and violinists, Ericsson et al. (1993) observed that even when individuals had access to similar training environments, large differences in their performance often still occurred. They also found that their *experience* in a domain was a weak predictor of their performance in that same domain. Rather than accepting these facts as evidence for innate differences in ability, they attempted to identify the nature and type of training activities that were most closely related to improvements in performance. They noticed that improvements were generally manifested when performers engaged in well-defined tasks with appropriate difficulty levels, informative feedback, and opportunities for repetition and corrections of errors. Ericsson et al. subsequently used the term deliberate practice to characterize these activities.

More specifically, deliberate practice refers to any highly structured, goal-directed, and effortful activity exclusively aimed at improving performance. Factoring in the dimension of quality, Ericsson et al. (1993) proposed that deliberate practice activities are distinct from recreation and spontaneous play, competition, work, and other forms of experience in a particular domain. They consist of activities, typically designed by teachers or coaches that involve high levels of concentration, problem solving, and the adoption of improved methods to perform specific tasks. According to Ericsson (1996), outstanding performers typically spend at least 10 years, or 10, 000 hours of deliberate practice, before reaching expert status.

Ericsson (1996) found that because high quality learning requires attention and the monitoring of goals and performance, it is usually facilitated by highly competent teachers or coaches. The author reported that "even if students are assigned appropriate training tasks, the mere duration of practice will not be a perfect predictor of attained performance" (p. 34). Performers must thus work with qualified teachers or coaches who will give them the proper support, guidance, and feedback for continuous improvement. Furthermore, they must overcome the challenge of accessing adequate training materials and facilities for sufficient periods of time and coaches / teachers play an important role in setting up the environment for this to occur (B. S. Bloom, 1985; G. A. Bloom, Durand-Bush & Salmela, 1997; Côté, Salmela & Russell, 1995).

In his latest review of the concept of deliberate practice and the development of expert performance, Ericsson (2003) stated the following regarding the role of coaches:

> Only by better understanding the mechanisms that mediate the process of learning and physiological adaptation will coaches and teachers be able to guide athletes to acquire expert levels of performance safely and effectively. Expert performers simply need help to negotiate the many constraints for daily deliberate practice and to respect the essential need for intermittent rest and daily recuperation. (p. 80)

It is interesting that for having put considerable emphasis on the significance of support, guidance, feedback, and monitoring of goals, Ericsson (1996, 2003) only superficially discussed the role of teachers and coaches, and did not attempt to discuss how coaches or teachers should fulfill their role.

Salmela (1996) found that coaches play a significant role in identifying and training various skills that contribute to the achievement of exceptional performance. Using an inductive qualitative design, he conducted in-depth and open-ended interviews with 22 expert coaches and reported that one of their main goals was to create an environment that was most conducive to improving performance. Results showed that these coaches invested considerable time and effort into planning and structuring practices so that the highest quality of training would occur. In addition, they were concerned with creating opportunities for athletes to become more autonomous and self-directed. This is illustrated in the following citation from an expert basketball coach:

The idea is you want to develop independent thinking, creative, responsible individuals who can make decisions when they leave. Clearly, it's incumbent upon athletes to develop self-discipline and properly manage their time and priorities. There will be ups and downs, pitfalls along the way but in the end, if they've survived a rigorous, demanding, and intense athletic involvement, and if they've also done well academically, achieving their degree, what more rewarding experiences could you ask for? (Salmela, 1996, p. 50)

The previous citation suggests that there is a reduced dependence on external human resources at an elite stage, and athletes become more responsible for the course of their learning and actions. In order to best prepare athletes to engage in self-directed learning, it appears that coaches should start to provide them with opportunities to exert control over their training environment in earlier stages of talent development. Singer & Janelle (1999) reinforced the fact that:

The learner is more inclined to be actively involved in self-instruction when given the opportunity to do so ... Also, by directly involving the learner in the learning process, responsibility for acquiring the skill is assumed by the learner, leading to greater effort, persistence, and satisfaction. (p. 138)

Salmela's (1996) study was instrumental because very little research has focused on the development of expert coaches, more specifically, coaches of team sports. The coaches shared important information regarding the development and training of elite athletes. One limitation of this study, however, was that only the perspectives of coaches were examined. The perceptions of athletes must also be investigated and compared to those of their coaches if the development of expert performance in sport is to be truly understood.

A seminal study that has shed light on the development of expertise and the role of coaches and teachers in this process was conducted by B. S. Bloom (1985). Bloom was particularly concerned with the process of talent development in young people from their early involvement in a field to the culmination of their career as expert performers. Using a retrospective and inductive approach, he interviewed 120 talented performers including Olympic swimmers, world-class tennis players, concert pianists, sculptors, research mathematicians, and research neurologists. A significant finding of his study was that talent development requires years of commitment, and central to this process is the amount and quality of support and instruction children receive from their teachers / coaches.

B. S. Bloom (1985) was innovative in that he identified three distinct stages of talent development: Early Years-Stage of Initiation, Middle Years-Stage of Development, and Late Years-Stage of Perfection. These stages provide excellent guidelines for performers as well as for their teachers or coaches who attempt to create appropriate training environments. However, B. S. Bloom indicated that these stages are only "signposts along a long and continuous learning process" (p. 537).

EARLY YEARS - STAGE OF INITIATION

B. S. Bloom (1985) discovered that the participants in his study first went through an initiation stage, in which they were engaged in fun, playful activities. As children, they were excited about their participation at this stage and relied heavily on their teacher or coach for guidance and support. It was predominantly during this early stage that parents and/or teachers noticed certain children appearing to be gifted, talented or "special" in some way. These attributions of special qualities affected both the expectations for the children and the methods used for teaching. Starkes, Deakin, Allard, Hodges, and Hayes (1996) also found that coaches in their study claimed to be able to detect talent even though they had a difficulty articulating how this was accomplished.

Teachers or coaches in B. S. Bloom's (1985) stage of initiation also generally adopted a process-oriented approach in their teaching, and thus encouraged and rewarded the young children for the process of effort rather than the outcome of achievement. Although teachers and coaches were not necessarily more knowledgeable and technically advanced at this stage, they provided the love and positive reinforcement the children needed to keep learning and performing activities.

MIDDLE YEARS - STAGE OF DEVELOPMENT

Eventually, the participants moved on to a stage of development where they became, as B. S. Bloom (1985) termed it, "hooked" on their particular activity. For example, they were "gymnasts" rather than "children who did gymnastics." Their pursuits evolved to a more serious nature and consequently, higher levels of dedication and training were witnessed. The participants became more achievement-oriented as practice time significantly increased and competition became the yardstick for measuring progress. Teachers or coaches at this stage were usually more technically skilled than those at the previous level. They emphasized the development of proper technique, provided children with opportunities to evaluate their performance, and expected results through discipline and a hard work ethic. B. S. Bloom found that teachers and coaches took a strong personal interest in the participants at this stage, and the loving relationship the children had with them during the initial stage was often replaced by one of respect.

LATE YEARS - STAGE OF PERFECTION

According to B. S. Bloom (1985), it was in the final stage, the one of perfection, that the participants became experts. They were radically obsessed by their chosen activity, which dominated their lives at this point. The emphasis was now placed upon the development of high-level skills through deliberate practice, and the participants were willing to invest the necessary time and effort required to achieve their ultimate performance goals. Furthermore, there was a shift in the responsibility for training and competition from the teachers or coaches to the performers. The performers had to be autonomous and extremely knowledgeable. B. S. Bloom revealed that because the mentors or master teachers / coaches at this level placed enormous demands on the performers, they sometimes became feared, but always respected.

In sum, B. S. Bloom (1985) largely contributed to the advancement of knowledge in the field of expertise. By using a qualitative approach with expert performers in different fields, he elicited data on the global process of talent development from the early childhood years to the later and more demanding years of talent perfection. He also provided important empirical information on the role of coaches and teachers in this process. In light of the topic of sport expertise, one potential limitation of his research is that the stages he outlined were not sport-specific. Although his sample consisted of 120 performers, he only included 18 tennis players and 21 swimmers. Nonetheless, his research has had a tremendous impact on the work of several other scholars including Côté (1999), Ericsson (1996), and Csikszentmihalyi et al. (1993).

Durand-Bush (2000) studied the perceptions of expert athletes, their coaches, and parents regarding the development and maintenance of expertise in sport. Specifically, the purpose of this study was to investigate the factors that contributed to the development and maintenance of performance of 10 athletes having won at least two Olympic gold medals or two World Championship titles, or a combination of both. In-depth, open-ended, and semi-structured interviews were conducted with the athletes, coaches, and parents using Patton's (1987) qualitative methodology. The data were analyzed both inductively and deductively using Côté, Salmela, Baria, and Russell's (1993) procedures for organizing and interpreting unstructured qualitative data.

The results revealed that the athletes progressed through four stages throughout their athletic career: the Sampling, Specializing, Investment, and Maintenance Years. Several factors were perceived to be important across these stages, and it is noteworthy that these factors could be classified under similar components figuring in Côté, Salmela, Trudel et al.'s (1995) coaching model. Specifically, the factors in this study pertained to the athletes' context, personal characteristics, training, and competition, which partly lend empirical support to the Coaching Model. A few significant differences were that in Durand-Bush's (2000) study, factors concerning coaching were categorized under "Context" while "Organization" was not a major theme like it was in the research of Côté and colleagues. A common finding, however, was that coaches were perceived to be extremely valuable resources throughout the athletes' career.

During the sampling years, the coaches created a nurturing environment in which the athletes had fun, felt secure, and experienced success. The athletes noted that although the coaches helped them to develop a repertoire of skills, the most memorable aspect of their participation at that level was that they made it fun for them (Durand-Bush, 2000). This finding is extremely important and supports the recommendation of Ewing, Seefeldt, and Brown (1996) that coaches should create a fun atmosphere for children who participate in youth sports in order to motivate them to remain involved. Similar findings regarding the important role of coaches during the early years of development were also discussed by B. S. Bloom (1985), Csikszentmihalyi et al. (1993), Carlson (1993), and Côté and Hay (2002).

According to Durand-Bush (2000), the training in which the expert athletes engaged at a young age was not particularly structured and conformed more to what Côté and Hay (2002) termed "deliberate play." In other words, coaches were more concerned with providing opportunities to play with the intent to have fun than playing with the specific and conscious intention of improving certain aspects of performance. Regardless, the athletes did improve because most of them reported experiencing success in sports very early on. Ericsson et al. (1993) advocated the importance of engaging in extensive hours of deliberate practice as early as possible, yet the results of Durand-Bush's (2000) study and that of Côté and Hay (2002) indicate that deliberate play seems to be more predominant than deliberate practice during childhood. One question that should be answered in future research is, "To what extent does deliberate play contribute to the development of expert performance?" Results of such research would help coaches to optimize the type of play activities required for optimal performance at different stages of development.

At a more specialized level (i.e., specializing years), most of the athletes' coaches were supportive and provided a more structured environment for developing skills and technique (Durand-Bush, 2000). These findings corroborate those of B. S. Bloom (1985) and Côté and Hay (2002). Another interesting finding was that some of the athletes who were introduced to their sport of excellence at this stage mentioned that a coach noticed their potential to succeed.

The phenomenon of talent detection in sport has been widely cited in the literature (Durand-Bush & Salmela, 2001). While there is evidence to substantiate the ability of coaches to detect special characteristics and attitudes of future champions at an early stage (Thomas & Thomas, 1999), several researchers severely questioned the accuracy and usefulness of talent detection and prediction (Bartmus, Neumann, & de Marées, 1987). Carlson (1993) found that it was not possible to fully predict who would become top-level players based on performance and skills during the early teenage years. Bartmus and colleagues also reported that it is very difficult to predict talent in sport. They advocated that talent detection is discriminating because children who do not show promise at an early age are sometimes denied the support and resources to which they are entitled to fully develop their potential in a sport. From a pedagogical perspective, it could be surmised that the Pygmalion effect (Sinclair & Vealy, 1989) could inhibit the performance of children in cases where coaches only choose to believe in and challenge those who show talent or promise at an early age.

The athletes' training activities during the latter years of their career (i.e., investment and maintenance years) included physical, mental, technical, and tactical training (Durand-Bush, 2000). The athletes had access to several human and physical resources at this stage that helped them overcome motivational and effort constraints. They worked with excellent coaches who assisted them in refining skills in training and developing optimal strategies for competitions. In most cases, the athletes' coaches were extremely knowledgeable and well respected. Some coaches were held in such high regards that they were sometimes feared. This fear element was also noted by B. S. Bloom (1985).

Many athletes and coaches in Durand-Bush's (2000) study revealed that they worked with other support staff members such as strength training coaches, exercise physiologists, sport psychologists, nutritionists, physiotherapists, and massage therapists, particularly during the investment and maintenance years. These individuals were extremely valuable resources because they provided information in areas in which the coaches were not necessarily the most knowledgeable. Very little research has been conducted on the role of support staff members in the development of expertise in sport. However, in one particular study, Salmela (1996) found that support staff members, particularly assistant coaches, provided invaluable services, and were important team members. The coaches in his study reported that they worked with assistants who were competent, hardworking, compatible with other team members, and could be trusted. They reflected high standards, particularly at an elite level, and contributed to the creation of an environment conducive to high quality training. Researchers should further examine the contribution of support staff members in the development of expert performance, and determine if and how they can enhance the overall quality of experience of both the athletes and coaches.

Partington (1995) provided empirical evidence on the role of teachers or master coaches in the development of expertise. He interviewed 21 renowned performers including two concert pianists and 19 principal orchestra players to examine their career development, preparation for performance, practicing regimens, and ideal performance states. Partington found that sustained effortful practice was important for the development of skills and preparation for performance. One musician stated:

> The right way to practice is not to play just because it's the thing to do, or because your teacher tells you that it will help what you are doing. Everything should be done for a specific reason. You are doing it with a specific result in mind. (Partington, 1995, p. 106)

Partington (1995) found that during early stages of development, the performers were exposed to teachers who nurtured their creativity, taught them how to practice intelligently, gave them constructive feedback, and made learning fun. These teachers believed in their potential to succeed. They were committed to helping them improve and initiated them to deliberate practice early in their career. These findings are similar to those reported in aforementioned studies conducted with athletes.

In sum, research in this section has shown that training is a central component in the development of expert performance. Both the amount and quality of training appear to be significant determinants in this process. As the previous citation illustrated, it is one thing to practice and simply go through the motions; it is another to practice with a specific intention to improve personal performance. It is apparent that coaches and teachers play a crucial role in helping performers strive and maintain this type of quality training. Since athletes train or deliberately practice to compete at various levels, and coaches most often play an important role in this capacity as well, it is imperative that we examine the competition component of the coaching process.

COMPETITION: MAKING IT HAPPEN WHEN IT COUNTS

Competition is evidently an important part of the coaching process. According to G. A. Bloom (2002), coaches engage in a variety of activities on the day of a competition. They perform important tasks prior to, during, and after the competition. Interestingly, it has been demonstrated that the responsibilities of coaches during competition vary from individual to team sports. In the latter context, coaches play an active role, while in the former one, coaches were found to be more passive and act more or less as observers (G. A. Bloom, 2002).

According to expert Canadian coaches of team sports, game-day routines are important for maximizing the preparation and performance of athletes (G. A. Bloom et al., 1997; Salmela, 1996). These routines can include team-building activities (i.e., pre-game meal), a morning practice, common transportation to the competition site, and a fixed dressing room protocol. For many expert coaches, mental preparation is also key on the day of a competition. Consequently, they allow some time in the pre-game schedule for their athletes to engage in individual mental activities.

Mental training was found to be quite important to both expert athletes and coaches in Durand-Bush's (2000) study. Although the athletes began to develop mental skills during early stages of their development, they made a more conscious effort to improve them at higher levels (i.e., investment and maintenance years). It is noteworthy that mental training did not always involve formal and structured sessions. Most of the time, the athletes refined their psychological skills and strategies during daily activities and in conjunction with other training exercises. Many athletes reported that they thought a lot about their sport in an attempt to figure out ways to maximize their performance during training and competitions, and that this in itself contributed to the development of their performance. This is an interesting finding because many researchers and practitioners in the field of sport psychology assume that mental training has to be structured and involve the use of specific performance enhancement techniques in order to be effective.

Nonetheless, aside from benefiting from being cognitively engaged, many athletes reported using visualization and self-talk mainly to prepare for competitions and to remain focused during competitions. The expert coaches in Durand-Bush's (2000) study argued that in helping the athletes to develop competition plans, they encouraged the use of imagery, relaxation, and other performance enhancement strategies. Competition planning has been shown to be a valuable skill in the achievement of exceptional performance. Orlick and Partington (1988) found that successful athletes developed elaborate competition plans that helped them to focus and refocus before and during events, and to evaluate their performances after the event. Gould, Eklund, and Jackson (1990) found similar results in their study with Olympic wrestling champions. It thus appears that coaches can contribute to the readiness of athletes on the day of competitions by helping them develop sound performance plans prior to these events.

Expert coaches are concerned with creating pre-competition routines not only for athletes but also for themselves since the quality of their performance during a competition is often affected by the amount of preparation in which they engage that day (Salmela, 1996). Rest, physical activity (i.e., walk or run), and mental rehearsal of tactics are examples of strategies they use to prepare themselves.

The pre-game warm-up is also perceived to be a key component of the game day routine. Expert coaches invest time in organizing cohesive team warm-ups so the athletes feel well-prepared going into the competition. During this time, some coaches take the opportunity to scout the opposition by observing line combinations as well as weaknesses and tendencies (Salmela, 1996; G. A. Bloom et al., 1997). Following the pre-game warm-up, expert coaches often engage in a final pre-game talk in which they address a few key points that later guide the athletes during the competition. Contrary to popular belief, they only give emotional or fired-up pre-game speeches on selected occasions.

Aside from implementing pre-competition plans, expert coaches were found to play an active role during competition as they get athletes to perform the strategies they have taught them in training (Salmela, 1996; G. A. Bloom et al., 1997). From a coach's perspective, several factors come into play during a competition; for example, they must monitor the opposition, prepare athletes for substitutions, deal with referees, and motivate athletes to perform at their optimal level. Time-outs as well as intermissions must be carefully planned in order to maximize opportunities to defeat opponents (Salmela, 1996; G. A. Bloom et al., 1997).

Research shows that post-competition evaluation is crucial at a high level in sport (G. A. Bloom et al., 1997; Durand-Bush, 2000; Orlick & Partington, 1988; Salmela, 1996). Many coaches and athletes spend a considerable amount of time assessing their performance after events and drawing lessons to improve their performance in subsequent practices and competitions. The reputable coaches in Salmela's study revealed that it is important to evaluate performance based on both the quality of a performance and the outcome. They suggested taking the time to meet with athletes after a competition but to refrain from doing a detailed analysis right away. Conducting an elaborate post-game evaluation within 24 hours following a competition appears to be more suitable as it gives both the coaches and the athletes sufficient time to reflect, regain control of emotions, and identify areas of improvement.

Very often coaches do not have much time to reflect during and after competitive events. They are often compelled to make decisions under severe pressure situations, some of which are not always favorably looked upon. During the 1996 Summer Olympic Games in Atlanta, long time gymnastic coach, Bela Karolyi, was criticized for a decision he made, which led to much controversy. During her first vault, American gymnast Kerri Strug severely sprained and tore ligaments in her ankle (Washington Post, 1996). In order for her team to earn the gold medal, she had to perform and succeed her second vault. Strug became an immediate star after landing her vault, shedding tears of pain, collapsing, and crawling off the mat. At the medal ceremony, coach Karolyi had to carry her to the podium due to the severity of her injury. An important question that arose was: "Should Karolyi have let Strug perform the second vault, knowing that she was suffering and could potentially cause more damage to herself?" With many college scholarship possibilities and several impending agents waiting for her after the Olympic feat, it was not clear why Karolyi acted the way he did. The Karolyi-Strug case is one of many that raise questions concerning the extent to which athletes should be pushed. It is not uncommon to see coaches overplay their top athletes during competitions even when they are exhausted or injured.

An important factor in high level sport is "recovery." Recovery was a significant theme addressed in Durand-Bush's (2000) study. The athletes discussed some of the strategies they used to allow themselves to recover mentally and physically from competitions, and from the intense training they were engaged in before events. These included relaxing, taking naps, and engaging in activities outside of their sport. According to many researchers, the importance of recovery cannot be underestimated. Ericsson et al. (1993) noted that because deliberate practice activities are mentally and physically effortful, they should be balanced with adequate recovery periods in order to prevent exhaustion or burnout. Morgan, Brown, Raglin, O'Connor, and Ellickson (1987) noted that athletes who do not allow their bodies to recuperate are at risk of being overtrained and experience both psychological and physiological disturbances that could seriously affect their performance. It is interesting that several athletes in Durand-Bush's study wished they had more time to rest during the investment and maintenance years. These findings have important implications for coaches who have the responsibility of closely monitoring the athletes' training and performances. Levin (1991) reported that coaches should ask their athletes to share how they physically and mentally feel throughout their training season in order to detect any signs of exhaustion or overtraining states.

In sum, expert coaches have an important job to do before, during, and after competitions. Before an event, they must establish routines for both themselves and their athletes. During a game, they must strategically plan for time-outs and intermissions, as well as maintain a good rapport with officials. After a competition, coaches must engage themselves and the athletes in debriefing performances and drawing lessons for future training and competitions. Due to the physical and mental demands of high level sport, coaches should monitor athletes throughout their training and competitive season to ensure that they are getting adequate recovery periods to prevent overtraining, injuries, and burnout.

ORGANIZATION: METICULOUS WORK BEHIND THE SCENES

Although not as explicitly researched or discussed, organization is a fundamental step in the coaching process as this is what helps coaches prepare for training and competition. Côté and Salmela (1996) defined organization as "the knowledge used by coaches to establish optimal training and competition conditions by structuring and coordinating various coaching tasks" (p. 250). Studies have shown that organization depends mainly on the type of sport (i.e., individual vs. team) that is being coached (Côté & Salmela, 1996; Salmela, 1996), however, similar key organizational elements to both environments have been found. These pertain to: (a) working closely with support staff, (b) long and short term planning, (c) structuring practice sessions, and (d) dealing and working with concerns.

Salmela (1996) found that at a more conceptual level, expert coaches initiate organizational tasks based on a vision that they have for a particular season. One of the challenges they face is getting athletes to buy into this vision. In order to provide a sense of control and direction, high level coaches routinely devise seasonal, and sometimes, quadrennial training plans that are consistent with the team vision. The main purpose of this long-term planning is to provide a structure for practicing physical, technical, tactical, and mental skills. In many cases, long-term plans are segmented into monthly and weekly tasks. While season plans can be detailed for some expert coaches, they remain flexible and are adapted based on the specific demands of situations (Salmela, 1996).

Another organizational task performed by expert coaches and their support staff involves team selection. According to Salmela (1996), coaches often select athletes based on character rather than skill or talent, as it is quite important for them to form a cohesive team. Setting and monitoring goals with athletes by using logbooks and game statistics, and having individual meetings with them on a regular basis is also common practice among expert coaches.

Coaches at a high level must deal with additional organizational feats such as fundraising to overcome financial concerns, the media, travel plans, and disruptive athletes (Salmela, 1996). Although some organizational tasks are time consuming and not particularly interesting to perform, expert coaches accept them as part of their job and invest considerable time and effort into accomplishing them because most often, their organization directly affects training and competition, as well as the motivation and respect of athletes (G. A. Bloom, 1996; Salmela, 1996).

Expert Coaches' and Athletes' Personal Characteristics: Developing the Right Skills and Attributes

Many studies have attempted to unravel the personal characteristics, skills, and behaviors of expert coaches and athletes required to excel at a high level. Research has shown that teachers or coaches who have confidence and believe in their students or athletes have a positive impact on their performance. This phenomenon has been referred to as the Pygmalion effect (Horn & Cox, 1993; Sinclair & Vealy, 1989). The Pygmalion effect is the process by which the expectations of teachers or coaches lead to the actualization of these desired expectations. Essentially, their expectations are based on their observations and beliefs in certain characteristics and skills that make up the talent of individuals. As expectations are verbally and non-verbally communicated over time, the performance of these individuals conforms to initial expectations. Their expectations and beliefs thus become a self-fulfilling prophecy.

According to Durand-Bush (2000), the Olympic and World champions manifested self-confidence early on in their athletic career. Many of them attributed this to the fact that their parents and coaches believed in them. Thus the "Pygmalion effect" appeared to be instrumental in these cases. Once particular expert coach confirmed that the first and most important thing to nurture in athletes is belief. She did, however, stated that it is improper to mislead athletes if they clearly demonstrate a lack of ability to succeed at a certain level in their sport. The expert coaches in Salmela's (1996) study also discussed the importance of believing in their athletes.

It is critical for coaches to create an environment that avoids social comparison and encourages skill development (Chaumeton & Duda ,1988). From early to later stages of sport participation, athletes may become dependent and focus on either winning or improving based on the environment that coaches choose to create. Barber, Sukhi, and White (1999) found that the top reasons for young athletes participating in various sports are to have fun, learn new skills and improve old ones, enjoy the excitement, and surmount challenges. On the other hand, it was found that some competitive swimmers terminated their participation because they were not having enough fun and they were not as successful as they had wished (Gould, Feltz, Horn, & Weiss, 1982). This shows how the environment created by coaches can have either a positive or negative impact on the sport experiences of athletes.

Two of the 10 accomplished athletes in Durand-Bush's (2000) study reported dropping out of their sport at one point during their career; in one case because of a lack of enjoyment, and in the other because of the excessive focus on competition and pressure to succeed. The incidence of dropout in sport, particularly during adolescence, is a prevalent concern in our society (Csikszentmihalyi et al., 1993; Ewing et al., 1996; Weinberg & Gould, 1995). Consequently, many studies examined the factors that lead to drop out. Weinberg and Gould found that too much emphasis on outcomes and performance, and a lack of motivation and self-esteem were contributing factors. Results of Durand-Bush's (2000) study showed that although most of the athletes were not pressured to compete and to win during childhood, some of them did not always have the most favorable environmental conditions in which they could develop.

Partington (1995) examined the role of master teachers or coaches in his study. He found that during early stages of development, the performers were exposed to teachers who nurtured their creativity, taught them how to practice intelligently, gave them constructive feedback, and made learning fun. These teachers believed in the performers' potential to succeed. They were committed to helping them improve and initiated them to deliberate practice early in their career.

Some research in the field of education indicates that excellent teachers and coaches possess certain perspectives and characteristics that appear to maximize the effectiveness of their interventions with performers (Berliner, 1988). Some scholars argue that successful coaches adopt a more constructivist approach, which has been shown to be extremely valuable in teaching (Larochelle & Bednarz, 1994). In the constructivist view of learning, individuals use their own existing knowledge and prior experiences to understand new information. Furthermore, when they are actively involved in processing information and reconstructing it in personally meaningful ways, they are more likely to remember it and apply it to other situations.

In contrast to traditional teaching-learning models in which individuals are passive rather than active learners, the constructivist model "places students at the center of the process - actively participating in thinking and discussing ideas while making meaning for themselves" (King, 1993, p. 30). Teachers or coaches facilitate learning in less directive ways, allowing students to interact with information, manipulate, and relate it to what they already know. They organize the context, provide resources, and question the students to stimulate critical thinking and develop personal problem-solving approaches (Glasersfeld, 1985; King, 1993). Research has shown that teachers and coaches who have significantly contributed to the development of expert performance often adopt this style of teaching (G. A. Bloom, 1996; Durand-Bush, 2000; Durand-Bush & Salmela, 1996; Salmela, 1996).

In one particular study in which the perspectives of athletes were examined, it was found that athletes favor coaches who: (a) plan effective practices, (b) are themselves skilled, and (c) provide learning opportunities (Martin, Dale, & Jackson, 2001). Chouinard and Thompson (2002) reported that National Hockey League (NHL) players also prefer skilled coaches who have an advanced knowledge of the game. They also appreciate coaches with great leadership and sound interpersonal and communication skills. First and foremost though, they favor coaches who treat them with respect and believe in their abilities.

Several athletes in Durand-Bush's (2000) study revealed that they appreciated the fact that their coaches paid attention to their needs and adapted their communication strategies to suit their style of learning. Coaches who were most effective and highly regarded were those with whom the athletes connected and developed a good relationship based on trust and respect. All of the coaches in this same study highlighted the importance of communicating well with their athletes and giving them opportunities to share their input and be part of the decision-making processes. They stimulated their critical thinking by asking them many questions and involved them in solving problems. It was clear that they adopted a more constructivist approach in their coaching (Glasersfeld, 1985; King, 1993).

Csikszentmihalyi et al. (1993) conducted a longitudinal study over a period of four years with 208 high school students excelling in the domains of art, athletics, mathematics, music, and science. Their focus thus centered on performers who had reached what B. S. Bloom (1985) entitled the "middle years." According to the talented teenagers, the most influential and memorable teachers in their lives were those who: (a) loved their work, (b) perceived their emerging needs and interests, (c) provided a secure environment for extending their skills, (d) inspired them to recognize intrinsic rewards, (e) gave them the freedom to make choices and be creative, and (f) minimized extrinsic pressures like competition, grades, rules, and bureaucratic procedures.

These teenagers also demonstrated a preference for teachers who gave immediate and constant feedback that was informational rather than controlling. Csikszentmihalyi et al. (1993) stated that "the less students' egos are threatened [by controlling feedback], the more unself-consciously they can become immersed in their work" (p. 220), thus the more they can experience flow. They further suggested that "Only those teachers who translate their own interest into flow conditions for students will succeed in catalyzing talent development" (p. 185). Similarly, Salmela (1996) found that the expert coaches in his study created a nurturing environment in which their athletes could express themselves, feel confident, and perform skills with a high degree of quality and satisfaction.

In sum, several studies have shed light on the characteristics of expert coaches and athletes. Believing in athletes, developing relationships based on trust and respect, stimulating critical thinking, providing opportunities for enjoyment and creativity, keeping communication channels open, and involving athletes in the decision making and problem solving process appear to be important coaching perspectives and attributes that contribute to the development of expertise of athletes. By shaping positive sport experiences, coaches can increase the self-confidence of athletes and encourage positive social behaviors (Smoll, 1998), which can in turn, contribute to the physical, emotional, and intellectual development of athletes (Smith, 1998). According to the expert coaches in Salmela's (1996) study, one important guiding principle is that coaches should be concerned with helping athletes develop sound personal characteristics that lead them to fulfill not only athletic but also personal goals.

Contextual Factors: The Influence of Culture and Type of Sport on Coaching

G. A. Bloom (2002) defined contextual factors as situation-specific variables that can have an important impact on the primary components of the coaching process, that is, organization, competition, and training. Consequently, contextual factors should be monitored and considered in coaching plans (Côté et al., 1995). Examples of contextual factors are family life, educational environment, and work conditions of coaches and athletes. All of these factors have the potential to positively or negatively influence team performance and overall success (G. A. Bloom, 2002).

The Coaching Model (Côté, Salmela, Trudel et al., 1995) was developed based on the knowledge and experiences of Canadian coaches. Interestingly, some recent studies have shown that the context of coaching in developing countries is quite different than that in developed countries like Canada, and has implications on the coaching process. Moraes, Salmela, and Rabelo (2000) studied 22 pre-elite Brazilian soccer players aged from 16 to 18 years old, and found that prior to being selected to junior professional developmental teams, they had little family support and formal coaching. However, this lack of coaching appeared to be compensated for by the remarkable number of hours they practiced during their childhood in anticipation that they might someday reap the financial rewards of becoming professional athletes. Rabelo (2002) found that the current professional coaches of these selected soccer players had little formal coaching education; however, they were all former professional players. These coaches did not spend much time on organization but rather invested most of their time running practices in the morning and in the afternoon without the help of assistant coaches. These findings are different than those of Salmela (1996) and G. A. Bloom and Salmela (2000) who found that expert Canadian coaches spend valuable time organizing and planning their practice sessions.

In another study, Vianna (2002) examined tennis players from upper-middle-class Brazilian families. Compared to the aforementioned soccer athletes from lower socio-economic-class families, these tennis athletes received specialized coaching early on in their career, a finding similar to that of Durand-Bush (2000). This suggests that even within one country, the coaching process can vary significantly and can depend to some extent on the socio-economic status of families.

In the context of judo in France, it was found that some dimensions in the original coaching model vary considerable from the Canadian judo context (Moraes, 1998; Moraes & Salmela, 2001), particularly where coach and athlete characteristics are concerned (d'Arripe-Longueville, Fournier & Dubois, 1998). Within the French judo context, certain coaching behaviors such as verbally abusing athletes, giving them preferential treatment, creating conflict between them, and showing interpersonal difference were tolerated. These behaviors would be highly questionable within the Canadian judo context, for example, where coaches are expected to respect athletes and provide a nurturing environment for the development of both personal and athletic skills.

In sum, research indicates that the context within which coaches work to help athletes achieve excellence must be carefully considered because significant differences can exist between sports and countries, and even within the same country (Moraes et al., 2000;

Vianna, 2002; Salmela & Moraes, 2003). Although the Coaching Model (Côté, Salmela, Trudel et al., 1995) can be used as a framework for guiding expert coaches and athletes in their endeavours, the dimensions of its components (i.e., training, competition, organization, coach and athlete personal characteristics, and context) must be adapted to best fit the current reality of coaching worldwide.

CONCLUDING REMARKS

Important advancements have been made in the research on expert coaching and the intricacies of the coaching process at a high level. Côté, Salmela, Trudel et al. (1995) made a significant contribution by postulating a coaching model to guide the development of athletes, however, more research is warranted to examine its applicability in various contexts. Overall, more research must be conducted in the domain of sport to clearly identify the roles, responsibilities, and contributions of coaches in the talent development process. After all, coaches are some of the most influential people in the sporting career of athletes (B. S. Bloom, 1985; van Rossum, 1995). Whether this is during childhood in the sampling years, during adolescence in the specializing years, or during adulthood in the investment and maintenance years, coaches leave their mark on athletes at one point or another in their athletic career. Hopefully, coaches will touch athletes in multiple positive ways, and not just once they reach an expert level. It appears that this will be more likely to happen if coaches are knowledgeable and skilled for the level at which they coach, they believe in their athletes, and they are sensitive to contextual needs and realities.

REFERENCES

Barber, H., Sukhi, H. & White, S. A. (1999). The influence of parent-coaches on participant motivation and competitive anxiety in youth sport participants. *Journal of Sport Behavior 22(2)*, 162-180.

Bartmus, U., Neumann, E. & de Marées, H. (1987). The talent problem in sports. *International Journal of Sports Medicine, 8*, 415-416.

Berliner, D. C. (1988). *The development of expertise in pedagogy.* Charles W. Hunt Memorial Lecture. American Association of College Teacher Education, New Orleans, LA.

Bloom, B. S. (1985). *Developing talent in young people.* New York: Ballantine.

Bloom, G. A. (1996). *Characteristics, knowledge, and strategies of expert team sport coaches.* Unpublished doctoral dissertation, University of Ottawa, Ottawa, Ontario, Canada.

Bloom, G. A. (2002). Coaching demands and responsibilities of expert coaches. In J. M. Silva & D. Stevens (Eds.), *Psychological foundations of sport* (2nd ed., pp. 438-465). Boston: Allyn and Bacon.

Bloom, G. A., Durand-Bush, N. & Salmela, J. H. (1997). Pre- and post-competition procedures of expert coaches of team sports. *The Sport Psychologist, 11(2)*, 127-141.

Bloom, G. A. & Salmela, J. H. (2000). Personal characteristics of expert sport coaches. *Journal of Sport Pedagogy, 6(2)*, 56-76.

Carlson, R. (1993). The path to the national level in sports in Sweden. *Scandinavian Journal of Medicine & Science in Sports, 3*, 170-177.

Chaumeton, N. R. & Duda, J. L. (1988). Is it how you play the game or whether you win or lose?: The effect of competitive level and situation on coaching behaviors. *Journal of Sport Behavior 11(3)*, 157-174.

Chouinard, N. & Thompson, K. A. (2002, March). *Qualities of a good coach and preferred coaching behaviors as perceived by National Hockey League players.* Paper presented at the 6th Annual Eastern Canada Sport & Exercise Psychology Symposium (ECSEPS), Hamilton, ON, Canada.

Côté, J. (1999). The influence of family in the development of talent in sport. *The Sport Psychologist, 13*, 395-417.

Côté, J. & Hay, J. (2002). Children's involvement in sport: A developmental perspective. In J. M. Silva & D. Stevens (Eds.), *Psychological foundations of sport* (2nd ed., pp. 484-502). Boston, MA: Merrill.

Côté, J. & Salmela, J. H. (1996). The organizational tasks of high-performance gymnastic coaches. *The Sport Psychologist, 10*, 247-260.

Côté, J., Salmela, J. H., Baria, A. & Russell, S. J. (1993). Organizing and interpreting unstructured qualitative data. *The Sport Psychologist, 6*, 55-64.

Côté, J., Salmela, J. H., Trudel, P., Baria, A. & Russell, S. J. (1995). The Coaching Model: A grounded assessment of expertise gymnastic coaches' knowledge. *The Journal of Sport and Exercise Psychology, 17(1)*, 1-17.

Côté, J., Salmela, J. H. & Russell, S. J. (1995). The knowledge of high-performance gymnastic coaches: Competition and training considerations. *The Sport Psychologist, 9*, 76-95.

Csikszentmihalyi, M., Rathunde, K. & Whalen, S. (1993). *Talented teenagers: The roots of success and failure.* New York: Cambridge University Press.

d'Arippe-Longueville, F., Fournier, J. F. & Dubois, A. (1998). The perceived effectiveness of interactions between expert French judo coaches and elite female athletes. *The Sport Psychologist, 12,* 317-372.

Durand-Bush, N. (2000). *The development and maintenance of expert athletics performance: Perceptions of Olympic and World champions, their parents and coaches.* Unpublished doctoral dissertation, University of Ottawa, Ottawa, Ontario, Canada.

Durand-Bush, N. & Salmela, J. H. (1996). Nurture over nature: A new twist to the development of expertise. *Avante, 2(2),* 87-109.

Durand-Bush, N. & Salmela, J. H. (2001). The development of talent in sport. In R. N. Singer, H. A. Hausenblas & C. Janelle (Eds.), *Handbook of sport psychology* (2nd ed., pp. 269-289). New York: John Wiley.

Ericsson, K. A. (1996). *The road to excellence: The acquisition of expert performance in the arts and sciences, sports and games.* Mahwah, NJ: Lawrence Erlbaum Associates.

Ericsson, K. A. (2003). Development of elite performance and deliberate practice: An update from the perspective of the expert performance approach. In J. L. Starkes & K. A. Ericsson (Eds.), *Expert performance in sports* (pp. 49-83). Champaign, IL: Human Kinetics.

Ericsson, K. A., Krampe, R. T. & Tesch-Römer, C. (1993). The role of deliberate practice in the acquisition of expert performance. *Psychological Review, 100(3),* 363-406.

Ewing, M. E., Seefeldt, V. D. & Brown, T. T. (1996). *Role of organized sport in the education and health of American children and youth.* Lansing, MI: Michigan State University, The Institute for the Study of Youth Sport.

Gilbert, W. D. & Trudel, P. (2000). Validation of the Coaching Model (CM) in a team sport context. *International Sports Journal 4(2),* 120-128.

Glasersfeld, E. von (1985). Reconstructing the concept of knowledge. *Archives de psychologie, 53,* 91-101.

Gould, D., Eklund, R. C. & Jackson, S. A. (1990). *An in-depth examination of mental factors and preparation techniques associated with 1988 U.S. Olympic team wrestling excellence.* Unpublished final project report presented to USA Wrestling.

Gould, D., Feltz, D., Horn, T. & Weiss, M. (1982). Reasons for attrition in competitive youth swimming. *Journal of Sport Behavior 5(3),* 155-165.

Horn, T. S. & Cox, C. (1993). The self-fulfilling prophecy theory: When coaches' expectations become reality. In J. Williams (Ed.), *Applied sport psychology: Personal growth to peak performance* (pp. 68-81). Mountain View, CA: Mayfield.

King, A. (1993). From sage on the stage to guide on the side. *College Teaching, 41(1),* 30-35.

Larochelle, M. & Bednarz, N. (1994). À propos du constructivisme et de l'éducation. *Revue des sciences de l'éducation, 20(1),* 5-19.

Levin, S. (1991). Overtraining causes Olympic-sized problems. *Physician and Sports Medicine, 19,* 112-118

Martin, S. B., Dale, G. A. & Jackson, A. W. (2001). Youth coaching preferences of adolescent athletes and their parents. *Journal of sport behavior 24(2),* 197-212.

Moraes, L. C. (1998). *Beliefs and actions of expert Canadian judo coaches.* Unpublished doctoral dissertation, University of Ottawa, Ottawa, Ontario, Canada.

Moraes, L. C. & Salmela, J. H. (2001). Influences of the Canadian context on beliefs of expert Canadian, Japanese, and European judo coaches. In M. Pirritano & A. Cei (Eds.), *Psicologia dello sport (Psychology of sport)* (pp. 61-74). Rome: CONI (School of Sport).

Moraes, L. C., Salmela, J. H. & Rabelo, A. S. (2000). O desenvolvimento de desempenho exceptional de jogadores jovens do futebol mineiro [The development of performance of young Mineiro soccer players]. Anais do primeiro congresso cientifico Latino-Americano. Fundep: Sao Paulo.

Morgan, W. P., Brown, D. R., Raglin, J. S., O'Connor, P. J. & Ellickson, K. A. (1987). Psychological monitoring of overtraining and staleness. *British Journal of Sports Medicine, 21*, 107-114.

Orlick, T. & Partington, J. (1988). Mental links to excellence. *The Sport Psychologist, 2,* 105-130.

Partington, J. T. (1995). *Making music.* Ottawa, Canada: Carleton University Press.

Patton, M. Q. (1987). *How to use qualitative methods in evaluation.* Beverly Hills, CA: Sage.

Rabelo, A. S. (2002). *The role of families in the development of aspiring expert soccer players.* Unpublished master's thesis, Federal University of Minas Gerais, Brazil.

Salmela, J. H. (1996). *Great job coach! Getting the edge from proven winners.* Ottawa, Canada: Potentium.

Salmela, J. H. & Moraes, L. C. (2003). Development of expertise: The role of coaching, families, and cultural contexts. In J. L. Starkes & K. A. Ericsson (Eds.), *Expert performance in sports* (pp. 276-293). Champaign, IL: Human Kinetics.

Sinclair, D. A. & Vealey, R. S. (1989). Effects of coaches' expectations and feedback on the self-perceptions of athletes. *Journal of Sport Behavior, 12,* 77-91.

Singer, R. N. & Janelle, C. M. (1999). Determining sport expertise: From genes to supremes. *International Journal of Sport Psychology, 30,* 117-150.

Smith, R. E. (1998). A positive approach to sport performance enhancement: Principles of reinforcement and performance feedback. In J. M. Williams (Ed.), *Applied sport psychology* (3rd ed., pp. 28-40). Mountain View, CA: Mayfield.

Smoll, F. L. (1998). Improving the quality of coach-parent relationships in youth sports. In J. M. Williams (Ed.), *Applied sport psychology* (3rd ed., pp. 63-73). Mountain View, CA: Mayfield.

Starkes, J. L., Deakin, J., Allard, F., Hodges, N. J. & Hayes, A. (1996). Deliberate practice in sport: What is it anyway? In K. A. Ericsson (Ed.), *The road to excellence: The acquisition of expert performance in the arts and science, sports and games* (pp. 81-106). Mahwah, NJ: Lawrence Erlbaum.

Thomas, K. T. & Thomas, J. R. (1999). What squirrels in the trees predict about expert athletes. *International Journal of Sport Psychology, 30,* 221-234.

van Rossum, J. H. A. (1995). Talent in sport: Significant others in the career of top-level Dutch athletes. In M. W. Katzko & F. J. Mönks (Eds.), *Nurturing talent* (pp. 43-57). Assen, The Netherlands: Van Gorcum & Comp.

Vianna, N. S., Jr. (2002). *The role of families and coaches in the development of aspiring expert tennis players.* Unpublished master's thesis, Federal University of Minas Gerais, Brazil.

Washington Post. (1996, August 2nd). *Strug to sign with big agent.* Retrieved from [http://www.washingtonpost.com/wpsrv/sports/olympics/daily/gymnstcs/aug/02/strug.htm].

Weinberg, R. S., & Gould, D. (1995). Foundations of sport and exercise psychology. Champaign, IL: Human Kinetics.

SHIFTING TRAINING REQUIREMENTS DURING ATHLETE DEVELOPMENT: DELIBERATE PRACTICE, DELIBERATE PLAY AND OTHER SPORT INVOLVEMENT IN THE ACQUISITION OF SPORT EXPERTISE

JOSEPH BAKER AND JEAN CÔTÉ

CONTENTS

SUMMARY

Researchers consistently indicate that elite performance in any domain is not possible without a significant commitment to training and practice. However, there is debate over the benefits and costs associated with various types of training performed during different stages of biological and cognitive development. This chapter advocates that early forms of involvement in organized sport should focus on a varied experience in physical activities with an emphasis on fun and enjoyment rather than structured, effortful training. Emphasis on structured, effortful training during early development is associated with greater costs (physical and social) and, in most cases, is not associated with greater levels of proficiency compared to a diversified, enjoyable involvement. The amount and type of training performed during the various stages of development is clearly dependent on the specific demands or capacities underlying performance in the sport, as well as the age at which athletes reach their peak performance. Coaches and parents should be aware of the effect these factors can have on youth involvement in sport and physical activity.

Introduction

Elite sport performers have the ability to captivate our attention with the seeming ease at which they accomplish difficult tasks. For as long as exceptional performers have been amazing us with their ability, researchers have considered the elements underpinning their performance. While early examinations of exceptional ability focused on the relative importance of biological factors versus environmental factors, more recent investigations have considered the interaction of these factors in developing expertise (see Baker & Davids, in review).

Although our understanding of genetic and environmental variables in the acquisition of expert performance is still limited, researchers consistently indicate that elite sport performance is not possible without a considerable commitment to training and practice. However, the nature of the training performed during an athlete's development is a topic of much contention and has important implications for sport expertise and long-term involvement in sport and physical activity.

Relationship between Quantity of Training and Proficiency

Empirical examinations of skill development robustly support the relationship between training/practice and skill acquisition. A. Newell and Rosenbloom (1981) reviewed a considerable literature on rates of learning and indicated that performance increases according to a power function. This finding, better known as the power law of practice, states that learning is negatively accelerated with rapid improvements in performance at the onset of practice but decreases over time as practice continues. However, while the rate of learning may decline, the positive relationship between hours of training/practice is maintained.

Although the power law of practice has its critics (K. M. Newell, Liu & Mayer-Kress, 2001), the seemingly ubiquitous nature of the law has lead some researchers to conclude that the majority of inter-individual variation in performance could be explained solely by the amount of training performed. Simon and Chase (1973), in their classic study of chess expertise, suggested that a large proportion of the variation between performers was the result of differences in time spent practicing. Similarly, Ericsson and his colleagues (e.g., Ericsson, Krampe, & Tesch-Romer; 1993; Ericsson & Lehmann, 1996) advocate that increases in performance in any domain are the result of adaptation to task constraints through training or practice. Supporting this conclusion are numerous examples of the athlete's cognitive system 're-organizing' to meet task and training demands. For instance, because of the limited visual information available from their opponent 'post contact', expert performers in racquet or batting sports (e.g., cricket, badminton, squash) will use advance visual information (i.e., opponent's body position 'pre-contact') to predict their opponent's forthcoming actions (e.g., Abernethy, 1990).

The theory of deliberate practice developed by Ericsson et al. (1993) is based on the idea that proficiency in any domain is tied explicitly to the amount and type of training performed. However, they proposed that it was not simply training of any type, but the engagement in 'deliberate practice', that was necessary for the attainment of expertise. According to Ericsson et al. deliberate practice activities require effort and attention, do not lead to immediate social or financial rewards, and are performed for the purpose of performance enhancement rather than enjoyment. The ability to accumulate the quantity of training required for expert level performance is constrained by 1) the availability of essential resources (e.g., coaches and training facilities), 2) sufficient motivation to perform effortful training for an extended period of time, and 3) an optimal balance between the training stress necessary for positive performance adaptations and the time necessary for recuperation.

Furthermore, while the power law of practice is based on the notion that the relationship between training and proficiency is negatively accelerated, the theory of deliberate practice is grounded in the belief that this negative acceleration can be averted through attention to 'deliberate practice'. According to Ericsson et al.'s (1993) *monotonic benefits assumption*, there is a linear relationship between the number of hours of deliberate practice and the performance level achieved. In a review of studies on skill acquisition and learning, Ericsson (1996) concluded that, with few exceptions, level of performance was determined by the amount of time spent performing a "well defined task with an appropriate difficulty level for the particular individual, informative feedback, and opportunities for repetition and corrections of errors" (pp. 20-21). By continually modifying the level of task difficulty, future experts are faced with opportunities to prevent learning plateaus and perpetuate adaptation to higher amounts of training stress.

Data from Ericsson et al.'s (1993) study of expert musicians supports the relationship between number of hours of deliberate practice and level of performance. They found that expert level musicians spent in excess of 25 hours per week in deliberate practice activities (i.e., training alone) whereas less successful musicians spent considerably less time in deliberate practice (e.g., amateurs < 2 hours per week). These notable differences in weekly training accumulate to become enormous divisions after years of training. Expert accumulated over 10, 000 hours in deliberate practice by age 20 while amateurs accumulated about 2000 hours at that age.

Although the theory of deliberate practice was developed through research with musicians, Ericsson and colleagues (Ericsson et al., 1993; Ericsson, 1996) have indicated that the theory also applies to expertise in sport. To date, researchers applying the theory of deliberate practice to sport have investigated figure skating (Starkes, Deakin, Allard, Hodges, & Hayes, 1996), karate (Hodge & Deakin, 1998), wrestling (Hodges & Starkes, 1996), soccer (Helsen et al., 1998), middle distance running (Young & Salmela, 2002), field hockey (Baker, Côté & Abernethy, 2003a; 2003b; Helsen et al., 1998), triathlon (Baker, Côté & Deakin, in press), and basketball and netball (Baker et al., 2003a; 2003b). By and large, the relationship between hours spent in sport-specific practice and level of attainment is consistent with the tenets of deliberate practice theory. Expert athletes accumulated more hours of training than non-experts (Helsen et al., 1998; Starkes et al., 1996; Hodge & Deakin, 1998), although the monotonic relationship has been criticized (see Baker et al., in press). Moreover, not only do experts spend more time overall in practice, they also devote more time to participating in the specific activities most relevant to developing the essential skills for expert performance (Baker et al., 2003b; Deakin & Cobley, 2003).

However, while the positive relationship between training and elite performance is consistently upheld in sport research, several other tenets of the theory of deliberate practice have not been supported (Abernethy, Farrow, & Berry, 2003). Most relevant to the present discussion is the lack of corroboration for deliberate practice as the single most valuable form of training an athlete can perform throughout his or her development. For example, Baker et al. (2003b) found that athletes rated involvement in competition as the most useful form of training for developing decision-making skills and physical fitness, yet the value of competitive experience is not addressed by the deliberate practice framework. Furthermore, there is significant research indicating that involvement in structured, intensive training during early development may be counter-productive to the development of expertise (see Baker, 2003; Côté, Baker, & Abernethy, 2003). Côté and his colleagues (Côté et al., 2003; Côté & Hay, 2002) advocate that reducing the acquisition of expert performance in sport to a single dimension (i.e. deliberate practice) fails to acknowledge important developmental and social aspects of human abilities.

A DEVELOPMENTAL APPROACH TO EXPERTISE DEVELOPMENT IN SPORT

Various researchers (Bloom, 1985; Côté, 1999; Wylleman, De Knop, Ewing, & Cumming, 2000) have conducted qualitative examinations of the development of expertise in sport. Common to their proposed models of development are important transitions that demarcate the stages in athletes' paths to expertise (Durand-Bush & Salmela, 2001). For example, Bloom (1985) suggested that elite performers moved through three qualitatively different stages, which he characterized as the early years, middle years, and later years. Wylleman et al. (2000) proposed four stages of sport participation that are based on the changing structure of organized sport. The first three stages evolve from initial contact to organized sports to intensive level of training, and finally to high level of involvement into competitive sport. The fourth stage is representative of athletes' discontinuing competitive sports. Côté and colleague (Côté, 1999; Côté et al. 2003; Côté & Hay, 2002) extended this work by developing an empirically based model specific to athlete development. The Developmental Model of Sport Participation (DMSP; Figure 1) considers three different outcomes of sport participation: 1) elite participation, 2) recreational participation, and 3) drop out. Where a sport participant ultimately ends up is determined by the types of activities and contexts they experience at different stages of development (Côté et al., 2003; Côté & Hay, 2002).

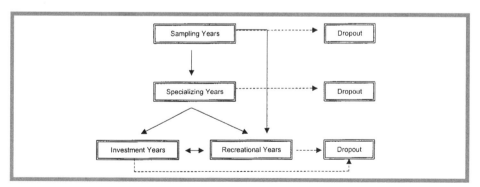

Figure 1 The Developmental Model of Sport Participation (DMSP) developed by Côté and colleagues. This model outlines te different paths youth sport participants can follow leading to 1) elite performance, 2) recreational performance, or 3) dropout from sport. At each stage of development different conditions are essential for maximized participation.

Strength of the DMSP is that a procedure has been developed to systematically assess the theoretical assumptions underlying the theory (Côté, Ericsson, & Beamer, in press). This interview procedure can be used to directly test the conditions of the sampling, specializing, and investment year by tracking longitudinal changes of sport participation patterns and various playing and training activities. The procedure also allows researchers to assess the optimal amount and structure of sport practice and play-related activities at each stage of development. The careful analysis of the lives of athletes that have achieved different performance levels in sport has uncovered valuable information about the conditions necessary to maximize participation and learning at different stages of sport involvement. All in all, the DMSP is consistent with other models of sport development (e.g. Bloom, 1985; Wylleman et al., 2000) and has specific determinants and outcomes that can be tested for their scientific validity.

Bronfenbrenner (1999) provided an operational model allowing the scientific study of development. His propositions can be applied to the development of expertise in sport. He proposed that in order for development to occur individuals must engage in the activity on a fairly regular basis over an extended period of time. Moreover to be developmentally effective the activity must increase in complexity; simple repetition is insufficient. Bronfebrenner and other developmental psychologists (e.g. Larson & Verma, 1999) proposed that measuring the activities children engage in throughout their development provides a useful assessment of the learning environments that lead to various developmental outcomes. In the DMSP, the activities of play, practice, and other sporting activities have been presented as measurable behaviors affecting the development of sport expertise and long-term sport participation. The sampling, specializing, and investment years are differentiated by the amount of deliberate practice and deliberate play performed, and the athlete's involvement in activities other than their main sport. The sampling years are characterized by a low frequency of deliberate practice and a high frequency of deliberate play; the specializing years are marked by similar amounts of deliberate play and deliberate practice; and the investment years are characterized by a high frequency of deliberate practice and a low frequency of deliberate play (Côté et al., 2003; Côté & Hay, 2002). Further, the sampling years are presented as an important period to "sample" different sporting activities instead of specializing in one sport. The DMSP also provides age ranges for each stage that are consistent with general theories of child development such as those identified by Piaget (1962) and Vigotsky (1978). An underlying similarity between these theories is the notion that plays and early diversification are important building blocks of children's physical, cognitive, and emotional development. Because of its focus on developmentally appropriate training, the DMSP allows policy makers and sport educators to make informed decisions in an effort to maximize children's sport participation and development while reducing costs (e.g. overtraining, injuries, drop out).

THE NEGATIVE CONSEQUENCES OF EARLY SPECIALIZATION

An important discrepancy between the deliberate practice model advocated by Ericsson et al. (1993) and the developmental model presented by Côté and colleagues (Côté, 1999; Côté et al., 2003; Côté & Hay, 2002) is the type of activities performed during early stages of development. The deliberate practice approach is based on the monotonic relationship between performance and time spent in deliberate practice. According to Ericsson et al. (1993) "the higher the level of attained elite performance, the earlier the age of first exposure as well as the age of starting deliberate practice" (p. 389). However, focus on deliberate practice at a young age is associated with significant costs (Baker, 2003; Wiersma, 2000). For instance, an early focus on structured training can have considerable negative effects on developing athletes' physical health. Excessive forms of training during crucial periods of biological development can significantly increase the risk of over-training injuries (Dalton, 1992). An example of this is often seen in the knees of developing athletes. Due to rapid bone growth of the femur, tibia and/or fibula (as seen during a 'growth spurt') the knee joint becomes less flexible because muscles and tendons do not increased in length at the same rate as the bones. Under periods of physical training, this imbalance increases the amount of stress applied to the knee and connective tissues, thereby increasing the risk of injury from repetitive microtrauma and associated conditions such as tendonitis, apophysitis, and stress fractures (Dalton, 1992).

One sport where early specialization is commonplace is gymnastics. Due to the specific requirements of gymnastics competition, early specialization *appears* to be a requirement for future elite performers. Beamer, Côté and Ericsson (2004) found that more successful international gymnasts specialized earlier than less successful international gymnasts. However, this earlier specialization was associated with a higher prevalence of injury. Indeed, the excessive training stress of high-level gymnastics involvement coupled with the rapid growth occurring during this period of biological development create an environment conducive to higher rates of overuse injuries (Caine, Cochrane, Caine, & Zemper, 1989; Zetaruk, 2000)

Early specialization is also associated with shorter sport careers than early diversification (Bompa, 2000). A study of elite Russian swimmers (Barynina & Baitsekhovskii, 1992) found that athletes who began specialized training early (age 9-10) spent less time on the National team and ended their sports careers earlier than athletes who started specialized training later (age 12-13). In fact, there is reasonable empirical support for the notion that early specialization is associated with higher levels of attrition at all levels of ability (Gould, 1987; Weiss & Petlichkoff, 1989). Gould, Udry, Tuffey, and Loehr's (1996) study of burnout in tennis players suggested that a singular focus on tennis at an early age contributed to withdrawal from the sport. More recently, Wall (2004) interviewed parents of active and dropout male high-level ice hockey players to examine possible differences in the hockey players' training activities between the ages of 6 and 13 years of age. While both groups invested similar amounts of time in organized training the dropout players began off-ice training (i.e., aerobic training and strength training) at a younger age and invested significantly more hours per year in off-ice training at ages 12-13 than the active players. This type of physical training activity has always been rated by expert athletes as being low in enjoyment (Hodge & Deakin, 1998; Hodges & Starkes, 1996; Helsen et al., 1998).

Based on these findings it is reasonable to suggest that the emphasis on structured, effortful training indicative of the early specialization approach may have forgotten an extremely salient factor in youth sport involvement - fun. Participants withdrawing from sport consistently indicate that lack of fun or enjoyment is a predominant motive for discontinuing participation (Ewing & Seefeldt, 1996). In a recent retrospective investigation of drop out from competitive youth sport, Butcher, Lindner, and Johns (2002) found that during early stages of involvement, "lack of enjoyment" was the most important reason for transfer to a different sport or withdrawal from sport altogether.

A cost-benefit analysis (Bjorklund & Pellegrini, 2001) can be used to establish the functional significance of early specialization and early involvement in deliberate practice. Cost-benefits analyses assume that for a particular option to be endorsed, benefits should outweigh the costs. Benefits with respect to early involvement in deliberate practice and early specialization score high on the skill acquisition dimension of expertise. However, one has to weigh the physical (injuries) and psycho-social (lack of fun, drop-out, burn out) costs before promoting early specialization as the only path towards the development of expertise in sport. Next, we review some functions of play and early diversification that would provide a path to expertise with lower costs and similar benefits to early specialization.

THE VALUE OF PLAY DURING EARLY DEVELOPMENT

A significant component of the early sport experiences of elite athletes is widespread involvement in a range of organized sports and "deliberate play" activities. Côté and colleagues (Côté, 1999; Côté & Hay, 2002; Côté et al., 2003) defined deliberate play as activities in sport designed to maximize inherent enjoyment. Deliberate play activities are regulated by flexible rules adapted from standardized sport rules and are set up and monitored by the children or by an adult involved in the activity. For example, children typically modify the rules of the sport to find a point where it most resembles the sport and yet allows them to play it at their level. Children will regularly change soccer and basketball rules to suit their needs for playing in the street, on a playing field, or in someone's backyard. When involved in deliberate play activities children are less concerned with the outcome of their behavior than with the behavior per se.

Given that the amount of deliberate practice is a consistent factor differentiating elite and non-elite players in a multitude of sports (Helsen et al., 1998; Starkes et al., 1996; Hodge & Deakin, 1998) a number of questions remain: From a skill acquisition perspective, should we encourage early specialization and sole involvement in deliberate practice at a young age? Is it a waste of time to get involved in play activities during the sampling years? Authors have considered play as a specific adjustment to the context of childhood (Bjorklund & Green, 1992). The sense of control and self regulation associated with children's sustain involvement in deliberate play may result in sustained involvement in sporting activities, which, in turn, affords greater opportunities for learning specific skills.

Although play is often described as having no readily observable immediate benefits, it has been defended as having an important function in children's development (Pellegrini & Smith, 1998). Bjorklund and Pellegrini (2001) argued that this paradox can be reconciled by suggesting that the apparent lack of immediate benefits associated with play reveals either a benefit that is delayed in development or an immediate benefit that the participant (or the observer) may be unaware of. For example, deliberate play in sport can have immediate value in terms of motivation to stay involved in sport or it may have differed benefits and relate to later ability to process information in various sporting situations.

Motivational theories based on self regulation (Ryan & Deci, 2000; Vallerand, 2001) support this idea and predict that early intrinsically motivating behaviors (e.g. deliberate play) have a positive effect over time on an individual's overall motivation, and ultimately the individual's willingness to engage in more externally controlled activities (e.g. deliberate practice). In a retrospective longitudinal examination of baseball players' training, the amount of deliberate play during the sampling years was positively related to the amount of specific baseball training during the specializing years ($r = .55$, $p < .05$) and the investment years ($r = .67$, $p < .05$; Gilbert, Côté, Harada, Marchbanks, & Gilbert, 2002). The authors suggested that early deliberate play activities could be beneficial in the development of motivation to pursue intense training in a specific sport. In other words, involvement in deliberate play during the sampling years engages young athletes in activities that are enjoyable and intrinsically regulated. This type of engagement during the sampling years subsequently helps young athletes become more self-determined and committed in their future sport participation. High amounts of deliberate play activities at a young age may provide children with a motivational advantage that early involvement in deliberate practice activities would not provide.

From a skill acquisition perspective deliberate play may serve as a way for youth to explore their physical capacities in various contexts. Qualitative analyses of children's early involvement in sports such as tennis (Carlson 1988; Côté, 1999), rowing (Côté, 1999), and baseball (Hill, 1993) show that deliberate play-like activities were important in the first few years of elite athletes' engagement in sport. Soberlak and Côté (2003) recently showed that elite hockey players spent slightly more time in deliberate play activities than deliberate practice activities before age 20. In another study of elite and recreational baseball players Gilbert et al. (2002) showed that elite players were involved more deliberate play hours than recreational players from age 6 to 12.

A recent study (Berry & Abernethy, 2003) investigated the early development of Australian Rules football players, comparing 17 elite players classified as expert decision-makers and 15 elite players classified as non-expert decision makers. Their results showed that experts invested a significantly greater amount of time in all deliberate play activities. Moreover, qualitative analyses allowed the authors to provide some insight into the context in which deliberate play took place. For example, Berry and Abernethy (2003) reported the following quotes from the expert players (p. 52-53):

She'd (mum) have four or five hockey sticks, you know, a couple of them were oldies, a couple were broken, we'd just smash around with those. And then we'd play with her basketball or something and then we'd go and have a kick with the footy, so you're getting three different sort of balls in a space of two hours and they're all different. (E3)

We used to play out in the backyard, backyard footy, backyard cricket, backyard basketball, soccer. All types of sport you know, if someone's outside it would be one on one marking competition, stuff like that. Where you do it, time and time again. And even the old man would be out there with soccer ball and would set up goals and try and put them through. (E15)

We used to do it (play football) at home like every day, every day we were out playing straight away, straight home from school, dropped the bag, there's four on four, lets go and (we) used to smash each other you know to get the ball. (E16)

A key area where involvement in deliberate play and structured practice are considerably different is in the amount of time that youth spend actively engaged in the activity. Deliberate play activities involve an engagement of time in physical activities that is difficult to match with any kind of structured practice. When youth play street basketball two on two for one hour there are few periods of waiting or "off task" time such as one would find in a structured practice. The athletes "time on task" or actual engagement in physical activities in practices has been investigated in sports such as volleyball (Brunelle, Spallanzani, Tousignant, & Martel, 1989; McKenzie, 1986; Wuest, Mancini, Van der Mars, & Terrillion, 1986), ice hockey (Trudel & Brunelle, 1985), soccer (Boudreau & Tousignant, 1991) and taekwon-do (Brunelle et al, 1989). These authors reported that athletes' time on task rates varied between 25 and 54 percent of the total practice time. The time "off task" during practices usually include athletes' waiting around to perform the next drill, coaches setting up equipment, or athletes transitioning from one drill to another. Although there are obvious advantages of having a coach provide athletes with feedback about their performance, monitor success, and provide immediate instruction, it is unclear whether, during early stages of development, the benefits of this structured environment are superior to the benefits one gains from engagement in deliberate play activities.

It is plausible that deliberate play activities during the sampling years establish a range of cognitive and motor experiences that become beneficial for sport specific performance and later involvement in deliberate practice activities. Repeated sport experiences during the sampling years, in various contexts, will ultimately provide children with a broad foundation of skills that will help them overcome the physical and cognitive challenges of various sports as well as their main sport. As sport around the world becomes more institutionalized and organized (De Knop, Engström, Skirstad, 1996) it is important to provide youth with opportunities to get involved in deliberate play activities. It is also important to think twice before modifying children's environments to achieve a more concentrated focus on deliberate practice at a young age at the expense of play.

EARLY DIVERSIFIED INVOLVEMENT AND ADULT EXPERTISE

Support for the early specialization approach to expertise acquisition is based on two assumptions. The first is that during early stages of development, future experts distinguish themselves from future non-experts with regard to training quantity and quality. However, research indicates that differences between these groups do not occur until later in the development. For instance, Hodges and Starkes (1996) found that training based differences between elite and non-elite wrestlers did not occur until approximately 18 years of age. Further comparisons of expert and non-expert athletes in soccer (Helsen et al.,

1998), field hockey (Helsen et al., 1998), and triathlon (Baker et al., in press) found that training-based differences did not occur until 13, 15, and 20 years of age, respectively. Prior to these ages the groups appeared quite similar with respect to training exposure.

The early specialization approach is also based on the assumption that in early stages of development, deliberate practice is superior to other forms of training. However, there is evidence that athletes who had a diversified sport background were not at a disadvantage compared to athletes who specialized early. In a recent study of expert decision-makers from the sports of basketball, netball, and field hockey, Baker et al. (2003a) found a significant negative relationship between athletes' involvement in additional sporting activities and the amount of sport-specific training needed to achieve expertise. In other words, as the number of additional sporting activities athletes were involved in increased, the number of hours of sport-specific training prior to national team selection decreased. Baker et al. indicated that participation in other relevant activities (e.g., other sports where dynamic decision-making is necessary) during early phases of development augmented the physical and cognitive skills necessary in their primary sport. Stevenson (1990) also found that elite field hockey, rugby, and water polo players who had a diversified early involvement were not at a disadvantage compared to those who specialized early.

However, there are notable exceptions that limit us from completely advocating diversification during early stages of expertise development. Sports where peak performance occurs at early ages (i.e., before biological maturation) such as women's gymnastics (Beamer et al., 2004) and women's figure skating (Deakin & Cobley 2003) indicate differences in sport specific training between elite and less elite athletes as early as age 7. However, as outlined earlier, this level of involvement during early periods of development can have significant consequences.

Apart from these particular cases, diversified training during early development in elite athletes is quite common. Nevertheless, our understanding of the mechanisms by which diversification influences skill development is limited. Research examining transfer of learning and cross training may provide some insight. Thorndike (1914) suggested that "identical elements" between tasks were transferable (see Singley & Anderson, 1989 for a more recent application of Thorndike's theory). Building on this concept, Schmidt and Wrisberg (2000) suggested that transferable elements could be categorized into movement, perceptual, and conceptual elements. Movement elements refer to the biomechanical and anatomical actions required to perform a task. For example, throwing a baseball overhand and an overhand serve in tennis share movement elements. Perceptual elements refer to environmental information that individuals interpret to make performance related decisions. Field hockey and soccer, both require participants to accurately interpret the actions of their opponents in order to be successful; therefore, these sports share this perceptual element. Lastly, conceptual elements refer to strategies, guidelines, and rules regarding performance. Gymnastics and diving share conceptual elements (e.g., similar rules), as do basketball and netball (e.g., similar strategies).

There is evidence that a "physical conditioning" category should be added to this list of transferable performance elements. Researchers (e.g., Loy, Hoffman, & Holland, 1995) examining the physiological effects of "cross-training" provided support for the notion that general cardiovascular effects can be transferred. Over the past three decades, exercise physiologists have considered the transfer of cardiovascular training effects across similar and dissimilar modes of activity. Typically, cross-training effects occur between sports that share similar modes rather than between dissimilar modes. For example, short-term interventions of combined run-cycle training, which share similar muscle groups (i.e., similar modes), are as effective as running alone in increasing physiological parameters such as aerobic capacity (Flynn et al., 1998; Mutton et al., 1993), while combined run-swim training was not as effective as running alone (Foster et al., 1995). In a recent examination of transfer of training in triathletes, Millet et al. (2002) found that cross-training effects occurred between cycling and running but not for swimming (i.e., a dissimilar mode of activity).

Studies also suggest that the effects of cross-training and/or transfer are most pronounced during early stages of involvement (Loy et al., 1995). For instance, any form of aerobic exercise can cause the general physiological adaptations that occur at the onset of a physical training program; however, the more trained an athlete becomes, the smaller the relative improvement from cross-training. By this reasoning, a variable participation during early stages of development may be equally beneficial to specific forms of training in achieving the physiological adaptations necessary for increases in cardiorespiratory fitness.

A diversified approach to early athlete development may not be at odds with the power law of practice. During initial stages of development increases in performance occur due to rapid improvement in general capabilities. With prolonged practice and training over time, improvements become much more specific in nature and more difficult to attain. During initial exposure to the task, however, the same general adaptations may be produced through similar activities that share the same 'elements.' For instance, childhood involvement in running or cycling will produce the same general physiological adaptations (e.g., increases in blood volume and maximal cardiac output). Once these general adaptations have been made, training should become more specific; however until that point there may be equal benefit in both types of training on the development of the aerobic performance system. A proposed model of this relationship is presented in Figure 2.

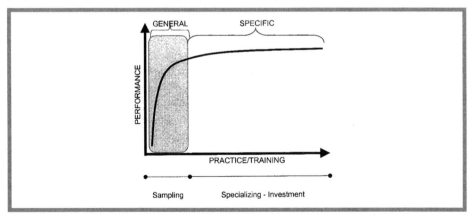

Figure 2 Proposed role of diversified early involvement in the developmemt of sport experise. The power law of practice proposed by A. Newell and Rosenbloom (1981) is represented by the solid line. During the sampling stage (i.e., the shaded area) adaptations are general in nature. Once these general adaptations have taken place, training should become more specific so that positive adaptations are perpetuated (i.e., during the specializing and investment stages).

GENERAL CONCLUSIONS: SPORT DEMANDS AND CONSTRAINTS ON THE DEVELOPMENT OF EXPERT PERFORMANCE IN SPORT

Côté, Deakin, Baker, and Horton (2003) concluded that sport-specific demands and constraints determine the type of training performed during different stages of expertise development. Sport demands include physical demands such as muscular endurance or power, movement demands such as precision and esthetics, and cognitive demands such as perception, memory or strategic capabilities. Understanding the task demands underpinning expert performance in a specific sport is essential for understanding the types and amount of training necessary at different stages.

To illustrate this relationship, we will discuss a series of studies (see Table 1) examining the development of expert performance in gymnasts (Beamer et al., 2004), team sport athletes (Baker et al., 2003a; 2003b), and triathletes (Baker et al., in press). These sports are ideal for comparisons of this nature since successful performance in each requires the mastery of different skills and/or capacities. For instance, successful performance in triathlon places high demands on endurance abilities and relatively little demand on memory abilities while gymnastics places high demands on memory abilities and very little on endurance. The team sports being examined fall somewhere between gymnastics and triathlon in relation to demands on memory and endurance, but place high demands on decision-making abilities. Further, gymnastics is unique in this group of sports because it also involves an aesthetic component not required in the other sports.

Table 1 Training-related variables during different stages of development.

	Gymnastics	Team Ball Sports	Triathlon
Pre-adolescence (5-12 years)			
Training Hours/Week	14-23	4	0
# of Other Sports	0	6	4
Adolescence (13-18 years)			
Training Hours/Week	38-50	8-16	4-7
# of Other Sports	0	2-5	4-6
Early Adulthood (19-35 years)			
Training Hours/Week	0[a]	22	20
# of Other Sports	N/A	0-2	0-3

[a] – gymnasts have typically retired by this stage.

As mentioned earlier, gymnastics is a sport where early specialization is a normal occurrence. Gymnasts can be involved in as much as 23 hours of sport-specific training per week during the pre-adolescent period (between 5 and 12 years of age). In contrast, team sport athletes performed an average of 4 hours of sport-specific training and triathletes reported performing no sport-specific training during this time. During adolescence (13 to 18 years of age), all groups reported increased involvement in sport specific training. However, for the gymnasts this level rose to an amazing average of 50 hours of training per week compared to averages of 16 hours per week and 7 hours per week in the team sport athletes and triathletes respectively.

Involvement in a range of sports (i.e., sampling) during pre-adolescence was found in the team sport athletes and the triathletes. The team sport athletes were involved in an average of 6 sports before 12 years of age while the triathletes were involved in four different sports during this time. As these athletes moved into adolescence, involvement in these activities typically decreased, which is indicative of moving into the "specializing" stage. Conversely, no evidence of sampling was found for the gymnasts. They were involved only in a single activity - gymnastics - throughout their development.

The differing age of peak performance in these sports may be a critical constraint on the type of training performed during an athlete's development. In their examination of peak performance in track and field, baseball, swimming, tennis, and golf, Schulz and Curnow (1988) speculated that different sporting abilities peaked at different times of life. For example, reaction time, flexibility, power and gross body coordination peak relatively early in life while precision, rate control, arm-hand steadiness, aiming, and endurance peak later (Schulz & Curnow, 1988). Ages of peak performance in our groups support this conclusion; specifically, gymnasts peak earliest (15-17 years of age) followed by team sport athletes and triathletes (peak performance between 21 and 35 years of age for both of these groups).

The esthetic requirement of gymnastics may also contribute to the early age of peak performance. Highest levels of performance for gymnasts are almost exclusively seen before biological maturation takes place. In some instances, considerable measures are taken to prevent the onset of biological maturation in developing gymnasts so that their performance careers can be lengthened (Ryan, 1996).

Given the early age of peak performance for gymnastics, the window of time to amass the quantity of practice necessary for expert performance is smaller compared with sports with later ages of peak performance. Therefore, future expert gymnasts must devote all of their training time to structured forms of training regardless of the negative consequences associated with this approach (e.g., increased risk of injury, shorter performance careers and dropout; Barynina & Baitsekhovskii, 1992; Beamer et al., 2004; Caine et al., 1989). Sports with later ages of peak performance have more flexibility with regard to the type of activities performed during early development. Given that the age of peak performance in the team sport athletes and triathletes had a wider age range and occurred later, training during early development can focus on the sort of diversified, play-like involvement necessary for the development of intrinsic motivation without sacrificing adult expertise. While more research remains to be done, the relationship between later ages of peak performance and opportunities for participation during mid and late adulthood (i.e., masters level participation) may not be coincidental. Given the negative consequences associated with early specialization, participants in these activities may not have the opportunity or the desire to participate beyond early adulthood.

What is clear is that the amount and type of training performed throughout an expert athlete's development is dependent on the specific demands or capacities underlying performance in the sport as well as the age at which performance of these abilities reach their peak. Sports underpinned with abilities that peak later in development can allow greater flexibility during early development than sports with abilities that peak earlier. But eventually, all future expert athletes must adopt a program of training that focuses on deliberate practice. Without a long term commitment to high quality training athletes will be unable to attain elite levels of performance. However, coaches and parents should consider the consequences of structured training during early development as these experiences have a profound influence on involvement in sport and physical activity across the lifespan.

REFERENCES

Abernethy, B. (1990). Anticipation in squash: Differences in advance cue utilization between expert and novice players. *Journal of Sports Sciences, 8,* 17-34.

Abernethy, B., Farrow, D. & Berry, J. (2003). Constraints and issues in the development of a general theory of expert perceptual-motor performance. In J. L. Starkes and K. A. Ericsson (Eds.) *Expert performance in sports: Advances in research on sport expertise* (pp. 349-369). Champaign, IL: Human Kinetics.

Baker, J. (2003). Early specialization in youth sport: A requirement for adult expertise? High Ability Studies, 14, 85-94.

Baker, J., Côté, J. & Abernethy, B. (2003a). Sport specific training, deliberate practice and the development of expertise in team ball sports. *Journal of Applied Sport Psychology, 15,* 12-25.

Baker, J., Côté, J. & Abernethy, B. (2003b). Learning from the experts: Practice activities of expert decision-makers in sport. *Research Quarterly for Exercise and Sport, 74,* 342-347.

Baker, J., Côté , J. & Deakin, J. (in press). Expertise in ultra-endurance triathletes: Early sport involvement, training structure and the theory of deliberate practice. *Journal of Applied Sport Psychology.*

Baker, J. & Davids, K. (in press). Genetic and environmental constraints on variability in sport performance. In K. Davids, S. J. Bennett & K. M. Newell (Eds.), *Variability in the Movement System: A Multidisciplinary Perspective.* Champaign, IL: Human Kinetics.

Barynina, I. I. & Vaitsekhovskii, S. M. (1992). The aftermath of early sports specialization for highly qualified swimmers. *Fitness and Sports Review International, 27(4),* 132-133.

Beamer, M., Côté, J. & Ericsson, K. A. (2003). *What Does it Take to be an Olympic Champion in Rhythmic Gymnastics?* Manuscript submitted for publication.

Berry, J. & Abernethy, B. (2003). Australian Football League Research Board. (2003, June). *Expert game-based decision-making in Australian Football: How is it developed and how can it be trained?* Brisbane, Australia: The University of Queensland, School of Human Movement Studies.

Bjorklund, D. F. & Green, B. L. (1992). The adaptive nature of cognitive immaturity. *American Psychologist, 47,* 46-64.

Bjorklund, D. F. and Pellegrini, A. D. (2001). *The origins of human nature: Evolutionary developmental psychology.* Washington, DC: American Psychological Association.

Bloom, B. S. (1985). *Developing talent in young people.* New York: Ballantine

Bompa, T. O. (2000). *Total training for young champions.* Champaign, IL: Human Kinetics.

Boudreau, P. & Tousignant, M. (1991). L'efficacité de l'intervention d'entraîneurs bénévoles en formation. *Canadian Journal of Sport Sciences, 16,* 134-141.

Bronfenbrenner, U. (1999). Environments in developmental perspective: Theoretical and operational models. In S. L. Friedman & T. D. Wachs, *Measuring environment across the life span: Emerging methods and concepts* (pp. 3-30). Washington DC: American Psychological Association.

Brunelle, J., Spallanzani, C., Tousignant, M., Martel, D. & Gagnon, J. (1989). Effets d'une stratégie d'auto-supervision sur les composantes du temps d'apprentissage dans l'enseignement de deux sports. *Revue Canadienne de l'Education, 14,* 189-201.

Butcher, J., Lindner, K. J. & Johns, D. P. (2002). Withdrawal from competitive youth sport: A retrospective ten-year study. *Journal of Sport Behavior, 25,* 145-163.

Caine, D., Cochrane, B., Caine, C. & Zemper, E. (1989). An epidemiologic investigation of injuries affecting young competitive female gymnasts. *American Journal of Sports Medicine, 17,* 811-820.

Carlson, R. C. (1988). The socialization of elite tennis players in Sweden: An analysis of the players' backgrounds and development. *Sociology of Sport Journal, 5,* 241-256.

Côté, J. (1999). The influence of the family in the development of talent in sports. *The Sports Psychologist, 13,* 395-417.

Côté, J., Baker, J. & Abernethy, B. (2003). From play to practice: A developmental framework for the acquisition of expertise in team sports. In J. Starkes & K. A. Ericsson (Eds.) *Expert performance in sports: Advances in research on sport expertise* (pp. 89-110). Champaign, IL: Human Kinetics.

Côté, J., Deakin, J., Baker, J. & Horton, S. (August, 2003). *Towards a lifespan model of sport development.* Paper presented at the 2003 Congress of the American Psychological Association (August, 2003), Toronto, Canada.

Côté, J., Ericsson, K. A. & Beamer, M. (in press). Tracing the development of elite athletes using retrospective interview methods: A proposed interview and validation procedure for reported information. *Journal of Applied Sport Psychology.*

Côté, J. & Hay, J. (2002). Children's involvement in sport: A developmental perspective. In J. M. Silva & D. Stevens (Eds.), *Psychological foundations of sport* (2nd Edition). Boston, MA: Merrill.

Dalton, S. E. (1992). Overuse injuries in adolescent athletes. *Sports Medicine, 13,* 58-70.

Deakin, J. M. & Cobley, S. (2003). An examination of the practice environments in figure skating and volleyball: A search for deliberate practice. In J. Starkes & K. A. *Ericsson (Eds.) Expert performance in sports: Advances in research on sport expertise* (pp. 90-113). Champaign, IL: Human Kinetics.

De Knop, P., Engström, L-M. & Skirstad, B. (1996). Worldwide trends in youth sport. In P. De Knop, L-M. Engström, B. Skirstad & M. Weiss (Eds.), *Worldwide trends in youth sport* (pp. 276-281). Champaign, IL: Human Kinetics.

Durand-Bush & Salmela (2001). The development of talent in sport. In R. N. Singer, H. A. Hausenblas & C. M. Janelle (Eds.), *Handbook of sport psychology* (2nd ed.) (pp. 269-289). New York: John Wiley.

Ericsson, K. A. (1996). The acquisition of expert performance: An introduction to some of the issues. In K. A. Ericsson (Ed.), *The road to excellence: The acquisition of expert performance in the arts and sciences, sports and games* (1-50). Mahwah NJ: Erlbaum.

Ericsson, K. A., Krampe, R. T. & Tesch-Römer, C. (1993). The role of deliberate practice in the acquisition of expert performance. *Psychological Review, 100,* 363-406.

Ericsson, K. A. & Lehmann, A. C. (1996). Expert and exceptional performance: Evidence of maximal adaptation to task constraints. *Annual Review of Psychology, 47,* 273-305.

Ewing, M. E. & Seefeldt, V. (1996). Patterns of participation and attrition in American agency-sponsored youth sports. In F. L. Smoll & R. E. Smith (Eds.), *Children and youth in sport: A biopsychosocial perspective* (pp. 31-45). Madison: Brown and Benchmark.

Flynn, M. G., Carroll, K. K., Hall, H. L., Bushman, B. A., Brolinson, P. G. & Weideman, C. A. (1998). Cross training: Indices of training stress and performance. *Medicine & Science in Sports and Exercise, 30,* 294-300.

Foster, C., Hector, L. L., Welsh, R., Schrager, M., Green, M. A. & Snyder, A. C. (1994). Effects of specific versus cross-training on running performance. *European Journal of Applied Physiology, 70,* 367-372.

Gilbert, J. N., Côté, J., Harada, C., Marchbanks, G. & Gilbert, W. D. (2002, October-November). *Comparison of developmental activities of NCAA Division 1 and recreational baseball players.* Paper presented at the meeting of the Association for the Advancement of Applied Sport Psychology, Tucson, Arizona.

Gould, D. (1987). Understanding attrition in children's sport. In D. Gould & M. R. Weiss (Eds.), *Advances in pediatric sports sciences* (pp. 61-85). Champaign, IL: Human Kinetics.

Gould, D., Udry, E., Tuffey, S. & Loehr, J. (1996). Burnout in competitive junior tennis players: 1. A quantitative psychological assessment. *The Sport Psychologist, 10,* 322-340.

Helsen, W. F., Starkes, J. L. & Hodges, N. J. (1998). Team sports and the theory of deliberate practice. *Journal of Sport & Exercise Psychology, 20,* 12-34.

Hill, G. M. (1993). Youth participation of professional baseball players. *Sociology of Sport Journal, 10,* 107-114.

Hodge, T & Deakin, J. (1998). Deliberate practice and expertise in the martial arts: The role of context in motor recall. *Journal of Sport & Exercise Psychology, 20,* 260-279.

Hodges, N. J. & Starkes, J. L. (1996). Wrestling with the nature of expertise: A sport specific test of Ericsson, Krampe and Tesch-Römer's (1993) theory of <deliberate practice>. *International Journal of Sport Psychology, 27,* 400-424.

Larson & Verma (1999). How children and adolescents spend time across the world: Work, play, and developmental opportunities. *Psychological Bulletin, 125,* 701-736.

Loy, S. F., Hoffmann, J. J. & Holland, G. J. (1995). Benefits and practical use of cross-training in sports. *Sports Medicine, 19,* 1-8.

McKenzie, T. L. & King, H. A. (1982). Analysis of feedback provided by youth baseball coaches. *Education and Treatment of Children, 2,* 179-188.

Millet, G. P., Candau, R. B., Barbier, B., Busso, T., Rouillon, J. D. & Chatard, J. C. (2002). Modelling the transfers of training effects on performance in elite triathletes. *International Journal of Sports Medicine, 23,* 55-63.

Mutton, D. L., Loy, S. F., Perry, D. M., Holland, G. J., Vincent, W. J. & Heng, M. (1993). Effect of run vs combined cycle-run training on aerobic capacity and running performance. *Medicine and Science in Sports and Exercise, 25,* 1393-1397.

Newell, A. & Rosenbloom, P. S. (1981). Mechanisms of skill acquistion and the law of practice. In J. R. Anderson (Ed.). *Cognitive skills and their acquisition* (pp. 1-55). Hillsdale, NJ: Erlbaum.

Newell, K. M., Liu, Y.-T. & Mayer-Kress, G. (2001). Time scales in motor learning and development. *Psychological Review, 108,* 57-82.

Pellegrini, A. D. & Smith, P. K. (1998). Physical activity play: The nature and function of neglected aspect of play. *Child Development, 69,* 577-598.

Piaget, (1962). *Play, dreams, and imitation in childhood.* New York: W. W. Norton.

Ryan, J. (1996). *Little girls in pretty boxes: The making and breaking of elite gymnasts and figure skaters.* New York, NY: Warner Books.

Ryan, R. M. & Deci, E. L. (2000). Self-determination theory and the facilitation of intrinsic motivation, social development, and well-being. *American Psychologist, 55,* 68-78.

Schmidt, R. A. & Wrisberg, C. A. (2000). *Motor learning and performance: A problem-based learning approach.* Champaign, IL: Human Kinetics.

Schulz, R. & Curnow, C. (1988). Peak performance and age among superathletes: Track and field, swimming, baseball, tennis, and golf. *Journals of Gerontology: Psychological Sciences, 43,* P113-P120.

Simon, H. A. & Chase, W. G. (1973). Skill in chess. *American Scientist, 61,* 394-403.

Singley, M. K. & Anderson, J. R. (1989). *The transfer of cognitive skill.* Cambridge, MA: Harvard University Press.

Soberlak, P. & Côté, J. (2003). The developmental activities of elite ice hockey players. *Journal of Applied Sport Psychology, 15,* 41-49.

Starkes, J. L., Deakin, J. M., Allard, F., Hodges, N. J. & Hayes, A. (1996). Deliberate practice in sports: What is it anyway? In K. A. Ericsson (Ed.), *The road to excellence: The acquisition of expert performance in the arts, sciences, sports and games* (pp. 81-106). Mahwah, N. J.: Erlbaum.

Stevenson, C. L. (1990). The athletic career: Some contingencies of sport specialization. *Journal of Sport Behavior, 13,* 103-113.

Thorndike, E. L. (1914). *Educational psychology: Briefer course.* New York: Columbia University Press.

Trudel, P. & Brunelle, J. (1985). Les situations d'apprentissage offertes aux joueurs inscrits dans des ligues de hockey mineur. *L'Association Canadienne pour la Santé, l'Education Physique et le Loisir, 51,* 18-25.

Vallerand, R. J. (2001). A hierarchical model of intrinsic and extrinsic motivation in sport and exercise. In G. C. Roberts (Ed.). *Advances in motivation in sport and exercise* (pp. 263-319). Champaign IL: Human Kinetics.

Vygotsky, L. S. (Ed.). (1978). *Mind in society: The development of higher psychological processes.* Cambridge, MA: Harvard University Press.

Wall, M. (2004). *The early activities and parental involvement of elite active and drop out hockey players.* Unpublished master's thesis. Queen's University, Kingston, Ontario, Canada.

Weiss, M. R. & Petlichkoff, L. M. (1989). Children's motivation for participation in and withdrawal from sport: Identifying the missing links. *Pediatric Exercise Science, 1,* 195-211.

Wiersma, L. D. (2000). Risks and benefits of youth sport specialization: Perspectives and recommendations. *Pediatric Exercise Science, 12,* 13-22.

Wuest, D. A., Mancini, V. H., Van der Mars, H. & Terrillion, K. (1986). The Academic Learning Time-Physical Education of high-, average-, and low- skilled female intercollegiate volleyball players. In M. Piéron & G. Graham (Eds.), *The 1984 olympic scientific congress proceedings* (vol. 6): sport pedagogy. (pp. 123-129). Champaign, IL: Human Kinetics.

Wylleman , P., De Knop, P., Ewing, M. E. & Cumming, S. P. (2000). Transitions in youth sport: A developmental perspective on parental involvement. In D. Lavallee & P. Wylleman (Eds.). *Career transitions in sport: International perspectives* (pp. 143-160). Morgantown, WV: Fitness Information Technology.

Young, B. & Salmela, J. (2002). Perceptions of training and deliberate practice of middle distance runners. *International Journal of Sports Psychology, 33,* 167-181.

Zetaruk, M. N. (2000). The young gymnast. *Clinics in Sports Medicine, 19,* 757-780.

Does Cardiorespiratory Fitness Moderate Stress Responses and Recovery?

Rod K. Dishman

Contents

Summary

A few studies indicate that people report they feel less stressed or cope better with stressful situations when they have been physically active. Also, laboratory studies suggest that people who have high cardiorespiratory fitness recover more quickly physiologically after stress despite having a greater response during stress. However, there have been very few scientific studies of how exercise training affects either coping with stress or physiological stress responses among athletes.

Also, there has been little use of the traditions and methods of biological psychology and neuroscience in the study of physical activity, fitness, and stress. Whether, or under what conditions, cardiorespiratory fitness or regular exercise leads to blunted or augmented physiological responses during stress cannot be determined by a sole reliance on social-cognitive models of stress. Though yet to be demonstrated by the cumulative evidence, it remains plausible that moderate exercise might mitigate certain stress responses in some circumstances. In contrast, vigorous exercise training could increase the capacity of the sympathoadrenal medullary and the HPA cortical systems to respond to intense stressors, such as athletic competition, that evoke a hypothalamic defense mechanism similar to heavy exercise. Therefore, future studies of how exercise training affects stress responses by athletes must clearly characterize the physiological patterns of response elicited by different stressor tasks. The purpose of this chapter is to characterize the current evidence about whether cardiorespiratory fitness moderates stress responses and recovery. Stress will be defined and the methods used to study it will be described. Some directions for future research will also be suggested.

INTRODUCTION

The ability to cope with acute and chronic stress is important for athletic performance and public health. Stress can impair concentration, judgment, and motor skills during competition, and it can lengthen the recovery period after athletic injury. It can lead to painful physical symptoms such as muscle tension, headache, and stomach upset; physiological signs such as a racing or irregular heart beat, high blood pressure, sweating, flushing, tremor, and dry mouth; and behaviors ranging from aggression to hyperactivity to withdrawal. Those signs and symptoms can occur alone or together with the experience of stress emotions, which include the physiological and behavior responses, but are experienced subjectively by the person (e.g., fear, anxiety, anger, confusion, fatigue, and despair). Stress is also linked to leading causes of death, such as heart disease, cancer, accidents, and suicide. Stress can occur during a crisis of high impact and either short or long duration, or during the smaller, brief hassles of daily living. Positive life events or daily uplifts in spirit can also be stressful, but in a good way because they reduce boredom and offset negative emotions. Athletic competition can be a potent elicitor of stress responses.

WHAT IS STRESS?

Lazarus (1993) has recognized three sources of stress: *harm, threat,* and *challenge.* Harm is psychological damage such as an irrevocable loss. Threat is the anticipation of harm. Challenge occurs when one is confident about successfully overcoming difficult circumstances. Responses to stress can be active (resistance or avoidance) or passive (taking it without resistance). Lazarus has also identified two main ways that people cope with stress, namely problem-focused coping and emotion-focused coping. Problem-focused coping involves the identification and removal of the sources of stress. Emotion-focused coping involves changing the way that stressful events are attended to or interpreted. For example, harm or threats are diminished if they are not thought about. Similarly, reevaluation of the meaning or consequences of harm or a threat can remove the cognitive source of stress; rationalizing, denying, and distancing are examples of emotion-focused coping.

Though some people are exposed to more events that cause stress or strain (e.g., family conflicts, money problems, loss of a loved one, athletic injury), personality, coping skills, and social support can lessen one's vulnerability to stress. People who view change as a challenge or an opportunity for success, who feel in control, and who have a strong commitment to a purpose in their life (e.g., career, other people, spirituality) seem to deal better with misfortune than people whose outlook interprets change as a threat, who feel out of control, and who lack a guiding purpose in their lives.

HE **E**XERCISE **C**ROSS-**S**TRESSOR **A**DAPTATION **H**YPOTHESIS

Recent evidence supports the notion that people who are physically active say that they experience fewer symptoms of distress than inactive people regardless of their exposure to undesirable life events or illness, and regardless of their social support from others (Ensel & Lin, 2004). Sources of perceived stress (Fletcher & Hanton, 2003), and the use of problem-focused and emotion-focused coping (Anshel, 1996; Anshel, Jamieson, & Raviv, 2001) has been described among athletes. Also, fluctuations in mood states have been used (e.g., Morgan et al., 1987) to monitor responses to male and female athletes during the stress of heavy training (see Dishman, 1992 for a review) and during recovery from injury (Manuel et al., 2002). Perceived stress and coping styles have also been included in models used to understand the risk and recovery of athletic injury (Wiese-Bjornstal et al., 1998; Williams & Andersen, 1998). Although perceived stress is important for health and human performance (Lazarus, 1993), physiological and biochemical responses during stress provide the biological mechanisms whereby such perceptions directly influence pathophysiology and skilled performance. For example, stress management techniques have been used in attempts to improve sport performance by controlling acute symptoms of stress (Dishman, 1983). Because there is no experimental evidence that exercise training or fitness changes the way people appraise events as threatening or challenging, it is important to determine whether physical activity or fitness alters physiological responses to events that elicit stress.

A study of professional judo and handball athletes (22-23 years of age) having below average peak oxygen uptake ($VO_{2peak} \sim 40$ ml.kg^{-1}.min^{-1}) reported a similar response, but quicker recovery, of HR to laboratory mental stress after an acute, maximal cycling exercise test (Moya-Albiol et al., 2001). Also, a few studies have described changes in levels of stress-related hormones such as cortisol and testosterone (Gonzalez-Bono, 1999; Passelergue & Lac, 1999; Passelergue et al., 1995; Suay et al., 1999) among athletes during or after competition in judo, basketball, wrestling, and weight lifting. However, it is not known whether cardiorespiratory fitness moderates such stress responses among athletes, especially athletes in sports where success does not depend upon high cardiorespiratory fitness or aerobic exercise training. The purpose of this chapter is to discuss existing evidence about the influence of cardiorespiratory fitness on responses to stressors other than exercise, and provide some directions for future studies that might include competitive athletes.

It has been hypothesized (Hocking-Schuler & O'Brien, 1997; Michael, 1957; Sothmann et al, 1996; Van Doornan & De Geus, 1993) that regular exercise or increased cardiorespiratory fitness might confer health protective effects by reducing stress responses such as elevations in heart rate, blood pressure, and catecholamines and cortisol in the blood, which can acutely alter decision making and motor control, and can be chronically pathogenic. Do cardiorespiratory fitness or regular exercise result in cross-stressor adaptations, such that physiological responses during non-exercise provocation are blunted, or otherwise altered? Likewise, does aerobic fitness modify physiological responses during stress among athletes? Those possibilities are plausible, but this chapter discusses whether the available scientific evidence supports that cardiorespiratory fitness or aerobic exercise lead to such a cross-stressor tolerance. The current evidence actually supports a small augmentation of stress responses, but quicker recovery after stress, among men and women who are fit (Jackson & Dishman, 2004). However, the approaches taken and the methods used need improvement for future study in order to fully understand the topic, especially among athletes who have received little research attention.

A Brief History of Exercise Studies

A meta-analysis of 25 studies conducted nearly 20 years ago concluded that the mean, cumulative effect of chronic exercise on physiological reactivity to psychosocial stressors was about a half standard deviation reduction that was similar regardless of the type of stressors used or the physiological responses measured (Crews & Landers, 1987). However, there is not a scientific consensus that agrees with that early conclusion (Blumenthal, 1989; Claytor, 1991; Hocking-Schuler & O'Brien, 1997; Peronnet & Szabo, 1993; Sothmann et al., 1996; Van Doornen & De Geus, 1993). The lack of consensus is mainly explainable by four main factors: (a) Early studies had done a poor job defining or measuring fitness or exercise (see Caspersen et al., 1985 for conventional definitions), so it was hard to determine whether people differed enough to permit a strong test of the influence of fitness or exercise habits on stress responses. Also, the use of HR to estimate peak oxygen uptake confounded the use of HR as both an independent and dependent variable in several studies. A test-anxious person could have exaggerated HR responses to the exercise test and to the other stressors, and be mis-classified as unfit because of the emotional elevation in HR during exercise, (b) the manner of reporting the methods used to measure physiological variables and for computing their change in response to stressors made it difficult to determine whether the procedures in many studies met international standards for psychophysiological research (e.g., Fowles et al., 1981; Fridlund & Cacioppo, 1986, Jennings et al., 1981; Pivik et al., 1993; Shapiro et al., 1996). The accuracy of the measures were questionable in some studies, and the influence of pre-test baselines on the stress variables measured during stress and recovery was not accounted for in several studies, likely giving a false measure of responsiveness, (c) about two-thirds of the studies had used a cross-section of time to compare stress responses among groups classified according to levels of fitness or exercise, rather than comparing responses after a change in fitness or exercise, and without matching the groups on other factors known to influence stress responses, such as temperament, behavior patterns, or reproductive hormone status, and (d) studies generally failed to compare standardized stressor tasks of equal novelty or difficulty and did not choose tasks according to their common or unique features that induce specific or general stress responses (e.g., different sympathovagal and sympathoadrenal medullary responses). Exercise adaptations might extend to certain types or intensities of stressors but not to others.

We recently performed a meta-analytic review of studies published in the English language from 1965 through 2003, that had examined the effect of cardiorespiratory fitness on cardiovascular reactivity during and after acute laboratory stressor tasks (Jackson & Dishman, 2004). There were 327 effects for reactivity measures and 98 effects (expressed as a standard deviation, SD) for recovery measures derived from 60 studies. Potential moderator variables were selected based on characteristics of the stressors, dependent variables, people, and study design that have been reported to influence reactivity. Small, heterogeneous effects of cardiorespiratory fitness were found for augmented reactivity (0.12 SD, 95 % CI, 0.05 to 0.20) but quicker recovery (-0.24, 95 % CI, -0.15 to -0.32). Moderator analyses generally did not explain variation in the observed effects, but fitter people had higher heart rate increases, yet faster recovery, in response to active stressors.

We located only 8 studies of athletes (Boutcher et al, 1995; Brandon et al., 1991; Keller & Seraganian, 1984; Lake et al., 1985; Spalding et al., 2000; Steptoe et al., 1993; Szabo et al., 1994; van Doornen & DeGeus, 1989). Their results paralleled the findings of the overall meta-analysis. Four of those studies were on distance runners or cyclists who have high cardiorespiratory fitness, thus it is unclear whether athletes from sports that emphasize other types of fitness respond differently during stress.

Nonetheless, the quantitative analysis did not support the idea that increased cardiorespiratory fitness is associated with an attenuation of stress reactivity or a substantial improvement in the recovery from stress. However, our review revealed a need for theory-based selection and standardization of stressor tasks that elicit different patterns of physiological reactivity and recovery. Also, studies of the autonomic nervous and its associated neuroendocrine responses that regulate integrated stress responses are needed.

Studies failed to adequately consider physiological mechanisms (Bennett & Whitehead, 1983; Persson, 1996) that explain variations in integrated responses such as HR, BP, or circulating stress hormones such as norepinephrine (NE), epinephrine (EPI), and cortisol. For example, HR responses to a stressor might be similar between people of different fitness levels, but for different reasons. A fit person might have less withdrawal of parasympathetic nerve inhibition of the heart, despite a similar or greater sympathetic nerve stimulation of the heart. Though the integrated HR might not differ from an unfit person, the different pattern of cardiac sympatho-vagal balance would be important, as it is known to have health consequences. Similarly, integrated blood pressure responses might not differ between fit and unfit people, but the groups might differ on factors influencing cardiac output or vascular resistance in ways important for performance or health.

Hence, it has not been possible to determine the specific contributions made by fitness or regular exercise to adaptations in regulatory physiology during stress. Most researchers in this area have assumed that cross-stressor adaptations in physiological responses after chronic exercise would be plausible without first understanding how those physiological responses adapt to exercise. Understanding adaptations to repeated exercise is necessary in order to explain how the hypothesized cross-stressor adaptations after chronic exercise might differ according to the degree of fitness, the type and difficulty of the stressor used, and the dependent stress responses which are elicited by different neurophysiological signals depending upon the nature and intensity of stressors. For those reasons, this chapter is organized to (a) describe the fundamental regulatory physiology of the major stress responses, (b) describe those responses and their adaptations during exercise, (c) discuss the evidence about possible cross-stressor adaptations by cardiorespiratory fitness or regular exercise, and (4) introduce newer methods that can be used to study the central nervous system during and after stress. The specificity and generalizability of physiological responses to various stressors will also be compared with physiology during exercise. Recommendations for future studies are provided.

Despite the widespread use of biological psychology in the study of stress (Chrousos, 1998), and the rapid advances in neuroscience techniques during the past 20 years (Feldman et al., 1997; Kandel et al., 1995), the research strategies employed by exercise psychology have focused on the assessment of self-reports of stress and on integrated physiological responses that are more likely to be signs, not explanations of the stress response. For that reason, the rest of this chapter focuses on the physiological basis of stress. The goal is to provide encouragement and guidance for future research in the field.

A BRIEF HISTORY OF STRESS

In the mid 1800s, the French physiologist Claude Bernard understood that life depended upon maintaining the "milieu interieur" in a constant state during changes in the environment (Bernard, 1867). For example, it is now known that mammalian cells can exist only when certain ranges of temperature and acid-base balance are maintained and when water, nutrients, and oxygen are available. Systems of cells also depend on such balances. In the 1920s, Harvard physician-scientist Walter Cannon formalized Bernard's views by introducing the term "homeostasis" with his research on the roles of adrenaline (i.e., epinephrine) and the autonomic nervous system in regulating and maintaining a physiological steady state during rage and fear (Cannon, 1929). In the early 1930s, Hartman et al. (1932) extended those views by proposing a general tissue hormone theory, which stated that adrenal cortical steroids were needed by all cells for resisting infection, muscular and nervous fatigue, and for regulating body temperature and fluid volume. Each of these events was credited by Hans Selye in forming his theory of a generalized adaptation syndrome (GAS) and the diseases of adaptation (Selye, 1936, 1950).

To Selye, altered homeostasis was not merely a passive response to changes in the environment. He believed that an animal's physiological systems could learn and maintain adaptive defenses against future exposure to stress. Hence, Selye theorized that many diseases resulted from maladaptations to the environments that were insufficient, excessive, or poorly regulated (Selye, 1950). He proposed that "conditioning factors," such as prior exposure and controllability of a stressor, could alter the GAS. Also, Selye believed that stressors, including muscular exercise, might lead to cross-stressor adaptations that would enhance resistance to psychosomatic and neurotic diseases. His research provided a scientific basis for the development of the cross-stressor adaptation hypothesis of exercise whereby exercise training or increased levels of fitness have been postulated to be associated with an attenuation of stress responses in non-exercise situations (Michael, 1957; Sothmann et al., 1996).

ALLOSTASIS
Recently, McEwen (1998) has used the term *allostatic load* to describe the long-term effects of physiological response to stress (including activation of the autonomic nervous system, the hypothalamic-pituitary-adrenal cortical (HPA) axis, and the metabolic, cardiovascular, and immune systems). *Allostasis* means the ability to achieve stability through change (i.e., adaptation). Like Selye, McEwen believes that the price paid for such adaptation to stress

is allostatic load, the strain that results from over activity or under activity of these allostatic systems. Some people develop a *hypoactivity* or *hyperactivity* of the normal stress response. It is believed that *too small* a stress response can be just as harmful as *too much* of a response, because it may result in other responses that compensate. For example, cortisol stimulates blood glucose for energy but it also keeps the immune system in check by inhibiting inflammation. If cortisol does not rise during stress, inflammation can result even though there is no infection. On the other hand, too much cortisol can make a person susceptible to infection by overly suppressing the inflammation response, and it can lead to bone loss, muscle atrophy, and elevated insulin levels.

For unknown reasons, the stress response does not subside in some people after a stressful event has ended. For example, public speaking activates the HPA axis and increases blood cortisol in most people, but that response goes away after experience. However, about 1 in 10 people continues to show an elevated level of cortisol response when they speak in public, regardless of their experience. Likewise, it is not understood why some people lose their ability to mount a stress response after chronic exposure to stressful events. Many researchers are convinced that regular exercise of moderate intensity is one of the best ways to offset the allostatic load of chronic stress, because exercise is known to reduce insulin levels that can be raised by high cortisol, and exercise training lowers blood pressure and resting heart rate. There is also evidence that regular vigorous exercise or high fitness levels increase the capacity to respond to stress (both during maximal exercise and non-exercise stress), while enhancing recovery after the stress ends. Such responses seem adaptive for reducing allostatic load, but are contrary to the more traditional, simple view that exercise mitigates, rather than augments, stress responses.
Stress Responses and Adaptations to Exercise

AUTONOMIC NERVOUS SYSTEM

Primary functions of the sympathetic and parasympathetic branches of the autonomic nervous system (ANS) during exercise are to regulate the increases in HR and BP needed to increase cardiac output in order to support the increased metabolism of skeletal muscle cells. Secondary functions include the regulation of breathing and temperature regulation. The cardiovascular pressor response, which regulates systolic BP during exercise, is understood to depend on a central command of autonomic efferent neural activity in the region of the temporal sensory/motor cortex, which is integrated at the ventrolateral medulla of the spinal cord with a pressor reflex arising from mechanoreceptors (e.g., sensitive to muscle tension) and metaboreceptors (e.g., sensitive to hydrogen ions) in exercising muscle (Mitchell & Raven, 1994). Cardiopulmonary and arterial baroreflexes modulate the exercise pressor response, apparently by an upward and parallel resetting of the operating (i.e., set) point of the arterial baroreflexes resulting from central command (Rowell, 1993). Increased HR during exercise results from an initial withdrawal of cardiac-vagal inhibition of the heart followed by increased activation of the heart by sympathetic nerve activity, and by hormonal stimulation through catecholamines secreted from the adrenal medulla during intense exercise.

Heart rate depends on an algebraic product of intrinsic rate of the heart and autonomic balance of sympathetic and vagal innervation of the heart. Results of several cross-sectional and exercise training studies of men that examined HR after drug blockade of beta-adrenoreceptors (e.g., using propanolol), cholinergic receptors using atropine (acetylcholine is the neurotransmitter of the vagus nerve), or double-autonomic blockade (i.e., propanolol plus atropine) suggest that the bradycardia associated with cardiorespiratory fitness is explained by lowered intrinsic rate rather than by altered sympatho-vagal balance (Berntson et al., 1993). In contrast, other cross-sectional and exercise training studies of men that used similar pharmacologic blockade procedures have demonstrated that the bradycardia results from increased vagal tone and a small reduction in sympathetic activity. Using double autonomic blockade, Shi, Stevens, Foresman, Stern, and Raven, (1995) reported that the bradycardia observed after a 27 % increase in VO_{2peak} in young men who trained for 8 months was determined by increased vagal tone with no change in intrinsic rate.

Early studies of humans estimated sympathetic nerve activity by measuring levels of its major metabolite, MHPG, in urine, plasma or cerebrospinal fluid. Studies of urinary MHPG after a single session of physical activity found increased MHPG excretion or no change, but exercise levels were not quantified relative to fitness, or very low levels of physical activity were used (Morgan and O'Connor, 1988). Later studies quantified exercise intensity relative to fitness levels, but again the findings were mixed. Plasma MHPG typically increased, but urinary MHPG remained unchanged. The relative contributions of NE from peripheral sympathetic nerves were not determined in these studies. At rest, 20-60 % of MHPG in peripheral blood or urine comes from metabolism of brain NE. However, the increase in blood levels of NE during exercise comes mainly from sympathetic nerves innervating the heart and vessels that supply blood to skeletal muscles.

Blood levels of NE and EPI increase in an intensity dependent pattern during acute exercise, similar to the exponential increase in blood lactic acid (Kjaer, 1992). They partially adapt to exercise training. Human studies indicate that exercise training does not alter plasma levels of NE (Kjaer, 1992) or muscle sympathetic nerve activity (Ray & Mark, 1993) measured during resting conditions. Among exercise trained men, plasma NE and EPI levels are lower at a given absolute exercise intensity, unchanged at the same intensity relative to maximal aerobic capacity, but higher than normal at maximal exercise. Whether the higher maximal levels reported among highly trained men results from an upregulated sympathetic response to exercise, i.e., an increased capacity to secrete catecholamines, after exercise training or from higher absolute work is not clear. A comparison of NE or EPI at maximal exercise between people matched on VO_{2peak} but differing in training history could help resolve that question.

Rat studies have shown that exercise training increases tyrosine hydoxylase activity in the adrenal gland and liver (indicative of increased capacity to synthesize NE), but decreases tyrosine hydroxylase activity and NE turnover (i.e., storage of newly synthesized NE) in the heart (Mazzeo, 1991). Changes in the synthesis or turnover of NE in the brain after exercise has not been reported, but studies have shown increases (Tumer et al., 2002) and no change (Soares et al., 1999) in mRNA for tyrosine hydroxylase in the brain. Concentration levels of NE in the brain are decreased in rats after exhaustive swimming (Barchas & Friedman, 1963; Moore & Lariviere, 1964) and nonexhaustive swimming, running on a motorized treadmill, or voluntary running in an activity wheel (Dunn & Dishman, 1991). Conversely, chronic treadmill or activity wheel running increases levels of NE by about 1/2 to 1 SD in NE cell bodies found in the LC and its terminal fields in the frontal cortex, amygdala, hippocampus, and hypothalamus (Dishman et al., 1997, 2000; Dunn et al., 1996; Yoo et al., 2000).

Hypothalamic-Pituitary-Adrenal Cortical Axis Adrenal corticosteroids play roles in regulating blood plasma volume, BP, and glucose metabolism in humans. Levels of adrenocorticotrophic hormone (ACTH) and cortisol in circulating blood increase in an intensity- and duration-dependent manner during cycling and running. These responses during exercise appear to partially adapt after chronic exercise training. Endurance trained men have lower plasma levels of ACTH and cortisol during sub-maximal exercise when compared with less active men at an absolute intensity of exercise, but not when exercise intensity is expressed as a percentage of maximal oxygen uptake (Sutton & Farrell, 1990).

Levels of HPA hormones measured at rest and after maximal exercise or HPA challenge among highly trained men and women suggest an altered regulation of the HPA system after heavy exercise training. Levels of plasma ACTH at supra-maximal exercise intensity have been reported to be higher or similar in highly trained men compared with sedentary control subjects. In contrast, one study of highly trained males reported a hypo-responsiveness of plasma ACTH and cortisol after infusion of corticotrophin releasing factor (CRF), but a normal elevation in ACTH and cortisol during submaximal and maximal treadmill running. Amenorrheic and eumenorrheic female distance runners typically have mild hypercortisolism at rest and blunted ACTH and cortisol response to CRF infusion, despite normal resting levels of ACTH (See Dishman et al., 1998 for a review). Neuropeptides and hormones can synergize at the level of the hypothalamus or pituitary gland to augment the effect of CRF on ACTH secretion. The most studied hormones are arginine vasopressin (AVP) and oxytocin. Cross-sectional and prospective studies in humans have reported lower plasma levels of AVP after exercise in trained compared with sedentary men. Oxytocin inhibits ACTH in primates, but its response to exercise is not understood for either humans or rats.

STRESS RESPONSES AND ADAPTATIONS TO EXERCISE

CROSS-STRESSOR ADAPTATIONS AFTER CHRONIC EXERCISE

Exercise psychologists have failed to build on the aforementioned advances when studying stress, especially by not clearly characterizing the features of the stressor used, and not considering the regulatory mechanisms that govern physiological stress responses. Whereas Cannon placed primary importance on epinephrine secreted from the adrenal medulla, a conventional view today is that NE secreted by sympathetic nerves plays the primary role during most types of stress, with EPI and NE secreted by adrenal medulla playing secondary supportive roles during activation of the sympathetic nervous system. Also, activity in different branches of the sympathetic nervous system can dissociate during mild stress. For example, we found that during passive cold pressor stress, but not active mental stress, fitter women had smaller increases in blood pressure and muscle sympathetic nerve activity, but not cardiac-vagal activity estimated by heart rate variability, than less fit women (Dishman et al., 2003). To complicate matters, it has been known since the 1950s that there are stable differences among people on their patterns of HR and BP responses to the same mental stressor (Lacey, 1950). Thus, interactions between the type of stressor and individual differences among people in their characteristic responses must be considered in research on exercise, fitness, and stress.

In addition, mounting evidence now challenges early views that responses during stress by the hypothalamic-sympathetic-adrenal medullary nervous and cardiovascular systems and the hypothalamic-pituitary-adrenal cortical systems are uniform or generalizable across various types of stress. Rather, stress responses appear to have considerable specificity depending on the type, duration, and intensity of the stressor, which elicits them. For example, novel immobilization stress in rat results in large increases in plasma NE, EPI, and ACTH, which stimulate glucocorticoid release from the adrenal cortex. In contrast, relative to ACTH response, cold stress evokes large NE response, and hemorrhage evokes small NE and EPI responses (Pacak et al., 1998).

A similar specificity has been observed in studies of cardiovascular responses to stress among humans (Allen & Crowell, 1989). Blood pressure responses are greater during hand immersion in cold water (cold pressor) than during mental arithmetic, which elicits greater responses than does a psychomotor reaction time task. In contrast, cardiac output estimated by impedance elctrocardiography is greater during a reaction time task or mental arithmetic than during a cold pressor test. Heart rate increases the most during mental arithmetic compared to lower elevations during the cold pressor or reaction time task. Moreover, increased HR during mental arithmetic is explainable by vagal withdrawal, whereas it is more influenced by sympathetic innervation of the heart during a reaction time task. The hemodynamic patterns also differ according to type of stressor. Increased cardiac output during a reaction time task is mainly explained by increased stroke volume, whereas during mental arithmetic it is explained by increased HR. Cardiac output during the cold pressor is unchanged because the increased HR is offset by decreased stroke volume.

ANS AND CARDIOVASCULAR RESPONSES

There is controversy whether the bradycardia and reduced BP observed at rest and during submaximal exercise in highly fit men and women generalize to reduced HR and BP in response to non-exercise stressors. In addition to the measurement and research design problems discussed at the outset of this paper, the controversy can mainly be traced to confusion about plausible mechanisms explaining why cardiorespiratory fitness should be expected to attenuate HR and BP responses to non-exercise stressors. Because acute aerobic exercise is characterized by increased cardiac output, HR, and systolic BP, and by unchanged or reduced diastolic BP, most researchers in this area have assumed that cardiorespiratory fitness is associated with adaptations in adrenergic activation of cardiovascular responses that will generalize to reduced HR and BP during active coping tasks such as mental arithmetic and psychomotor reaction-time tasks. However, research conducted over 30 years ago found that exercise and mental arithmetic affect left ventricular time intervals differently (Franks & Cureton, 1967). Also, studies consistently have shown that plasma and urinary catecholamine levels after stressful tasks are similar between groups differing in cardiorespiratory fitness (Peronnet & Szabo, 1993; Sothmann et al., 1991). Nonetheless, because levels of circulating catecholamines can rise because of reduced clearance from the blood, in addition to release from sympathetic nerves or the adrenal gland, it is premature to conclude that fitness or physical activity has no effect on sympathetic nervous system responses during mental stress.

Morever, those null findings might be explained in large part by a restricted range in the increase of plasma catecholamines evoked by the stressors. Most of the stressors used have been mild and evoked small increases, typically yielding levels in a range approximating 300-500 pg/ml for NE and 40-80 pg/ml for EPI. Those levels are below thresholds for NE (1500-2000 pg/ml) and EPI (75-125 pg/ml) that reliably elicit increases in HR and systolic BP (Clutter et al., 1980; Silverberg et al., 1978). A five- to-ten-fold elevation in NE and two-fold increase in EPI are generally believed necessary for cardiovascular effects, yet the stressors used have seldom resulted in a doubling of catecholamines above basal levels. In contrast, moderate-to-heavy exercise induces a six- to-ten-fold increase in NE and a tripling of plasma EPI (Clutter et al., 1980).

Psychologists have proposed that increased sensitivity of adrenergic receptors might explain reduced HR and BP among aerobically fit humans during psychosocial stress (Crews & Landers, 1987). However, that hypothesis conflicts with knowledge in neuroscience (Fillenz, 1990, Stanford, 1990), and evidence from exercise studies (Maki et al., 1990; Mazzeo, 1991). Reduced, rather than increased, adrenergic sensitivity on heart and vessels, and in brain, could plausibly explain blunted cardiovascular responses. Human studies testing the cross-stressor adaptation hypothesis of exercise have not measured or manipulated adrenergic receptors.

In summary, it remains unclear why adrenergic adaptations to exercise would have the same form or function as the adrenergic adaptations to typical laboratory stressors. Exercise induces a high metabolic rate with low peripheral resistance to blood flow, but laboratory stressors are applied at a near-resting metabolic rate, and frequently induce increased peripheral resistance. Moreover, the roles of central command and reflexive control of cardiovascular responses seem to differ between exercise and affective behavior (Mitchell & Raven, 1994; Spyer, 1989). Cardiovascular adjustments that accompany behavioral responses are typically congruent with the motor and metabolic demands of the activity, i.e., they are coupled with somatic activity. However, owing to increased sympathetic activity and/or parasympathetic withdrawal during exposure to psychological stressors, physiological responses can exceed those required for energy expenditure. Oddly though, not much research has examined how the brain adapts to exercise in ways that would affect central motor command to stress organs in ways that might generalize to other types of stress. Such brain changes should be studied much more.

Brain Norepinephrine

In a series of studies using rats, we have reported a blunted NE depletion in the LC after repeated foot shock among activity wheel runners (Dishman, et al., 1997), consistent with the view that physical activity has a positive cross-stressor adaptation under certain circumstances. Subsequently we used microdialysis, which permits in vivo sampling of extracellular levels of neurotransmitters in discrete brain areas. We found that chronic wheel runners had a blunted release of NE in the frontal cortex in response to foot shock, despite no change in mRNA for tyrosine hydroxylase in the locus coeruleus (Soares et al., 1999). In contrast, we have found that treadmill exercise training led to augmented levels of NE in the hypothalamus and amygdala in response to the acute stress of immobilization (Dishman et al., 1999). We reported that chronic activity wheel running by rats led to a decreased density of ?adrenoreceptors in the brain frontal cortex when measured under basal conditions (Yoo et al., 2000), but after foot shock stress, the results were reversed. The number of receptors increased, but their sensitivity was decreased, after foot shock (Yoo et al, 1999). How these cross-stressor responses by the brain noradrenergic system might explain cardiovascular or endocrine responses during stress has not been determined, but increased NE levels in the hypothalamus and amygdala after treadmill exercise training are associated with hyper-responsiveness by ACTH to novel immobilization stress (Dishman et al., 1999; White-Welkley, et al., 1995). Also, the brain NE responses do not appear dependent upon exercise intensities sufficient to increase fitness but may differ according to whether the running is forced.

HPA CORTICAL RESPONSES

Cross-stressor adaptations of the HPA cortical system following chronic exercise have received very little study in humans or lower animals. Sinyor et al. (1983) reported that trained men had higher levels of cortisol at rest, under stress (mental arithmetic, a challenging quiz, and the Stroop word-color conflict test), and during recovery when compared to sedentary controls, but the rates of response and recovery were the same for the trained and untrained men. In other studies, men differing in fitness levels had similar levels of cortisol or ACTH in plasma after the Stroop word-color conflict test under novel (Sothmann et al., 1989) or familiar (Blaney et al., 1990) conditions. In animal studies, we have reported no effects of chronic activity wheel running on plasma levels of ACTH and cortisol after repeated footshock in female and male rats (Dishman et al., 1995,1997). Our findings differ from reports of an attenuated ACTH response after immobilization stress in male rats that were treadmill exercise trained (White-Welkley et al., 1996) and after cage-switch in male rats chronically trained by treadmill running (Watanabe et al., 1992).

Exercise studies usually have not measured or controlled reproductive hormones known to influence physiological responses to non-exercise stressors, despite evidence of an interaction between the HPA cortical and the HPA gonadal systems in highly trained women. We have found that treadmill exercise training of female rats treated with estrogen was accompanied by an attenuated ACTH response to familiar treadmill running but a hyperresponsiveness of ACTH to novel immobilization or footshock (White-Welkley et al., 1995, 1996). Whether this hyperresponsiveness of ACTH is a healthful adaptation and whether it is due to increased CRF or other factors that release ACTH is not known. The latter seems likely since treadmill exercise training is accompanied by reduced ACTH in male rats after immobilization stress with no change in brain CRF (White-Welkley et al., 1996). Those findings may indicate that the energy and neuromuscular demands of treadmill running lead to an increased potential for HPA responses to novel stressors.

STRESSOR TASKS

Some of the inconsistency in the results of exercise studies may be explained by the use of different types of stressors. In addition to the novelty vs. familiarity of a stressor, other characteristics of tasks that alter cardiovascular responses during stress include whether the task involves, (a) attention to external or internal sensory stimuli, (b) direct matching of cardiac output to the metabolic demands of the task, (c) active or passive coping, and (d) optimal difficulty to motivate performance. Early work by Lacey and Lacey (1974) led to an intake-rejection hypothesis that cardiovascular reflexes were shaped by attention to external events (sensory intake), leading to cardiac deceleration and hypotension, or by inattention to external events during cognitive tasks (sensory rejection), leading to cardiac acceleration and hypertension. Methodological controversy between this hypothesis and the cardiac-somatic coupling hypothesis of Obrist et al. (1974), which stated that HR and BP increased because the tasks increased metabolism, fueled concerns over the influence of task dimensions on cardiovascular responses during stress. For example, stressor tasks should have minimal motor components, as motor acts may provoke cardiovascular responses independently of an emotional response (Steptoe, 1985).

It is not apparent that cardiovascular adaptations to exercise should be expected to generalize to other stressors that do not have similar psychomotor demands. In contrast to exercise, most non-exercise stressors elicit little or no sensory afferent activity to regulate cardiovascular responses. Thus, much of any cross-stressor adaptation after exercise must involve central command (i.e., motor nerve discharge to the heart, vessels, or adrenal medulla) or altered responses by organs to central command (e.g., decreased number or sensitivity of receptor cells that bind with EPI).

Table 1 Characteristic features and physiological responses to common tasks used in human studies of stress and the ANS.

Task	Coping (Active vs. Passive)	Sensory Focus (Intake vs. Rejection)	Response Pattern	ANS Pattern
Mental arithmetic	active	rejection	88 HR, 88 SBP, 88 DBP,)SV, 88 CO,)TPR	strong vagal withdrawal, β-adrenergic
Psychomotor reaction time	active	intake/rejection	8 HR, 8 SBP, 8 DBP, 8 SV, 88 CO, 9 TPR	moderate vagal withdrawal, β-adrenergic
Stroop word-color conflict	active	intake/rejection	8 HR, 8 SBP, 8 DBP,)SV, 8 CO,)TPR	moderate vagal withdrawal, β-adrenergic
Forehead cold	passive	?	9 HR, 8 SBP, 8 DBP 9 SV,)CO, 8 TPR	vagal activity, α-adrenergic
Cold pressor	passive	?	8 HR,888 SBP, 888 DBP, 9 SV,)CO, 8TPR	vagal withdrawal, β-adrenergic(CA) α-adrenergic

ANS=autonomic nervous system, CA=coronary arteries, CO=cardiac output, DBP=diastolic blood pressure, HR=heart rate, SBP=systolic blood pressure, SV=stroke volume, TPR=total peripheral resistance, 8=increase, 9=decrease,)= little or no change. Sources: Allen & Crowell (1989); Lacey (1950); Dishman et al., (2002; 2003); Jackson & Dishman (2002)

Task features: ANS

Active vs. passive coping is a commonly used taxonomy that recognizes the importance of controllability of stressors and the way central motor commands to the hypothalamic defense system can differ according to different stressors (Spyer, 1989). Active coping is characterized by the availability of control over events (e.g., mental arithmetic, quizzes, reaction time tasks). Active coping typically results in increased β-adrenergic activation. Physiological responses include increases in HR, cardiac output, systolic BP, and withdrawal of vagal tone. Passive coping involves little or no opportunity to control an aversive situation. Passive coping can result in increased HR and an α-adrenergic response that increases peripheral resistance and diastolic BP. Atypical responses can also occur such that increased vagal tone results in decreased HR and decreased BP (a so-called "playing dead" response) (Spyer, 1989). A passive test that elicits a cardiac-vagal response in many people is application of cold to the forehead. Forehead cold can elicit increases in BP characteristic of α-adrenergic activation and muscle sympathetic activity, as well as reduced HR, similar to the mammalian diving reflex, which involves a vagally-mediated bradycardia and β-adrenergic vasoconstriction of the skin and viscera.

The intensity or difficulty of tasks have also been poorly controlled in studies of exercise and cross-stressor adaptations. Hence, comparisons of stress responsiveness between groups differing in fitness or exercise habits might be misleading if the difficulty of the tasks differed between the groups. In our quantitative analysis of the fitness and stress reactivity literature (Jackson & Dishman, 2004) we found that most studies had not reported a measure of actual or perceived difficulty of the task. Of the 60 studies included in the analysis, only about a third reported subjective measures of difficulty or stress. Additionally, only a third of the studies reported performance scores or a measure of the effort that subjects put into performing well on the task; each an indicator that the participants were engaged in the task. Effort is likely to vary if the task is too easy or too challenging. The social context of testing can also interact with task difficulty to influence whether certain physiological responses are evoked. Though real-life experiences that are threatening (e.g., an oral exam, race driving, pilot training) can evoke a large EPI response, sufficient to augment HR and BP responses through hormonal action, commonly used stressors such as mental arithmetic or the Stroop Color-Word conflict task are milder and usually increase HR by altered sympatho-vagal balance of the autonomic nervous system's innervation of the heart rather than by hormonal response. For example, during mental arithmetic heart transplant patients, who have had the autonomic nerves to the heart severed, experience increased BP (Sehested et al., 1995) without the increase in HR (Sehested et al., 1995; Shapiro et al., 1994, 1996) that is observed in people with innervated hearts. Those observations indicate that mental arithmetic does not evoke a sympatho-adrenal medullary response sufficient to alter HR. Thus, tasks like mental arithmetic and public speaking when applied in non-threatening circumstances appear to be too mild to detect differences among fit and unfit subjects on plasma NE or EPI responses (Moyna et al., 1999; Sothmann et al., 1991).

Such tasks might, however, evoke bigger changes in other measures of sympathetic activity. For example, a few studies have reported that MSNA is increased during mental arithmetic, hand immersion in cold water, and isometric exercise. But, I'm unaware of studies comparing subjects differing in cardiorespiratory fitness on MSNA during non-exercise stressors other than the cold pressor. We recently reported that fitness was unrelated to MSNA during mental arithmetic or the cold pressor among men, but fitter women had blunted MSNA and blood pressure responses during the cold pressor (Dishman et al., 2003).

EXERCISE STUDIES: ANS

It is plausible that the resting and exercise bradycardia common among people, who are physically fit, reflect an enhanced cardiac vagal tone that might generalize to other stressors (Porges, 1995). An early study with borderline hypertensive rats found that swim training led to decreased HR and plasma catecholamines, but elevated systolic BP, in response to novel footshock (Cox, 1991).The vagus antagonist, atropine, led to increased HR in the swim trained animals but had no effect on untrained animals. Thus, it appeared that the attenuation in HR after exercise training was explained by increased vagal tone that was maintained during sympatho-medullary stress rather than decreased sympathetic responses alone.

In studies of college-age men and women (Buckworth et al., 1994,1997; Graham et al., 1996), we have used the bradycardia induced by neck suction as an index of vagal tone to determine whether HR and BP responses to active compared with passive coping tasks. Stimulation of the carotid baroreceptors by negative pressure applied to the neck results in a reflexive increase in cardiac-vagal activity and a reduced HR for the few seconds of negative pressure.

In those studies, active coping tasks included a challenging oral quiz, mental arithmetic, and psychomotor reaction time. Each task increases cardiac output, by eliciting either cardiac-vagal withdrawal or adrenoreceptor activation and reduced peripheral resistance to blood flow. Passive tasks were used that either elicit an increase in HR with no increases in cardiac output or peripheral vascular resistance (i.e., hand immersion in cold water) or a decrease in HR and an increase in peripheral resistance presumably by 1-mediated vasoconstriction (i.e., forehead cold). In a cross-sectional comparison of young normotensive men who differed on cardiorespiratory fitness, we reported that high fit subjects had lower HR during all stressors, and in response to carotid negative pressure when compared to the low fit subjects (Graham, Zeichner, Peacock, & Dishman, 1996). However, the change from baseline in HR and BP responses to the stressor tasks did not differ between the groups.

In a cross-sectional study of normotensive women whose parents had hypertension, we reported that physical activity and cardiorespiratory fitness each were associated with bradycardia during mental arithmetic, forehead cold application, and during neck suction (Buckworth et al., 1994). As indicated in the study of men, however, the rate of change from baseline in response to the tasks did not differ according to fitness or activity level. In a third study, fit normotensive women with parental hypertension were detrained for eight weeks (Buckworth et al, 1997). We found no change in BP or HR responses to mental arithmetic, forehead cold, or neck suction after detraining, despite an elevation in resting BP.

Our studies have indicated that cardiorespiratory fitness is associated with lower resting HR that is maintained during and several minutes after different types of stress, and appears to be explainable by cardiac vagal tone. Fitness was not, however, associated with responses (i.e., change from baseline) by HR or BP to stress. Thus, our findings agree with other research (e.g., Claytor, 1991) that contradicts the view that fitness leads to altered HR and BP reactivity to stress. Rather, the lower HR response by fit men and women is accounted for by their lower HR at rest. Our findings are remarkably similar to null findings reported 30 years ago by Raab and Krzywanek (1965) in a classical, but largely ignored, study that used methods superior to most of the studies cited in support of reduced reactivity of HR and BP among active men (Crews & Landers, 1987).

Nonetheless, it remains plausible that increased cardiac-vagal tone after regular exercise might generalize to blunt responses to mild stressors, which elicit increases in HR and BP mainly by vagal withdrawal. In contrast, responses by the sympathetic nervous system seem to be unique to different stress organs during mild stressors. Hence, whether altered regulation of the sympathetic nervous system after regular exercise might lead to a generalizable response seems less clear and could depend upon the intensity of exercise and other stressors.

TASK FEATURES: HPA

The type of stressor also affects HPA cortical responses in rats. Whether the (a) intensity, (b) controllability, (c) novelty, or (d) physiological or psychological nature of stressors, including the type of exercise, affect cross-stressor adaptations after regular exercise has only recently been studied.

Repeated exposure to acute stressors (e.g., restraint, footshock, cold, injection, changes in housing, and forced swimming and treadmill running) commonly results in reduced (i.e., habituated) plasma levels of ACTH and corticosterone to the same stressor. In contrast, hyperresponsivness, or sensitization, of HPA hormonal responses in rats also has been observed after periods of repeated stress, depending upon the duration, type, or intensity of the acute and repeated stress. Even without electric shock, which is often used to motivate running, treadmill training confounds exertion with forced running, and swimming confounds forced exertion with exposure to water. Circadian activity wheel running under ad libitum feeding conditions is voluntary; hence, HPA adaptations may differ from those after forced exercise.

Neurosecretory influences on the release of ACTH differ for stressors, which are predominantly psychological when, compared with physical stressors or those, which combine physical and psychological stress such as footshock. AVP and oxytocin each potentiate CRF release of ACTH in non-primates. In rat, AVP in peripheral circulation increases during severe, physical stress (e.g., hemorrhage, electric foot shock, hypoglycemia), but not during milder behavioral stress (e.g., novel environment, restraint, tail shock, swimming), which increases oxytocin. Romero and Sapolsky (1996) concluded that psychological stressors such as novelty and fear evoke increases in oxytocin but not AVP, whereas footshock, which involves both psychological and physical stress, evokes increases in both oxytocin and AVP.

Exercise studies: HPA. Though we had previously reported that chronic activity wheel running did not alter plasma levels of ACTH or corticosterone in response to novel or repeated footshock in rats, we conducted another study of foot shock, but added the novelty of cage-switch stress. We thought that the added psychological stress might elicit HPA responses not found in previous studies of chronic wheel running, which used foot shock alone. We found that chronic activity wheel running blunted levels of plasma ACTH in response to repeated footshock combined with cage-switch stress (Dishman et al., 1998). Adding the psychological stress of the cage-switch condition to repeated footshock may reveal a unique adaptation in neurosecretory release of ACTH, which interacts with wheeling running. Oxytocin response is especially interesting, as it is elicited by both footshock and novelty.

FUTURE RESEARCH

Future studies of how exercise training affects stress responses by leisure exercisers and competitive athletes must clearly characterize the physiological patterns of response elicited by different stressor tasks. In addition to the novelty, controllability, intensity or difficulty, and duration of the stressor, the degree to which sympatho-vagal, sympatho-adrenal medullary, brain noradrenergic, and HPA cortical systems are provoked must be specified. Also, adaptations by these components of the stress response to types and intensities of exercise training must be better understood. The interaction of the immune system with the sympathetic nervous system and the HPA cortical system during stress also deserves more attention. We've reported that both activity wheel running and treadmill exercise training mitigate natural killer cell cytotoxicity after footshock stress (Dishman et al., 1995, 2000). This effect seems to be unrelated to cortisol responses to the stress, but may be partly dependent upon noradrenergic innervation of the spleen (Dishman, Hong et al., 2000), which is a main lymphoid storage area for natural killer cells.

Cross-sectional comparisons of groups that differ on fitness or exercise habits can be informative when other influences on stress responses are controlled. However, exercise-training studies that compare low and high intensities are needed to determine whether exercise can alter stress responses independently of increased fitness (Buckworth et al., 1994). We have recommended that training studies increase VO_{2peak} by 25 % or more among people who initially have low-to-average fitness in order to approximate the differences in cardiorespiratory fitness that we have reported in cross-sectional comparisons. Previous exercise training studies that found no differences in HR and BP responses to mental stress or cold application typically reported increases in VO_{2peak} of less than 20 %, or the studies used an indirect estimate of VO_{2peak} that had measurement errors of 10 % to 15 %.

Studies also should study people with major depression, panic disorder, hypertension, or other disorders that are accompanied by altered autonomic and endocrine responses. Other groups who should receive more study include obese people who can have hypoactive SNS and HPA responses and African-Americans who have more hypertension and different nocturnal BP patterns than do African blacks or white people of European ancestory. Each of those groups may have different autonomic influences on HR and BP than do young normotensive white men and women who have been studied the most. We have reported that obese African-American women had elevated resting BP, despite low cardiac output. During mental arithmetic, their level of cardiorespiratory fitness was associated with increased BP, which resulted from increased HR with no change in stroke volume or total peripheral resistance (Crabbe et al., 1998). Hence, it is possible that exercise could upregulate the sympathetic tone, relative to vagal withdrawal, of people who have hypoadrenergic syndrome.

It will also be important to learn more about vascular and endothelial responses (Harris & Matthews, 2004) during and after stress, especially among people at risk for cardiovascular disease. We recently reported that fitness had complex relationships with blood pressure and vascular resistance during stress among young black women with parental hypertension (Jackson & Dishman, 2002). Blood pressure, heart rate, stroke volume, cardiac output, total peripheral resistance, calf blood flow, and calf vascular resistance were assessed during exposure to forehead and hand cold pressors, and mental arithmetic, as well as during recovery after the tasks. Fitness was positively related to increases in the vascular resistance measures during each stressor. In contrast, fitness was positively related to blunted blood pressure during or after passive stress (i.e., hand or forehead cold) and enhanced recovery of blood pressure and peripheral resistance after the active stressor (i.e., mental arithmetic); effects of fitness on the vascular responses during and after mental arithmetic were stronger among women having a negative history of parental hypertension.

Because fitness can be associated with reduced intrinsic rate of the heart, with uncertain changes in sympathetic activity, we also have recommended that studies employ pharmacologic antagonists (Bernston et al., 1994) and agonists (Mills et al., 1994) of the ANS or concomitant measures of sympathetic activity (e.g., plasma catecholamines, systolic time intervals such as pre-ejection period, or muscle sympathetic nerve activity) and sympathovagal balance (e.g. spectral analysis of HR variability after chronic exercise. Laboratory responses to stress may not reflect naturalistic responses, so we also recommend that ambulatory measures of physiological variables be made outside experimental settings (e.g., Dishman, Nakamura, et al., 2000; Jackson et al., 1998).

Studies have not adequately examined the effects of gender and age. There is evidence that catecholamine and hypothalamic-pituitary-adrenal cortical responses to stressors differ according to menstrual or estrous status, but how exercise and fitness moderate estrogen-dependent stress responses is not known. Sapolsky (1992) has shown that chronic, excessive exposure to glucocorticoids after chronic stress is accompanied by death of hippocampal glucocorticoid receptors, which impairs the feedback by rising cortisol levels to inhibit further ACTH release. Activity wheel running increases mRNA for nerve growth factors in the hippocampus of adult rats (Neeper et al., 1996; Van Hoomissen et al., 2003), which might delay neuron death with stress and aging. Also, plasma NE responses to submaximal exercise and to mental stress have been reported to be higher in older human males. However, a recent study comparing young and old men of similar VO_{2peak} showed no difference in plasma NE or EPI during ~20 min of cyclng at 75 % of

VO_{2peak} (Kastello, Sothmann & Murthy, 1993). Thus, age differences in SNS responsiveness may be moderated by aerobic capacity or training history. Also, cardiorespiratory fitness has been inversely related to blood pressure and muscle sympathetic nerve activity during cold pressor stress among women but not men (Dishman et al., 2002; Dishman et al., 2003; Jackson & Dishman, 2002), so gender differences in stress reactivity and recovery need more study. Vascular responses associated with blood flow during stress are influenced both by the ANS and intrinsic factors that modulate vessel constriction and dilation. They require study to understand how fitness affects the vascular response during stress.

Finally, the acute response of increased brain blood flow during exercise is limited to brain regions involved with sensory, motor, and cardiovascular responses associated with the increased metabolism of exertion, and only those regions appear to have increased metabolic capacity after chronic exercise (McCloskey et al., 2001). Nonetheless, recent evidence suggests that cardiorespiratory fitness and aerobic exercise training influence brain cortical (i.e., anterior cingulate cortex) blood flow during cognitive tasks that involve executive function (Colcombe et al., 2004). Studies are needed that examine the moderating effect of cardiorespiratory fitness on brain blood flow during stress, especially tasks that require quick decision-making under competitive stress.

REFERENCES

Allen, M. T. & Crowell, M. D. (1989). Patterns of autonomic response during laboratory stressors. *Psychophysiology, 26,* 603-614.

Anshel, M. H. (1996). Coping styles among adolescent competitive athletes. *The Journal of Social Psychology, 136,* 311-323.

Anshel, M. H. Jamieson, J. J., & Raviv, S. (2001). Coping with acute stress among male and female Israeli athletes. *International Journal of Sport Psychology, 31,* 271-289.

Barchas, J. D. & Friedman D. X. (1963). Brain amines: Response to physiological stress. Biochemistry and. *Pharmacology, 12,* 1232-1233.

Bennett, G. W. & Whitehead, S.A. (1983). *Mammalian Neuroendocrinology.* New York: Oxford University Press.

Bernard, C. L. (1867). *Rapport sur les progres et la marche de la physiologie generale.* Bailliere, Paris.

Berntson, G. G., Caacioppo, J. T., Binkley, P. F., Uchino, B. N., Quigley, K. S. & Fieldston, A. (1994). Autonomic cardiac control .3. Psychological stress and cardiac response in autonomic space as revealed by pharmacological blockades. *Psychophysiology, 31,* 599-608.

Berntson, G., Cacioppo, J. & Quigley, K. (1993). Cardiac psychophysiology and autonomic space in humans: Empirical perspectives and conceptual implications. *Psychological Bulletin, 114,* 296-322.

Blaney, J., Sothmann, M., Raff, H., Hart, B. & Horn, T. (1990). Impact of exercise training on plasma adrenocorticotropin hormone response to a well learned vigilance task. *Psychoneuroendocrinology, 15,* 1-10.

Blumenthal, J. A. (1989). Response to Abbott and Peters. *Psychosomatic Medicine, 51,* 219-220.

Boutcher, S. H., Nugent, F.W., McLaren, P. F. & Weltman, A. L. (1998). Heart period variability of trained and untrained men at rest and during mental challenge. *Psychophysiology, 35,* 16-22.

Boutcher, S. H., Nugent, F. W., & Weltzman, A. L. (1995). Heart rate response to psychological stressors of individuals possessing resting bradycardia. *Behavioral Medicine, 21,* 40-46.

Brandon, J. E., Loftin, J. M. & Curry, Jr., J. (1991). Role of fitness in mediating stress: A correctional exploration of stress reactivity. *Perceptual and Motor Skills, 73,* 1171-1180.

Buckworth, J. B., Dishman, R. K. & Cureton, K. J. (1994). Autonomic responses of women with parental hypertension: effects of physical activity and fitness. *Hypertension, 24,* 576-584.

Buckworth, J. B., Convertino, V., Cureton, K. J. & Dishman, R. K. (1997). Increased finger arterial blood pressure after exercise detraining in women with parental hypertension: autonomic tasks. *Acta Physiologica Scandinavica, 160,* 29-41.

Cannon, W. B. (1929). Organization for physiological homeostasis. *Physiological Review, 9,* 399-431.

Caspersen, C. J., Powell, K. E. & Christenson, G. M. (1985). Physical activity, exercise, and physical fitness: definitions and distinctions for health-related research. *Public Health Reports, 100,* 126-131.

Chrousos, G. P. (1998). Stressors, stress, and neuroendocrine integration of the adaptive response: the 1997 Hans Selye memorial lecture. *Annals of the New York Academy of Sciences, 851,* 311-335.

Claytor, R. P. (1991). Stress reactivity: hemodynamic adjustments in trained and untrained humans. *Medicine and Science in Sports and Exercise, 23,* 873-881.

Clutter, W., Bier, D., Shah, S. & Cryer, P.E. (1980). Epinephrine: plasma metabolic clearance rates and physiologic thresholds for metabolic and hemodynamic actions in man. *Journal of Clinical Investigation, 66,* 94-101.

Cohen, M. S. & Bookheimer, S. Y. (1994). Localization of brain function using magnetic resonance imaging. *Techniques in Neuroscience, 17(7),* 268-277.

Colcombe, S. J., Kramer, A. F., Erickson, K. I., Scalf P., McAuley, E., Cohen, N. J., Webb, A., Jerome, G. J., Marquez, D. X. & Elavsky, S. (2004). Cardiovascular fitness, cortical plasticity, and aging. *Proceedings of the National Academy of Sciences, U S A, 101,* 3316-3321.

Cox, R. H. (1991). Exercise training and response to stress: Insights from an animal model. *Medicine and Science in Sports and Exercise, 23,* 853-859.

Crabbe, J. B., Jackson, E. M., Ray, C. A., DuVal, H. P. & Dishman, R. K. (1998). Cardiovascular responses to mental arithmetic in African-American women with hypertension. *Medicine and Science in Sports and Exercise, 30,* (5), Supple. S. 98, 1703.

Crews, D. J. & Landers, D. M. (1987). A meta-analytic review of aerobic fitness and reactivity to psychosocial stressors. *Medicine and Science in Sports and Exercise, 19* (Suppl.), S114-S120.

Dishman, R. K. (1997). Brain monoamines, exercise, and behavioral stress: animal models. *Medicine and Science in Sports and Exercise, 29,* 63-74.

Dishman, R. K. (1992). Physiological and psychological effects of overtraining. In K. D. Brownell, J. Rodin, J. H. Wilmore (Eds.). *Eating, Body Weight, and Performance in Athletes.* (pp. 248-271). Philadelphia: Lea & Febiger.

Dishman, R. K. (1983). Stress management procedures. In M. Williams (Ed.) Ergogenic Aids in Sport. (pp. 275-320). Champaign, IL: Human Kinetics.

Dishman, R. K., Bunnell, B. N., Youngstedt, S. D., Yoo, H. S., Mougey, E. H. & Meyerhoff, J. L. (1998). Activity wheel running blunts increased plasma ACTH after footshock and cage-switch stress. *Physiology & Behavior, 63,* 911-917.

Dishman, R. K., Hong, S., Soares, J., Edwards, G. L., Bunnell, B. N., Jaso-Friedmann, L. & Evans, D. L. (2000). Activity-wheel running blunts suppression of splenic natural killer cell cytotoxicity after sympathectomy and footshock. *Physiology & Behavior, 71,* 297-304.

Dishman R. K., Jackson E. M. & Nakamura Y. (2002). Influence of fitness and gender on blood pressure responses during active or passive stress. *Psychophysiology, 39,* 568-576.

Dishman, R. K., Nakamura, Y., Garcia, M. E., Thompson, R. W., Dunn, A. L., Wilkinson, W. J., Kampert, J. B. & Blair, S. N. (2000). Heart rate variability, trait anxiety, and perceived stress among physically fit men and women. *International Journal of Psychophysiology, 37,* 121-133.

Dishman R. K., Nakamura, Y., Jackson, E. M., Ray, C. A. (2003). Blood pressure and muscle sympathetic nerve activity during cold pressor stress: fitness and gender. *Psychophysiology, 40,* 370-380.

Dishman, R. K., Renner, K. J., White-Welkley, J. E., Burke, K. A. & Bunnell, B. N. (2000). Treadmill exercise training augments brain norepinephrine response to familiar and novel stress. *Brain Research Bulletin, 52,* 337-342.

Dishman, R. K., Renner, K. J., Youngstedt, S. D., Reigle, T. G., Bunnell, B. N., Burke, K. A., Yoo, H. S., Mougey, E. H. & Meyerhoff, J. L. (1997). Activity wheel running reduces escape latency and alters brain monoamines after footshock. *Brain Research Bulletin, 42,* 399-406.

Dishman, R. K., Warren, J. M., Hong, S., Bunnell, B. N., Mougey, E. H., Meyerhoff, J. L., Jaso-Friedmann L, Evans DL. (2000). Treadmill exercise training blunts suppression of splenic natural killer cell cytolysis after footshock. *Journal of Applied Physiology, 88,* 2176-2182.

Dishman, R. K., Warren, J. M., Youngstedt, S. D., Yoo, H., Bunnell, B. N., Mougey, J. L., Meyerhoff, L., Jaso-Friedmann, L. & Evans, D. L. (1995) Activity-wheel running attenuates suppression of natural killer cell activity after footshock. *Journal of Applied Physiology, 78,* 1547-1554.

Dunn, A. L. & Dishman, R. K. (1991). Exercise and the neurobiology of depression. *Exercise and Sport Sciences Reviews, 19,* 41-98.

Dunn, A. L., Reigle, T. G., Youngstedt, S. Y., Armstrong, R. B. & Dishman, R. K. (1996) Brain norepinephrine and metabolites after treadmill training and wheel running in rats. *Medicine and Science in Sports and Exercise, 28,* 204-209.

Ensel, W. M., & Lin, N. (2004). Physical fitness and the stress process. *Journal of Community Psychology, 32,* 81-101.

Feldman, R. S., Meyer, J. S. & Quenzer L. F. (1997). Principles of Neuropsychopharmacology. Sunderland, Mass: Sinauer Associates.

Fillenz, M. (1990). Noradrenergic neurons. New York: Cambridge University Press.

Fletcher, D. & Hanton, S. (2003). Sources of organizational stress in elite sports performers. *The Sport Psychologist, 17,* 175-195.

Fowles, D. C., Christie, M. J., Edelberg, R., Grings, W. W., Lykken, D. T., & Venables, P. H. (1981). Publication recommendations for electrodermal measurements. *Psychophysiology, 18,* 232-239.

Franks, B. D. & Cureton, T. K. (1968). Orthogonal factors of cardiac intervals and their response to stress. *American Association for Health, Physical Education, and Recreation: Research Quarterly, 39,* 524-532.

Fridlund, A. J. & Cacioppo, J. T. (1986). Guidelines for human electromyographic research. *Psychophysiology, 23,* 567-589.

Gonzalez-Bono, E., Salvador, A., Serrano, M. A. & Ricarte, J. (1999). Testosterone, cortisol, and mood in a sports team competition. *Hormones and Behavior, 35,* 55-62.

Graham, R. E., Zeichner, A., Peacock, L. J. & Dishman, R. K. (1996). Bradycardia during baroreflex stimulation and active or passive stressor tasks: cardiorespiratory fitness and hostility. *Psychophysiology, 33,* 566-575.

Harris, K. F. & Matthews, K. A. (2004). Interactions between autonomic nervous system activity and endothelial function: a model for the development of cardiovascular disease. *Psychosomatic Medicine, 66,* 153-64.

Hartman, F. A., Brownell, K. A. & Lockwood, J. E. (1932). Cortin as a general tissue hormone. *American Journal of Physiology, 101,* 50-56.

Hocking-Schuler, J. I. & O'Brien, W. O. (1997). Cardiovascular recovery from stress and hypertension risk factors: a meta-analytic review. *Psychophysiology, 34,* 649-659.

Jackson, E. M. & Dishman, R. K. (2002). Hemodynamic responses to stress among black women: fitness and parental hypertension. *Medicine and Science in Sports and Exercise, 34,* 1097-1104.

Jackson, E. M. & Dishman, R. K. (2004). The effects of cardiorespiratory fitness on physiological responses during stress: a quantitative synthesis. *Medicine and Science in Sports and Exercise, 36* (5, Suppl.), S720.

Jackson, E. M., Natarajan, A. & Dishman, R. K. (1998). Cardiorespiratory fitness and 24-h ambulatory blood pressure in women with family history of hypertension. *Medicine and Science in Sports and Exercise, 30* (5, Suppl.), S298.

Jansen, A. S. P., Nguyen, X. V., Karpitskiy, V., Mettenleiter, T. C. & Loewy, A. D. (1995). Central command neurons of the sympathetic nervous system: basis of the fight-or-flight response. *Science, 270,* 644-646.

Jennings, J. R., Berg, W. K., Hutcheson, J. S., Obrist, P., Porges, S. & Turpin, G. (1981). Publication guidelines for heart rate studies in man. *Psychophysiology, 18,* 226-231.

Kandel E. R., Schwartz, J. H. & Jessell, T. M. (Eds) (1995). *Essentials of neural science and behavior.* Norwalk, CT : Appleton & Lange.

Kastello, G. M., Sothmann, M. S. & Murthy, V. S. (1993). Young and old subjects matched for aerobic capacity have similar noradrenergic responses to exercise. *Journal of Applied Physiology, 74,* 49-54.

Keller, S. & Seraganian, P. (1984). Aerobic fitness level and autonomic activity psychosocial stress. *Journal of Psychosomatic Research, 28,* 279-287.

Kjaer, M. (1992). Regulation of hormonal and metabolic responses during exercise in humans. *Exercise and Sports Sciences Reviews, 20,* 161-184.

Lacey, J. I. (1950). Individual differences in somatic response patterns. *Journal of Comparative and Physiological Psychology, 43,* 338-350.

Lacey, B. C. & Lacey, J. I. (1974). Studies of heart rate and other bodily processes in sensorimotor behavior. In P. A. Obrist, A. H. Black, J. Brener & L. V. DiCara (Eds.) *Cardiovascular Psychophysiology* (pp. 538-564). Chicago: Aldine Publishing Company.

Lake, B. W., Suarez, E. C., Schneiderman, N. & Tocci, N. (1985). The type A behavior pattern, physical fitness, and psychophysiological reactivity. *Health Psychology, 4,* 169-187.

Lazarus, R. S. (1993). From psychological stress to the emotions. *Annual Review of Psychology, 44,* 1-21.

Le Bihan, D. (moderator) (1995). NIH conference: Functional magnetic resonance imaging of the brain. *Annals of Internal Medicine, 122,* 296-303

Maki, T., Kontula, K. & Harkonen, M. (1990). The beta-adrenergic system in man: Physiological and pathophysiological response. *Scandinavian Journal of Clinical Laboratory Investigation, 50* (Suppl 201), 25-43.

Manuel, J. C., Shilt, J. S., Curl, W. W., Smith, J. A., DuRant, R. H., Lester, L. & Sinal, S.H. (2002). Coping with sports injuries: an examination of the adolescent athlete. *Journal of Adolescent Health, 31,* 391-393.

Mason, J. W., Maher, J. T., Hartley, L. H., Mougey, E., Perlow, M. J. & Jones, L. G. (1976). Selectivity of corticosteroid and catecholamine response to various natural stimuli. In G. Serban (Ed.). *Psychopathology of Human Adaptation.* (pp. 147-171). New York: Plenum.

Mazzeo, R. S. (1991). Catecholamine responses to acute and chronic exercise. *Medicine and Science in Sports and Exercise, 23,* 839-845.

McCloskey, D. P., Adamo, D. S. & Anderson B. J. (2001). Exercise increases metabolic capacity in the motor cortex and striatum, but not in the hippocampus. *Brain Research, 891,*168-175.

Michael, E. D. (1957). Stress adaptations through exercise. American Association for Health, Physical Education, and Recreation: *Research Quarterly, 28,* 50-54.

Mills, P. J., Dimsdale, J. E., Nelesen, R. A., Jasiewicz, J., Ziegler, M. G. & Kennedy, B. (1994). Patterns of adrenergic agonists underlying cardiovascular responses to a psychological challenge. *Psychosomatic Medicine, 56,* 70-76.

Moore, K. E. & Lariviere, E. W. (1964). Effects of stress and d-amphetamine on rat brain catecholamines. *Biochemistry and Pharmacology, 13,* 1098-1100.

Morgan W. P., Brown, D. R., Raglin J. S., O'Connor P. J., Ellickson K. A. (1987). Psychological monitoring of overtraining and staleness. *British Journal of Sports Medicine, 21,* 107-114.

Morgan, W. P. & O'Connor, P. J. (1988). Exercise and mental health. In R. K. Dishman (Ed.). *Exercise Adherence: its impact on public health.* (pp. 91-121). Champaign, IL: Human Kinetics Publishers.

Moya-Albiol, L., Salvador, A., Costa, R., Martinez-Sanchis, S., Gonzalez-Bono, E., Ricarte, J. & Arnedo, M. (2001). Psychophysiological responses to the Stroop Task after a maximal cycle ergometry in elite sportsmen and physically active subjects. *International Journal of Psychophysiology, 40,* 47-59.

Moyna, N. M., Bodnar, J. D., Goldberg, H. R., Shurin, M. S., Robertson, R. J. & Rabin, B. S. (1999). Relation between aerobic fitness level and stress induced alterations in neuroendocrine and immune function. *International Journal of Sports Medicine, 20,* 136-141.

Neeper, S. A., Gomez-Pinilla, F., Choi, J. & Cotman, C. W. (1996). Physical activity increases mRNA for brain-derived neurotrophic factor and nerve growth factor in rat brain. *Brain Research, 726,* 49-56.

Obrist, P. A., Howard, J. L., Lawler, J. E., Galosy, R. A., Meyers, K. A., & Gaebelein, C. J. (1974). The cardiac-somatic interaction. In P. A. Obrist, A. H. Black, J. Brener & L.V. DiCara (Eds.) *Cardiovascular Psychophysiology.* (pp. 136-162). Chicago: Aldine Publishing Company.

O'Neal, H. A., Van Hoomissen, J. D., Holmes, P. V. & Dishman, R. K. (2001). Prepro-galanin messenger RNA levels are increased in rat locus coeruleus after exercise training. *Neuroscience Letters,* 69-72.

Pacak, K., Palkovits, M., Yadid, G., Kvetnansky, R., Kopin, I. J. & Goldstein, D. S. (1998). Heterogeneous neurochemical responses to different stressors: a test of Selye(s doctrine of nonspecificity. *American Journal of Physiology, 275* (4 Pt 2), R1247-R1255.

Pagliari, R. & Peyrin, L. (1995a). Norepinephrine release in the rat frontal cortex under treadmill exercise: a study with microdialysis. *Journal of Applied Physiology, 78,* 2121-2130.

Pagliari, R. & Peyrin, L. (1995b). Physical conditioning in rats influences the central and peripheral catecholamine responses to sustained exercise. *European Journal of Applied Physiology, 71,* 41-52.

Passelergue, P. & Lac, G. (1999). Saliva cortisol, testosterone and T/C ratio variations during a wrestling competition and during the post-competitive recovery period. *International Journal of Sports Medicine, 20,* 109-113.

Passelergue, P., Robert, A. & Lac, G. (1999). Salivary cortisol and testosterone variations during an official and a simulated weight-lifting competition. *International Journal of Sports Medicine, 16,* 298-303.

Peronnet, F. & Szabo, A. (1993). Sympathetic response to acute psychosocial stressors in humans: linkage to physical exercise and training. In P. Seraganian (Ed.), *Exercise Psychology: the influence of physical exercise on psychological processes.* (pp. 172-217). New York: John Wiley.

Persson, P. B. (1996). Modulation of cardiovascular control mechanisms and their interaction. *Physiological Reviews, 76,* 193-244.

Pivik, R. T., Broughton, R. J., Coppola, R., Davidson, R. J., Fox, N. & Nuwer, M. (1993). Guidelines for the recording and quantitative analysis of electroencephalographic activity in research contexts. *Psychophysiology, 30,* 547-558.

Porges, S. W. (1995). Cardiac vagal tone: a physiological index of stress. *Neuroscience and Biobehavioral Reviews, 19,* 225-233.

Raab, W. & Krzywanek, H. J. (1965). Cardiovascular sympathetic tone and stress response related to personality patterns and exercise habits. *American Journal of Cardiology, 16,* 42-53.

Ray, C. A. & Mark, A. L. (1993). Sympathetic adjustments to exercise: insights from microneurographic recordings. In R. Hainsworth & A. L. Mark (Eds). *Cardiovascular Reflex Control in Health and Disease.* (pp. 145-146). London: Saunders.

Romero, L. M. & R. M. Sapolsky. (1996). Patterns of ACTH secretagog secretion in response to psychological stimuli. *Journal of Neuroendocrinology, 8,* 243-258.

Rowell, L. B. (1993). *Human cardiovascular control.* New York: Oxford University Press.

Sapolsky, R. M. (1992). *Stress, the aging brain, and the mechanisms of neuron death.* Cambridge, Ma: MIT Press.

Sehested, J., Reinicke, G., Ishino, K., Hetzer, R., Schifter, S., Schmitzer, E. & Regitz, V. (1995). Blunted humoral responses to mental stress and physical exercise in cardiac transplant recipients. *European Heart Journal, 16,* 852-858.

Selye, H. (1936). A syndrome produced by diverse nocuous agents. *Nature, 138,* 32.

Selye, H. (1950). *Stress.* Montreal, Acta, Inc.

Shapiro, D., Jamner, L. D., Lane, J. D., Light, K. C., Myrteck, M., Sawadea, Y. & Steptoe, A. (1996). Blood pressure publication guidelines. *Psychophysiology, 33,* 1-12.

Shapiro P. A. Sloan R. P., Bigger, J. T., Jr., Bagiella, E. & Gorman, J. M. (1994) Cardiac denervation and cardiovascular reactivity to psychological stress. *American Journal of Psychiatry, 151,* 1140-1147.

Shapiro, P. A., Sloan, R. P., Bagiella, E., Bigger, J. T., Jr. & Gorman, J. M. (1996). Heart rate reactivity and heart period variability throughout the first year after heart transplantation. *Psychophysiology, 33,* 54-62

Shi, X., Stevens, G. H. J., Foresman, B. H., Stern, S. A. & Raven, P. B. (1995). Autonomic nervous system control of the heart: endurance exercise training. *Medicine and Science in Sports and Exercise, 27,* 1406-1413.

Silverberg, A. B., Shah, S. D., Haymond, M. W. & Cryer, P. E. (1978). Norepinephrine: hormone and neurotransmitter in man. *American Journal of Physiology, 234,* E252-E256.

Soares, J., Holmes, P. V., Renner, K. J., Edwards, G. L., Bunnell, B. N. & Dishman, R. K. (1999). *Behavioral Neuroscience, 113,* 558-566.

Sothmann, M. S., Buckworth, J., Claytor, R. P., Cox, R. H., White-Welkley, J. E. & Dishman, R. K. (1996). Exercise training and the cross-stressor adaptation hypothesis. *Exercise and Sport Sciences Reviews, 24,* 267-287.

Sothmann, M. S., Gustafson, A. B., Garthwaite, T. L., Horn, T. S. & Hart, B. A. (1988). Cardiovascular fitness and selected adrenal hormone responses to cognitive stress. *Endocrine Research, 14,* 59-69.

Sothmann, M. S., Hart, B. A. & Horn, T. S. (1991). Plasma catecholamine response to acute psychological stress in humans: relation to aerobic fitness and exercise training. *Medicine and Science in Sports and Exercise, 23,* 860-867.

Spalding, T. W., Jeffers, L. S., Porges, S. W. & Hatfield, B. D. (2000). Vagal and cardiac reactivity to psychological stressors in trained and untrained men. *Medicine and Science in Sports and Exercise, 32,* 581-591.

Spyer, K. M. (1989). Neural mechanisms involved in cardiovascular control during affective behaviour. *Trends in Neuroscience, 12,* 506-513.

Stanford, S. C. (1990). Central adrenoreceptors in response and adaptation to stress. In D. J. Heal & C. A. Marsden (Eds.) *The pharmacology of noradrenaline in the central nervous system.* (pp. 379-422). Oxford, England: Oxford University Press.

Steptoe, A. (1985). Theoretical basis for task selection in cardiovascular physiology. In A. Steptoe, H. Ruddel, & H. Neus (Eds.), *Methodological issues in cardiovascular psychophysiology* (pp. 11-15). Berlin: Springer-Verlag.

Steptoe, A. Kearsley, N. & Walters, N. (1993). Cardiovascular activity during mental stress following vigorous exercise in sportsmen and inactive men. *Psychophysiology, 30,* 245-252.

Suay, F., Salvador, A., Gonzalez-Bono, E., Sanchis, C., Martinez, M., Martinez-Sanchis, S., Simon, V. M. & Montoro, J. B. (1999). Effects of competition and its outcome on serum testosterone, cortisol and prolactin. *Psychoneuroendocrinology, 24,* 551-66.

Sutton, J. R., Farrell, P A. & Harber, V. J. (1990). Hormonal adaptations to exercise. In C. Bouchard, R. J. Shephard, T. Stephens, J. R. Sutton, & B. D. McPherson (Eds). *Exercise, fitness, and health: A consensus of current knowledge.* (pp217-257). Champaign, Il: Human Kinetics Books.

Szabo, A., Peronnet, F., Frenkl, R., Farkas, A., Petrekantis, M., Meszaros, J., Hetenyi, A. & Szabo, T. (1994). Blood pressure and heart rate reactivity to mental strain in adolescent judo athletes. *Physiology & Behavior, 56,* 219-224.

van Doornen, L. P. & DeGeus, E. J. (1989). Aerobic fitness and the cardiovascular response to stress. *Psychophysiology, 26,* 17-28.

van Doornen, L. J. P., & DeGeus, E. J. C. (1993). Stress, physical activity and coronary disease. *Work & Stress, 7,* 121-139.

Van Hoomissen, J. D., Chambliss, H. O., Holmes, P. V. & Dishman, R. K. (2003). Effects of chronic exercise and imipramine on mRNA for BDNF after olfactory bulbectomy in rat. *Brain Research. 974,* 228-235.

Watanabe, T., A. Morimoto, Y. Sakata, N. Tan, K. Morimoto & Murakami, N. (1992). Running training attenuates the ACTH responses in rats to swimming and cage-switch stress. *Journal of Applied Physiology, 73,* 2452-2456.

White-Welkley, J. E., Bunnell, B. N., Mougey, E. H., Meyerhoff, J. L. & Dishman, R. K. (1995). Treadmill training and estradiol moderate hypothalamic-pituitary-adrenal cortical responses to acute running and immobilization. *Physiology & Behavior, 57,* 533-540.

White-Welkley, J. E., J. A. Eisler, G. L. Warren, A. Cohen, J. Mulcahey, K. V. Thrivikraman, P. M. Plotsky & D. B. Neill. (1996). Effects of treadmill training on plasma ACTH and Brain CRF responses to heterotypic stress. *Medicine and Science in Sports and Exercise, 28* (5) Suppl.: S109.

White-Welkley, J. E., Warren, G. L., Bunnell, B. N., Mougey, E. H., Meyerhoff, J. L. & Dishman, R. K. (1996). Treadmill exercise training and estradiol increase plasma levels of ACTH and prolactin after footshock. *Journal of Applied Physiology, 80,* 931-939.

Wiese-Bjornstal, D. M., Smith, A. M., Shaffer, S. M. & Morrey, M. A. (1998). An integrated model of response to sport injury: psychological and sociological dynamics. *Journal of Applied Sport Psychology, 10,* 46-49.

Williams, J. M., & Andersen, M. B. (1998). Psychosocial antecendents of sports injury: review and critique of the stress and injury model. *Journal of Applied Sport Psychology, 10,* 5-25.

Yoo, H., O'Neal, H. A., Hong, S., Tackett, R. L. & Dishman, R. K. (1999). Brain β-adrenergic responses to footshock after wheel running. *Medicine and Science in Sports and Exercise, 31,* (5), Suppl. S109, 647.

Yoo, H. S., Tackett, R. L., Bunnell, B. N., Crabbe, J. B., & Dishman, R. K. (2000). Antidepressant-like effects of physical activity vs. imipramine: neonatal clomipramine model. *Psychobiology, 28,* 540-549.

Motivational and Self-Regulatory Factors and Sports Performance in Young Elite Athletes

Anne-Marie Elbe and Jürgen Beckmann

Contents

Summary

This chapter examines the relationship between personality factors and athletic performance, and presents recent findings about young elite athletes. The chapter shows that a theory-based evaluation of personality development can be applied to sports. Results concerning achievement motivation, volition, and action control are presented that indicate that certain personality factors show a unique development in young elite athletes. These personality factors are necessary for the young elite athletes to develop and to meet goals. Sports-specific achievement motivation seems to be a fairly stable personality factor in young elite athletes and also correlates with future athletic success. Action orientation and volition change over time, indicate adaptability and adjustment through time and practice. Some variations in these components are inherent in various sports; specific requirements demand different personality characteristics in different sports. Action orientation, for example, seems to be an important personality factor for athletic achievement in track and field. However, action orientation might not enhance performance for all sports, or in all positions in a team sport. The relationship between these self-regulatory factors and athletic achievement is described in this chapter. Furthermore, the importance of volitional personality factors in preventing dropout is shown. Finally, the chapter illuminates the conditions necessary for a positive development of these personality factors. Environmental factors like parents, peers, the boarding school, and leisure time can all contribute to a positive development of performance-relevant psychological factors in young adults. For positive personality development, athletes need opportunities for social interaction where they can get feedback from peers and adults, and in order for them to interact socially, they need sufficient leisure time. Sport psychologists can aid the talent development process by monitoring personality development and stress levels and by performing psychological skills training with the young athletes.

INTRODUCTION

The athletic training of young athletes focuses predominantly on the development of physical components. Personality factors are thought of as innate characteristics of an athlete, meaning that they either are present or not. This assumption is often based on the coaches' perceptions of the term talent. A common belief among coaches is that talent can be identified when individuals exhibit above average performance at one point in time (Letzelter, 1981). Furthermore, talent is described as being independent of environmental influence and development (Krämer, 1977). This restrictive and "static" definition suggests that personality factors are, in fact, innate and stable. Thus, little time is spent on training or enhancing mental factors of performance. Recently more open and dynamic definitions of talent have been offered (e.g., Seidel & Hohmann, 1999). These definitions incorporate the idea that the development of talent is a dynamic process, and that its development can be influenced by personality and environmental factors. Personality is also perceived as a dynamic factor that undergoes developmental changes.

Nonetheless, there are still many open questions concerning the relationship between sport performance and psychological factors. For example, which mental factors affect performance? Can they be identified in talented young athletes? Can their development be positively influenced?

Since talent identification is closely related to talent development, it is often assumed that only selected young athletes, shown to have the potential to achieve excellence, should be supported. Since early and effective talent identification lowers the cost of talent development programs, the limited funds and resources could be allocated for those athletes having high future potential. The development of performance-relevant personality factors could be encouraged in young elite athletes, to enhance future athletic performance.

This chapter examines the relationship between personality and athletic performance, and presents recent findings that support this view in young elite athletes. In addition, these findings indicate that certain personality factors show unique development in young elite athletes. Specifically, some of the personality characteristics alter with time and experience, which indicates adaptability and adjustment through time and practice. This chapter discusses which environmental factors can contribute to a positive development of performance-relevant psychological factors in young adults.

PERSONALITY AND ATHLETIC PERFORMANCE

In earlier research, personality was not the main focus of studies that estimated the relationship between personality factors and athletic performance. From the current perspective it appears that in the past only selected personality traits were considered in athletic samples, by applying available personality measures from the field of general or clinical psychology. The assumption that these "personality traits" should differ in athletes lacked theoretical foundation (Morris, 1995; 2000). To determine the presence of an athletic personality, cross-sectional methodology was employed. Successful and less successful athletes, or elite and non-elite athletes, were compared to each other at one point in time to determine personality differences (Kroll & Crenshaw, 1970; Morgan & Costill, 1972; Schurr, Ashley & Joy, 1977; Williams & Parkin, 1980). Researchers looked for connections (not causal ones) between personality and athletic involvement, and preference for specific sports or athletic achievement in these correlational studies.

The questionnaires applied mainly to adult samples were, for example, the Eysenck Personality Questionnaire (EPQ; Eysenck & Eysenck, 1975) or the 16 Personality Factor questionnaire (16 PF: Cattell, 1965). The Minnessota Multiphasic Personality Inventory (MMPI; Hathaway & Mc Kinley, 1967) was also used however, this was strongly criticized since these questionnaires were originally designed to identify persons with psychological abnormalities and its validity for psychologically healthy individuals was questioned (Morgan, 1980). Cox (1998) concluded, therefore, that this cross-sectionally designed research showed no clear relationship between sport performance and personality. Morris (2000) added that results concerning sport performance and personality factors were inconsistent even when the same measures were used in the same sport. According to Conzelmann (2001), the different theoretical and methodological approaches were the reason for such inconsistent results.

Furthermore, research on personality-related expertise employed a rather static trait concept. This concept postulated the existence of stable personality characteristics perceived as stable over time and contexts. However, this trait concept has been widely criticized in psychology for its very low predictive value (Mischel, 1968). The stability of personality characteristics over time and the nature in which personality traits are affected by contextual factors has also been questioned (Mischel & Shoda, 1995). Personality stability over time has not been demonstrated in the sport domain (Morris, 2000), because it ignores the effect of socialization through environmental interaction. Social learning theory assumes that long-term involvement in sport leads to changes in personality characteristics.

The aim of the German studies reported here was to test the socialization hypothesis versus the selection hypothesis. The selection hypothesis assumes that only individuals who show certain psychological characteristics become involved in sports, and/or remain successfully involved. This hypothesis implies that involvement in sport does not lead to a change in personality, and therefore contradicts the socialization hypothesis. Gabler's (1976) study with swimmers and Sack's (1980) with long-distance runners are longitudinal. A longitudinal design makes it possible to examine the extent to which personality characteristics change over long-term involvement in sports. The results of both studies confirmed the selection rather than the socialization hypothesis. Sack (1980) summarized his research concerning the two hypotheses as follows: "the world of (high -) achievement sport is structured in such a way that individuals with certain characteristics either remain in it or drop out of this system" (p. 223). Gabler (2002) also concluded that competitive sports fails to result in any changes in general personality factors. Since motivational aspects determine the duration and performance level of athletes involved in top level sports, they also appear to be relevant personality traits for sports performance. The achievement motive is an especially sound trait for predicting sport careers. According to Schneider, Bös and Rieder (1993), personality traits like achievement motivation, concentration, self-regulation and persistence are essential prerequisites for high athletic achievement in young athletes. This is in line with Ericsson, Krampe and Tesch-Römer's (1993) expertise theory that places much importance on such factors for achieving peak performance.

GENERAL AND SPORT SPECIFIC ACHIEVEMENT MOTIVATION

A current longitudinal research study of young elite athletes provides further insight into the relevance of the general and sport-specific achievement motive for athletic performance. The students studied in the research project, "Personality and achievement development of young elite athletes in Potsdam" (Beckmann, Elbe, Szymanski & Ehrlenspiel, in press) attended a high school designed exclusively for young elite athletes. Such schools were an important institution in the former GDR sports system. After Germany's reunification, these schools were strongly criticized. Students were forced to live away from home, had to undergo harsh training regimens and lacked opportunities for personal development. Many of these schools were closed in the early post-reunification period; a number of the schools were reopened in the mid-1990s, however, thanks to the athletic success of many former students.

Thirty-eight of these schools exist in Germany today. Similar schools are also found in France (Altmeyer, Beuchot & Staszak, 2002) and are being developed in Andorra and India. To be admitted to one of Germany's elite athletic programs, the young athletes are subject to a strict selection process, including several tests of athletic performance, and recommendation by the state sport organization. Once admitted to the school, students train daily, and frequently take part in weekend and vacation training camps and competitions. Many of the students board at the schools.

Students are monitored and compared to students not involved in competitive sports attending a regular high school in the same neighborhood. Testing started in grade 7, when students entered the sports school and continued through grade 12. The testing was carried out twice in grade 7, and then again at the beginning of each subsequent school year. Psychological and sociological measures, as well as sport motoric tests, were employed. One of the psychological measures was Gjesme and Nygard's (1970) Achievement Motives Scale, which measures the two components of the general achievement motive, namely, "fear of failure," and "hope for success." The main aim was to examine whether achievement motive

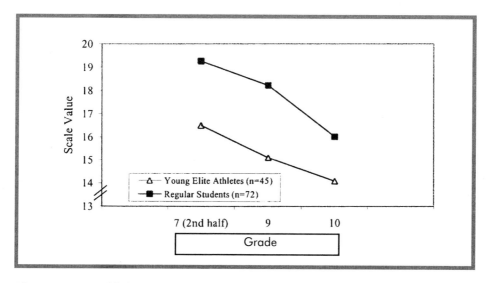

Figure 1 "Fear of failure" in young elite athletes and regular students in grades 7 -10.

would show a stronger development in the athletic sample. Figure 1 relates to "fear of failure," while Figure 2 relates to "hope for success" tested in grade 7 (2nd half), 9 and 10 in the athletic and non-athletic sample.

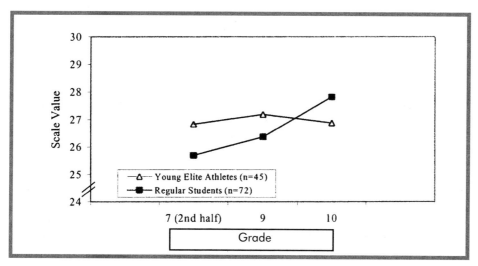

Figure 2 "Hope for Success" in young elite athletes and regular students in grades 7-10

The results indicate that "hope for success" remained stable over the course of three years. No significant differences were found between the young elite athletes and the regular students (Elbe, Beckmann & Szymanski, 2003b). "Fear of failure," however, decreased over time in both samples, but it was less pronounced in the elite athletes. No gender differences were identified at any age.

In addition, Elbe et al. (2003b) examined the link between motivational components and athletic success in athletes from individual sports. A scale from 1 to 8 was used to rate the athletes' placements in regional and national competitions. One point, for example, was assigned to placement among the first eight in a regional competition, and eight points for winning the German championships. No meaningful correlations were obtained between the current or future competition results and the scales "fear of failure or "hope for success." Correlations ranged from -.35 - .23. Furthermore, the sport-specific achievement motivation was also assessed in the athletic and non-athletic samples. A revised version of the sport-specific achievement motivation questionnaire (SLM) developed by Allmer (1973) was used to measure sport-specific achievement motivation. This questionnaire consists of sub-scales such as success/failure motivation, training motivation, arousal, competition motivation, and competition anxiety (emotional instability). No significant change in sport-specific achievement motivation was noted over the course of three years. This indicates that the sport-specific achievement motivation is a stable personality aspect, which does not change in young male or female elite athletes. However, there were significant correlations between competition performance and scales of the sport-specific achievement motivation (Elbe et al., 2003b). More specifically, a significant correlation between the success motivation in grade 7 and the competition results in the same year ($r = .58$) was revealed. In addition, training motivation in grade 9 correlated significantly ($r = .38$) with the competition results in the following year (grade 10). The correlation between the success motivation in grade 7 with athletic success in grade 10 ($r = .48$) is meaningful for the field of talent identification, as it indicates that success motivation is a valid predictor of athletic performance in line with Gabler's (1976) conceptualization of the relevance of the achievement motive for peak performance. Similarly, Seidel (in press) performed a study similar to the Potsdam project with young elite swimmers, track and field athletes, and team handball players at a school for young elite athletes in Magdeburg. She examined the development of motivational, volitional and cognitive personality aspects over a period of two years, using Allmer's (1973) sport-specific achievement motivation questionnaire as one of the instruments. Results confirmed that for the sample of track and field athletes, high success motivation predicted athletic success.

A further indication that sport specific achievement orientation seems to be of predictive value is Hellandsig's (1998) results in a longitudinal study with young Norwegian competitive athletes. In this study, sports orientation (Gill & Deeter, 1988) was measured in top-level male and female athletes, aged 15 - 16, in a wide range of sports. The results revealed that a high competitiveness and low win orientation predicted future athletic success in all the sports over a period of three years.

In conclusion, results of the current research projects indicate that a sport-specific measurement of achievement motivation seems to show moderate relation to actual athletic performance, and that it has a predictive value. However, motivation alone is not sufficient to maintain athletic training over the long period of time required to achieve expertise. Motivation is a dynamic process, and in some cases competing motivation may work against the completion of an action (Atkinson & Birch, 1970). Meta-motivational processes are required to stabilize motivation in order to maintain the intended action, especially when immediate rewards are not available. These meta-motivational or volitional processes are influenced by personality factors. Additional personality factors are needed to secure a complete athletic accomplishment.

ACTION CONTROL AND VOLITION

High skill-level and high motivation are often not sufficient to achieve a goal. Auxiliary, self-regulatory processes, referred to as action control or volition, are also required. Volition consists of meta-motivational processes, i.e. knowing how to motivate oneself. When higher-level action control processes fail, volition may consist of increasing vigor (Beckmann, 1987a). The concept of action control refers to both implicit and explicit processes. Most research has focussed on explicit processes that ensure that a current action is successfully screened off from motivations competing against this action. This way, an intended action is not interfered with by action alternatives, and can actually be executed (Sahre, 1991). The concept has been shown to be of great relevance for the field of sports (Beckmann & Kazén, 1994; Sahre, 1991; Seidel, 2002).

The theory of action control (Kuhl, 1983) distinguishes between "action oriented" and "state oriented" individuals. Action oriented individuals are characterized by their ability to successfully transform their intentions into actions. Furthermore, they can "down-regulate unwanted affect in a highly efficient, non-repressive and flexible manner" (Koole & Jostmann, 2003, p.53). State oriented individuals, on the other hand, often ruminate about current, past or future situations (states). After a failure, their thoughts circle around the current state, and possibly around the success initially hoped for. In that case, their thoughts are not followed by actions unless they think about the action to follow with the same intensity as they think about their failure. State oriented individuals are less able to restore positive affect in stressful situations, and therefore show less self-motivation. In addition, in state oriented individuals, the time needed to make a decision and to deactivate an intention is prolonged (Beckmann, 1994).

Three different aspects are differentiated with action- and state orientation (Kuhl, 1983): (a) failure-related, (b) decision-related, and (c) performance-related action versus state orientation. Kuhl (1983) postulated an interaction model of personality and situational factors in the generation of an actual state of action or state orientation. Only this actualized state is supposed to produce behavioral effects. State orientation can be caused by frequent experiences of failure or the experience of a lack of control. Action orientation is mediated by everything that focuses attention on the action such as specific goals with feedback (Antoni & Beckmann, 1989).

Action control during the performance of activities (AOP) seems to be especially important for sport activities. AOP, i.e., how strongly a person "can lose" himself in an activity, is fundamental for maintaining athletic training as well as for achieving peak performance. Action control during the performance of activities (AOP) correlated significantly with athletic achievement (r = .33) in a study of 91 track and field athletes (Beckmann, 1987b). In addition, the combination of failure-related state orientation and action orientation showed to be advantageous for track and field disciplines that call for short maximal force (Beckmann, 1987b). In other disciplines (endurance sports, martial arts) this combination fails to positively affect performance (Beckmann & Kazén, 1994) because the consequence is a lack of self-regulation due to state orientation. This combination furthers the maximal utilization of resources, but also causes quicker fatigue. Roth (1991, 1993) and Sahre (1991) identified different action control patterns in team sport athletes. They found that state orientation was an advantageous disposition for players responsible for setting up the plays (e.g. guard in basketball), but disadvantageous for those players responsible for scoring points (e.g. forwards and centers in basketball). According to Beckmann and Strang (1991), the action control disposition can even be applied to position young athletes in team sports. Up until now, no research exists on how action control develops in youth in general or in young talents in particular.

Kuhl (1994a), however, identified different circumstances, which affect the development of action and state orientation. The action control disposition, for example, is considered an alterable personality trait. This means that a change of control processes can be achieved through intervention. Kuhl (1994b) postulated that even the relatively stable components of a disposition towards state orientation could be altered through experience and personal growth.

Recent research has begun to focus on the development of action control dispositions. It is assumed that action and state orientation are mediated by a personality disposition acquired through socialization that begins in early childhood (Kuhl 1994b; Beckmann, 1996). An upbringing that leaves the child little initiative, is overprotective or too controlling, and hinders the development of a strong conflict- free individual is said to further the development towards state orientation (Kuhl, 1994a). Brunstein (2001) reported on the relationship between the striving for need-congruent goals and action control. Situations in which chosen achievement situations are mastered actively and independently seem to further the development of action orientation.

The results of the Potsdam research project (Beckmann et al., in press) provide a clue to the relevance of action and state orientation in youth sports, and show how its components develop in this age group. To measure the three components of action control, Kuhl's (1990) Action Control Scale was applied. The development of young elite athletes was again compared to that of non-athletic students.

Action control subsequent to failure (AOF) was found to be a stable personality factor. Action orientation during (successful) performance (AOP) and prospective and decision-related action orientation (AOD) showed a significant increase in the athletic sample (Elbe, Beckmann & Szymanski, 2003c). The results indicate that as early as seventh grade, the action orientation during (successful) performance (AOP) is already significantly more developed in the elite athletes. This indicates that action orientation during (successful) performance (AOP) is not only of relevance for adult performance, but can also be a contributing factor in athletic performance in youth sports. However, the correlations between the three action control scales and current or future athletic competition results were low and non-significant. These results contradict Seidel's (in press) results in which a higher action control subsequent to failure (AOF), and prospective and decision-related action orientation (AOD), were predictors of athletic success in young track and field athletes and swimmers.

The inconsistent results of the two similar research projects concerning the relationship between action orientation and future sport performance may possibly be attributed to the fact that Seidel (in press) applied a sport specific version of Kuhl's Action Control Scale (1990), and that it is the sport-specific action orientation that is relevant for achieving athletic success, not the general action orientation. This explanation is in line with the findings about the general and sport-specific achievement motive.

Another personality component that is important for completing an action is volition. Kuhl (1987) argued that motivational processes lead only to the decision to act. Once an individual is engaged in an action, however, volitional processes determine whether the intention is fulfilled or not. Volition deals with processes that are responsible for initiating an action despite internal and external resistance and for maintaining the action until the goal has been reached (Kuhl, 1983). Volition involves cognitive, motivational and emotional control strategies; not giving up when things get difficult, not letting oneself be distracted, not losing one's confidence and staying positive, are few examples of self-regulatory processes.

VOLITION AND SPORT PERFORMANCE

It is generally accepted that self-regulation abilities and skills are important for maintaining long-term life goals. In recent years, scientific interest concerning volition and its underlying regulatory processes has increased in the field of sport psychology. Numerous studies have examined the relationship between volitional skills and athletic achievement (for example, Beckmann & Strang, 1991; Beckmann & Kazén, 1994; Beckmann, 1999; Beckmann, Szymanski & Elbe, 2004). Schneider, Bös and Rieder (1993) claimed that among other personality factors, self-regulation and persistence are essential prerequisites for attaining high athletic achievement in young elite tennis players. Volition is especially important for performing long, intense training loads during the course of an athletic career or for adhering to regular exercise regiments.

Not much is known, however, about how volition develops in youths. What is known is that the two most important developmental tasks are maintaining both one's goals and the integrity of one's self. Self-control (Kuhl, 1992) is merely maintaining one's goal. The more favorable process is self-regulation, which is "maintaining one's actions in line with one's integrated self" (Kuhl & Fuhrmann, 1998, p.15). The development of an independent, conflict-free self is necessary for efficient self-regulation. To achieve favorable volitional control, specific socialization conditions must be present (Kuhl, 1994a): (a) unrealistic goals should be avoided, and (b) rigid adherence to rules and chronic frustrations must be minimized. Kuhl and Kraska (1989) identified a set of determinants, which are necessary for the development of volition, such as the freedom to take self-determined action, and the opportunity to try oneself out in social interaction with the immanent chance of failure.

The Systems Conditioning Model (Kuhl & Völker, 1998) further describes how social interaction should be designed to enhance volitional development. The interaction needs to occur within a certain time window, and has to be responsive to and in concert with the child's needs. Once the individual expresses sadness or discouragement, for example, the interaction partner needs to address positive feelings and to encourage the child. The feedback has to fit the individual's needs at that certain moment. Only then can the young athlete make a connection between his or her self-system and the self-regulation system. If these specific socialization conditions are present, a favorable self-regulation is most likely developed.

In the Potsdam project (Beckmann et al., in press) young elite athletes maintained higher values of self-optimization and held higher levels during grades 7 - 10 than students of regular schools. Self-optimization includes positive volitional skills necessary for reaching goals like self-motivation and initiative. Self-impediment, on the other hand, addresses skills in stress situations like negative emotionality and procrastination. Self-impediment, which continually increases in the students of a regular school, stayed stable in the athletic sample. The living conditions of the athletes were more positive in self-optimization than those of athletes living at home with their parents.

Elbe, Beckmann and Szymanski (2003a) further examined the athletic sample by comparing the volitional development of athletes dropping out of competitive sports despite of good performance results, to those who remain active. At the beginning of this study, self-impediment was less developed in the dropout athletes. Until grade nine self-impediment increased in the dropouts, whereas it remained unchanged in the adhering athletes. The negative development of self-impediment was indicated by lack of energy, procrastination, and intrusions. Figure 3 shows the differences between the two samples through the three years study concerning "lack of energy".

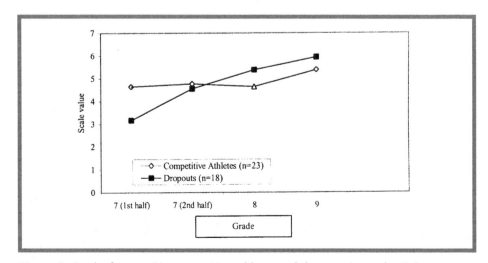

Figure 3 "Lack of energy" in competitive athletes and dropouts in grades 7-9.

Furthermore, the dropouts were significantly lower on "procrastination" at grade 7, but became similar to the adherers in grades 8 to 9 (see Figure 4).

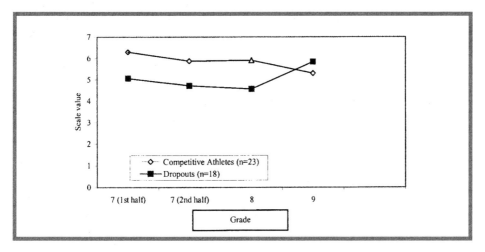

Figure 4 "Procrastination" in competitive athletes and dropouts in grades 7-9.

"Intrusive thoughts" were higher in competitive athletes at grade 7 (1st half), but increased sharply in the dropout athletes in grade 7-9 (2nd half; see Figure 5) .

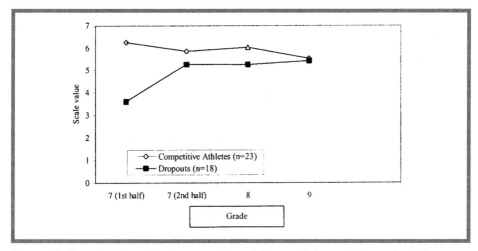

Figure 5 "Intrusive thoughts" in competitive athletes and dropouts in grades 7-9.

According to Kuhl (1994a) experiencing failure can be a cause for suboptimal volitional development. To test this assumption, the investigation performed a comparison of the competition results in the two groups. The results indicated clearly that the dropout was not related to athletic failure. Other factors, therefore, need to be identified which might have led to the dropout.

Results from different studies show that psychological factors account for athletic success and dropping out of youth competitive sports (e.g., Elbe et al., 2003b; Elbe et al. 2003c, Hellandsig, 1998; Seidel, 2002). Sport-specific achievement motivation, action and state orientation, and stable volitional development seem to be prerequisites for young elite athletes' maintaining athletic training over a long period of time, and for achieving athletic success. In addition, the sport-specific achievement motive seems to be a fairly stable personality component that is especially relevant in accounting for athletic talent.

ENHANCING PERSONALITY DEVELOPMENT IN YOUNG ELITE ATHLETES

The main concern here is how personality development can be supported and enhanced in the form of motivational and self-regulatory aspects. Our findings indicate that the sport-specific achievement motive is a relatively stable personality factor. However, studies have proven that this personality factor can change via intervention programs. Kleine (1980) and Wessling-Lünnemann (1985) showed that through training a reduction of fear of failure and an increase in the hope for success component can be obtained. Action orientation and volition alter and develop in young elite athletes. Positive development of these volitional personality skills seems to be important for athletic success. In the following section the environment of young elite athletes is described, and the conditions that must be met to create a positive influence on personality development are outlined.

PARENTS

Parents are the most important and influential agents during childhood, and thus play a substantial role in structuring the motivational and volitional personality factors of their children. For example, providing the child feedback according to Kuhl and Völker's (1998) Systems Conditioning Model can further the development of self-regulation. An upbringing that is overprotective or too controlling, on the other hand, can negatively influence personality development. Heim (2002) found that parents' relationship with their competitively active children is generally very supportive. However, he also described a less than optimal situation when the parents' expectations are too high. Parents demanding too much of the young athletes can lead to dramatic negative consequences. A "demanding" parent-child relationship can hinder the child's motivational and volitional personality development.

PEERS

During adolescence the importance of peer contacts greatly increases. Kaminski, Mayer and Ruoff (1984) showed that the peer contacts of young athletes are restricted to members of the team or training group. Contacts to peers outside of the sport domain are comparatively minimal. Bona (1996) added that having a restricted group of friends applies mainly to boys. Girls have a larger network of friends including peers outside of the sports domain. Peer relations with fellow athletes for boys and girls can be of different quality, though. These relations can be supportive when communication centers on training or school issues, which enhance need responsive feedback, and result in personality growth. Peer contacts, especially in the same team or training group, however, can also be characterized by competition and jealousy, can be experienced as stressful, and can result in negative personality development.

BOARDING SCHOOL

The boarding school is a place of manifold and plentiful peer contacts. These contacts have positive effects on personality development, especially when students enter this new environment, and become adjusted to the new situation. Here the role of the context comes into play as indicated by several motivation theorists (Urdan, 1999). Recent work has shown that the school environment and school context can greatly influence motivation (Stipek, 1998). Eccles and Wigfield (2002) maintained that "it is difficult if not impossible to understand students' motivation without understanding the contexts they are experiencing" (p.130). Up to now the context of the boarding school in competitive sports has been strongly criticized. It has been described as having a negative influence on personality development among young elite athletes because of its ghetto-like nature (Franke, 1998; Funke, 1983).

However, the personality development of boarding school inhabitants has never been longitudinally assessed and/or compared to the development in other environments. Our results showed that athletes living at the boarding school had more positive psychological development than those living at home with their parents. The boarding school students profited especially at the beginning of their high school career. These students were confronted with a special situation when entering the new school. They made new friends, not only in school and in practice but also in the dormitories. Having to assert themselves in all areas, they were forced to question their own position. According to Kuhl and Kraska (1989) these new and challenging situations are the conditions for the development of a conflict-free self that enable efficient self-regulation. Cookson and Persell's (1985) study showed that boarding school inhabitants had a strong desire to find a group of friends rather quickly, in order to receive a feeling of belonging and security. This intense confrontation with one's social role (Sturzbecher & Lenz, 1997), which possibly takes place after entering the boarding school context, is favorable for the volitional development. The integration into the new environment of the boarding school, which allowed the athletes to try themselves out in social interaction, also included the inherent chance of failure. In addition, the boarding school offers more chances for interaction that is contingent with the athlete's needs. It can be concluded that the boarding school offers the chance of a favorable development in the area of self-regulation (see Kuhl, 1994a). However, this positive development cannot be achieved by peer contacts alone. Further environmental factors are needed in the boarding school to ensure that athletes develop in a positive manner.

The role of the caretakers in the boarding schools therefore should not be neglected. Richartz (2002) showed the importance of caretakers in providing support, stimulation, solving conflicts and developing competencies. Caretakers must be professionally trained and devote much time to meeting the needs of the young elite athletes. Only under such conditions are they able to contribute to the athletes' personal growth. The caretakers represent valuable social interaction partners who, along with other adults like parents, teachers, and coaches, are important for delivering feedback according to the Systems Conditioning Model (Kuhl & Völker, 1998).

LEISURE TIME

Another important factor for personality development is the amount and the quality of leisure time. Leisure time, important for recovery, also allows time for necessary social interaction. In the Potsdam project, Elbe and Beckmann (2002) showed that the ninth grade regular students had an average of 6.2 hours of leisure time during a weekday, whereas the young elite athletes had an average of 3.8 hours of free time a day. In addition, the leisure activities that involve social interaction (e.g. spending time with friends / spending time with girlfriend- boyfriend) and which could contribute to personality growth, decreased from grade 7-9. Competitions and longer training sessions limited their leisure time on weekends. Even during vacations, young athletes had less free time because they took part in training camps. This was especially the case in sports in which intensive training begins at a very young age (e.g. gymnastics) or in sports with large training loads (e.g. rowing, swimming, and triathlon). Athletes in team sports had more time available. The young athletes maintained that because of their dual academic and athletic responsibilities, the little free time they do have is used for recovery and not for social activities.

Lack of free time can lead to under-recovery, stress, and ultimately to dropping out of competitive sports. The relevance of stress becomes evident in the results concerning volition and dropout. Reasons for dropout described by the athletes were:

> The reason was the stress, the pressure to perform by the coaches. And I don't know, that was just too tough for me. Yes, and mostly the stress .... (female, 10th grade, track and field).
> All that pressure. There is school, practice, two practices a day, two sessions of school a day and all that training. Then you are finished for the day and you do your homework until about midnight and all that pressure to perform. That is the main reason (male, 10th grade, canoeing).
> The increase in pressure to perform ... And that I could not keep up with my school work... (male, 10th grade, rowing). (Elbe et al., 2003a)

Stress and pressure were the main reasons for dropout. It became apparent that by trying to fulfill their demands in school and completing daily training, these athletes were experiencing too much stress. This despite the fact that the German sport schools were designed to optimally balance school and training loads. The school schedule was adjusted to the training schedule, and as many students lived on campus, not much time was wasted on traveling in between school, training facilities and home. Nonetheless the double load of school and training had negative consequences.

The overall results of the Potsdam project (Beckmann et al., in press), however, indicate positive effects on athletes' personalities. These positive effects are further supported by results from Hackfort and Birkner (2003) who studied elite athletes attending a school to become federal police officers. Hackfort and Birkner's results indicated that athletes can benefit from having two responsibilities at the same time. Similarly, Kellmann (2002) postulated that changing stress systems, i.e. from motor to mental activities, actually promotes recovery. Thus, having two responsibilities may help athletes find a better balance; this is the more overall or distal perspective. From a more proximal perspective, an optimal coordination of duties is necessary. Although an alpine skier may profit from activities other than skiing to care about in the long run, she or he will not be able to efficiently prepare for a math exam after a strenuous training camp with a high training load because of physical fatigue.

SPORT PSYCHOLOGIST

A person able to scientifically monitor the stress levels of young athletes is the sport psychologist. However, sport psychologists are often contacted too late, namely when the student has put up with high stress levels for a long time, and has already made the decision to drop out. A sport psychologist can be more effective when integrated into the entire talent development process. Continuous assessment of stress and recovery, and monitoring of the young athletes' personality development, is crucial in the effort to achieve athletic goals. In this way, negative developments can be identified at an early stage and solutions can be sought. Williams and Reilly (2000) state, "the prevention and detection of injury and overuse should be a constant concern in any system of selection and player development" (p. 663). Only this way can over-exertion and burnout be prevented. The sport psychologist can also be addressed in crisis situations (for example injuries, unsuccessful competitions, conflicts on the team, etc.). However, the role of the sport psychologist should not be reduced to monitoring and crisis intervention. According to Beckmann's (2003) model for systematic sport psychological counseling (see Figure 6), a very important part of the counseling process is the training of performance-relevant psychological skills.

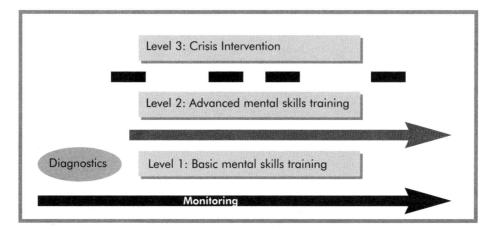

Figure 6 Beckmann's model of systematic sport psychological counseling.

The performance-relevant skills include strategies like relaxation techniques, positive self-talk, and activation regulation. Beckmann's (2003) model combines the aspects of basic mental skills training, advanced mental skills training, crisis intervention, and monitoring. The monitoring process includes the assessment of stress and recovery levels with the Recovery and Stress Questionnaire for Athletes (Kellmann & Kallus, 2001) or the improvement of mental skills, which can be assessed, for example, with the Ottawa Mental Skills Assessment Tool (Durand-Bush, Salmela & Green-Demers, 2001).

Sport psychologists can also aid the school education process. Developing programs for e-learning can contribute to stress reduction for the young elite athletes when they are away from schools for long periods of times (Hackfort & Schlattmann, 2002). This is often the case during competitions or training camps. Through these programs the athletes can keep up with their school work via internet even when they are away for longer periods of time, minimizing the pressure resulting from having to catch up with school work when they return.

In conclusion, many environmental factors including parents, peers and the boarding school environment play roles in the development of young elite athletes. Paying attention to these influential environmental aspects can contribute to healthy personality development, which also can contribute to athletic performance and aid the long process of deliberate practice.

It is the hope of the authors that more attention will be paid in the future to the psychological development of young elite athletes. The chapter has shown how the field of sport psychology can aid the process of talent identification. More important though, is the way in which sport psychology supports the talent development process in order to further personality development in young elite athletes.

REFERENCES

Allmer, H. (1973). *Zur Diagnostik der Leistungsmotivation - Konstruktion eines sportspezifischen Motivationsfragebogens [Measuring achievement motivation - construction of a sport-specific motivation questionnaire]*. Ahrensburg: Czwalina.

Antoni, C. & Beckmann, J. (1989). An action control conceptualization of goal setting and feedback effects. In U. E. Kleinbeck, H. H. Quast, H. Thierry & H. Häcker (Eds.), *Work Motivation* (pp. 1-52). Englewood Cliffs, N. J.: Erlbaum.

Atkinson, J. W. & Birch, D. (1970). *A Dynamic Theory of Action*. New York: Wiley.

Altmeyer, L., Beuchot, P. & Staszak, A. (2002). Das Forbacher Leistungszentrum für Geräteturnen [The Forbach center for top level gymnastics]. In A.-M. Elbe & J. Beckmann (Eds.), *Dokumentation der 1. Tagung der Eliteschulen des Sports "Lebenskonzepte für Sporttalente"* (pp. 80-88). Frankfurt: DSB-Presse.

Beckmann, J. (1987a). Metaprocesses and the regulation of behavior. In F. Halisch & J. Kuhl (Eds.), *Motivation, Intention and Volition* (pp. 71-386). Berlin, Heidelberg: Springer-Verlag.

Beckmann, J. (1987b). Höchstleistungen als Folge missglückter Selbstregulation [Peak Performance as a consequence of unsuccessful self-regulation]. In J. P. Janssen, E. Hahn & H. Strang (Eds.), *Handlungskontrolle und soziale Prozesse im Sport* (pp. 52-63). Köln: bps.

Beckmann, J. (1994). Volitional correlates of action and state orientations. In J. Kuhl & J. Beckmann (Eds.), *Volition and Personality: Action and State Orientation* (pp. 155-166). Seattle, WA: Hogrefe & Huber Publishers.

Beckmann, J. (1996). Aktuelle Perspektiven der Motivationsforschung [Current perspectives in motivation research]. In N. E. Witte (Ed.), *Sozialpsychologie der Motivation und Emotion* (pp. 3-33). Lengerich: Pabst.

Beckmann, J. (1999). Volition und sportliches Handeln [Volition and physical activity]. In D. Alfermann & O. Stoll (Eds.), *Motivation und Volition im Sport - Vom Planen zum Handeln* (pp. 13- 26). Köln: bps.

Beckmann, J. (2003). *Modell zur systematischen sportpsychologischen Betreuung. [A model for systematic sport psychological counseling]*. University of Potsdam: unpublished manuscript.

Beckmann, J. & Kazén, M. (1994). Action and state orientation and the performance of top athletes. In J. Kuhl & J. Beckmann (Eds.), *Volition and Personality: Action and State Orientation* (pp. 439-451). Seattle: Hogrefe.

Beckmann, J. & Strang, H. (1991). Handlungskontrolle im Sport [Action control in sport]. *Sportpsychologie, 5*(4), 5-10.

Beckmann, J., Szymanski, B. & Elbe, A.-M. (2004). Erziehen Verbundsysteme zur Unselbständigkeit? Entwicklung von Sporttalenten an einer Eliteschule des Sports. Sportwissenschaft [Do school systems for young elite athletes promote helplessness? The development of young elite athletes attending a sport school]. *Sportwissenschaft, 34*, 65-80.

Beckmann, J., Elbe, A.-M., Szymanski, B. & Ehrlenspiel, F. (in press). *Chancen und Risiken vom Leben im Verbundsystem von Schule und Leistungssport - Psychologische, soziologische und Leistungsaspekte [Chances and risks of life in a school system for young elite athletes - psychological, sociological and achievement aspects]*. Köln: Sport und Buch Strauß.

Bona, I. (1996). Soziale Unterstützung durch Gleichaltrige [Social support by peers]. In W. Brettschneider & A. Richartz (Eds). *Weltmeister werden und die Schule schaffen* (pp. 130-187). Schorndorf: Hofmann.

Brunstein, J. C. (2001). Persönliche Ziele und Handlungs- versus Lageorientierung: Wer bindet sich an realistische und bedürfniskongruente Ziele? [Personal goals and action versus state orientation: Who builds a commitment to realistic and need-congruent goals?]. *Zeitschrift für Differentielle und Diagnostische Psychologie, 22,* 1-12.

Cattell, R. B. (1965). *The Scientific Analysis of Personality.* Baltimore: Penguin.

Conzelmann, A. (2001). *Sport und Persönlichkeit. Möglichkeiten und Grenzen von Lebenslaufanalysen [Sport and personality. Prospects and limits of life-span evaluation].* Schorndorf: Hofmann.

Cookson, P. W. & Persell, C. H. (1985). *Preparing for Power - American's Elite Boarding Schools.* New York, NY: Basic Books.

Cox, R. H. (1998). *Sport Psychology: Concepts and Applications* (4th ed.). Madison, WI: Brown & Benchmark Publishers.

Durand-Bush, N., Salmela, J. H. & Green-Demers, I. (2001). The Ottawa Mental Skills Assessment Tool (OMSAT-3*). *The Sport Psychologist, 15,* 1-19.

Eccles, J. S. & Wigfield, A. (2002). Motivational beliefs, values, and goals. *Annual Review of Psychology, 53,* 109-132.

Elbe, A.-M. & Beckmann, J. (2002). Lebenskonzepte für Sporttalente: Schlussfolgerungen und Perspektiven [Life concepts for athletic talents: Conclusions and perspectives]. In A.-M. Elbe & J. Beckmann (Eds.), *Dokumentation der 1. Tagung der Eliteschulen des Sports "Lebenskonzepte für Sporttalente"* (pp. 97-102). Frankfurt: DSB-Presse.

Elbe, A.-M., Beckmann, J. & Szymanski, B. (2003a). Das Dropout Phänomen an Eliteschulen des Sports - ein Problem der Selbstregulation? [The drop out phenomenon in young elite athletes - a problem of self regulation?]. *Leistungssport, 33,* 46-49.

Elbe, A.-M., Beckmann, J. & Szymanski, B. (2003b). Entwicklung der allgemeinen und sportspezifischen Leistungsmotivation von SportschülerInnen [Development of the general and sport specific achievement motivation of young elite athletes]. *Psychologie und Sport, 10,* 134-143.

Elbe, A.-M., Beckmann, J. & Szymanski, B (2003c). *Development of action control in young elite athletes.* Manuscript submitted for publication.

Ericsson, K. A., Krampe, R. T. & Tesch-Römer, C. (1993). The role of deliberate practice in the acquisition of expert performance. *Psychological Review, 100,* 363-406.

Eysenck, H. J. & Eysenck, S. B. G. (1975). *Eysenck Personality Inventory manual.* London: Hodder & Stoughton.

Franke, E. (1998). Bedeutung und ethische Konsequenzen sportlicher Höchstleistungen im Kindes- und Jugendalter [Significance and ethic consequences of sport peak performance in childhood and youth]. In R. Daugs, E. Emrich & C. Igel (Eds.), *Kinder und Jugendliche im Leistungssport* (pp. 50-68). Schorndorf: Hofmann.

Funke, J. (1983). Was sich früh krümmt, wird auf Dauer krumm. Über das falsche und richtige Sporttreiben von Kindern [What is crooked at an early age, will always be crooked. About correct and incorrect physical activity of children]. *Die Zeit, 41,* 72.

Gabler, H. (1976). Zur Entwicklung von Persönlichkeitsmerkmalen bei Hochleistungs-sportlern [Development of personality traits in peak performance athletes]. *Sportwissenschaft, 6*(3), 247-276.

Gabler, H. (2002). *Motive im Sport [Motives in sport]*. Schorndorf: Hofmann.

Gill, D. L. & Deeter, T. E. (1988). Development of the sport orientation questionnaire. *Research Quarterly for Exercise and Sport, 59*, 191-202.

Gjesme, T. & Nygard, R. (1970). *Achievement - related motives: Theoretical considerations and construction of a measuring instrument*. Unpublished manuscript, University of Oslo, Norway.

Hackfort, D. & Birkner, H.-A. (2003). *Werdegang von Sportlern der BGS-Sportschule Bad Enddorf [The career of athletes attending the sport school for federal police officers in Bad Endorf]*. Unpublished manuscript, Bundeswehr University Munich, Germany.

Hackfort, D. & Schlattmann, A. (2002). Externe Unterrichtsbeteiligung im virtuellen Klassenzimmer [External classroom participation in the virtual classroom]. In A.-M. Elbe & J. Beckmann (Eds.), *Dokumentation der 1. Tagung der Eliteschulen des Sports "Lebenskonzepte für Sporttalente"* (pp. 7-76). Frankfurt: DSB-Presse.

Hathaway, S. R. & Mc Kinley, J. C.(1967). *Minnesota Multiphasic Personality Inventory manual*. New York: Psychological Corporation.

Heim, R. (2002). Entwicklung und Perspektiven sportpädagogischer Jugendforschung [Development and perspectives of sport pedagogical youth research]. In G. Friedrich (Ed.), *Sportpädagogische Forschung* (pp1-50). Hamburg: Czwalina.

Hellandsig, E. T. (1998). Motivational predictors of high performance and discontinuation in different types of sports among talented teenage athletes. *International Journal of Sport Psychology, 29*, 27-44.

Kaminski, G., Mayer, R. & Ruoff, B.A. (1984). *Kinder und Jugendliche im Hochleistungssport? Eine Längsschnittuntersuchung zur Frage eventueller Auswirkungen [Children and teenagers in competitive sports? A longitudinal study concerning the question of its implications]*. Schorndorf: Hoffmann.

Kellmann, M. (2002). *Enhancing Recovery: Preventing Underperformance in Athletes*. Champaign, IL: Human Kinetics.

Kellmann, M. & Kallus, K.W. (2001). *Recovery-Stress Questionnaire for Athletes; user manual*. Champaign, IL: Human Kinetics

Kleine, W. (1980). *Leistungsmotivschulung im Grundschulsport. Eine motivations-psychologische Studie unter sportpädagogischen Aspekten [Improving achievement motivation in elementary physical education. A motivation psychological study with a sport pedagogical perspective]*. Schorndorf: Hofmann.

Koole, S. L. & Jostmann, N. (2003). *Getting a Grip on Your Feelings: Effects of Action Orientation and Social Demand on Intuitive Affect Regulation*. Manuscript, Free University of Amsterdam, The Netherlands.

Krämer, K. (1977). *Zur Problematik einer Talentsichtung. Informationen zum Training, 12 [Concerning the problem of identifying talents]*. Berlin: Bartels & Wernitz.

Kroll, W. & Crenshaw, W. (1970). Multivariate personality profile analysis of four athletic groups. In G. S. Kenyon (Ed.), *Contemporary Psychology of Sport: Second International Congress of Sport Psychology*. Chicago: The Athletic Institute.

Kuhl, J. (1983). *Motivation, Konflikt und Handlungskontrolle [Motivation, conflict and action control]*. Berlin: Springer-Verlag.

Kuhl, J. (1987). Motivation und Handlungskontrolle: Ohne guten Willen geht es nicht. [Motivation and action control: It does not work without good will]. In H. Heckhausen, P. M. Gollwitzer & F. E. Weinert (Eds.), *Jenseits des Rubikon: Der Wille in der Humanwissenschaft* (pp. 01-120). Berlin: Springer.

Kuhl, J. (1990). *Fragebogen zur Erfassung der Handlungs- und Lageorientierung [Questionnaire to measure action and state orientation]*. München: Soziologische Forschung.

Kuhl, J. (1992). A theory of self-regulation: Action versus state orientation, self-discrimination, and some applications. *Applied Psychology: An International Review, 41*, 95-173.

Kuhl, J. (1994a). A theory of action and state orientation. In J. Kuhl & J. Beckmann (Eds.), *Volition and Personality: Action and State Orientation* (pp. 9-46). Seattle, WA: Hogrefe & Huber Publishers.

Kuhl, J. (1994b). Motivation and volition. In G. d'Ydevalle, P. Bertelson & P. Eelen (Eds.), *Current Advances in Psychological Science: An International Perspective*. Hillsdale, NJ: Erlbaum.

Kuhl, J. & Fuhrmann, A. (1998). Decomposing self-regulation and self-control: The volitional components inventory. In J. Heckhausen & C. Dweck (Eds.), *Lifespan Perspectives on Motivation and Control* (pp. 15-49). Hillsdale, NJ: Erlbaum.

Kuhl, J. & Kraska, K. (1989). Self-regulation and metamotivation: Computational Mechanisms, development and assessment. In R. Kanfer, P. L. Ackermann & R. Cudek (Eds.), *Abilities, Motivation, and Methodology: The Minnesota Symposium on Learning and Individual Differences* (pp. 343-374). Minnesota: Erlbaum.

Kuhl, J. & Völker, S. (1998). Entwicklung und Persönlichkeit [Development and personality]. In H. Keller (Ed.), *Lehrbuch der Entwicklungspsychologie* (pp07-240). Bern: Huber.

Letzelter, M. (1981). Der Beitrag der Trainingswissenschaft zur "Theorie des sportlichen Talents" (Problematik - Strategie - Lösungen) [The contribution of training science to the theory of athletic talent (Problem - Strategy - Solution)]. In D. Augustin & N. Müller (Eds.), *Leichtathletiktraining im Spannungsfeld von Wissenschaft und Praxis,* (pp. 38-52). Niedernhausen: Schors.

Mischel, W. (1968). *Personality and Assessment*. New York: Wiley.

Mischel, W. & Shoda, Y. (1995). A cognitive-affective system theory of personality: Reconceptualizing situations, dispositions, dynamics, and invariance in personality structure. *Psychological Review, 102*, 246-268.

Morgan, W. P. (1980). The trait psychology controversy. *Research Quarterly for Exercise and Sport, 17*, 94-100.

Morgan, W. P. & Costill, D. L. (1972). Psychological characteristics of the marathon runner. *International Journal of Sports Medicine, 8*, 124-131.

Morris, T. (1995). Psychological characteristics and sports behaviour. In T. Morris & J. Summers (Eds.), *Sport Psychology* (pp. 3-28). Milton, Queensland: John Wiley & Sons.

Morris, T. (2000). Psychological characteristics and talent identification in soccer. *Journal of Sport Science, 9*, 715-726.

Richartz, A. (2002). Unterstützen - Anregen - Konflikte bewältigen: Grundlagen einer modernen Internatspädagogik [Support - Motivate - Cope with conflicts: The basics of a modern boarding school pedagogy]. In A.-M. Elbe & J. Beckmann (Eds.), *Lebenskonzepte für Sporttalente* (pp. 54-66). Frankfurt: DSB Presse.

Roth, K. (1991). Entscheidungsverhalten im Sportspiel [Making decisions in team sports]. *Sportwissenschaft, 21*, 229-246.

Roth, K. (1993). Entscheidungsverhalten im Sportspiel in Abhängigkeit von situations- und personenbezogenen Merkmalen [Making decisions in team sports: situational and personal aspects]. In J. Beckmann, H. Strang & E. Hahn (Eds.), *Aufmerksamkeit und Energetisierung. Facetten von Konzentration und Leistung* (pp. 155-175). Göttingen: Hogrefe.

Sack, H.-G. (1980). *Zur Psychologie des jugendlichen Leistungssportlers [Psychology of the young competitive athlete]*. Schorndorf: Hofmann.

Sahre, E. (1991). *Handlungskontrolle im Basketball [Action control in basketball]*. Aachen: Meyer & Meyer Verlag.

Schneider, W., Bös, K. & Rieder, H. (1993). Leistungsprognose bei jugendlichen Spitzensportlern [Performance prediction in young top athletes]. In J. Beckmann, H. Strang & E. Hahn (Eds.), *Aufmerksamkeit und Energetisierung. Facetten von Konzentration und Leistung* (pp. 277-299). Göttingen: Hogrefe.

Schurr, K. T., Ashley, M. A. & Joy, K. L. (1977). A multivariate analysis of male athlete characteristics: sport type and success. *Multivariate Experimental Clinical Research, 3,* 53-68.

Seidel, I. (2002). Die Handlungskontroll-Disposition als Unterscheidungskriterium unterschiedlich talentierter Nachwuchsathleten im Handball und Schwimmen? [Does the action control disposition distinguish between differently talented young athletes]. In A. Hohmann, D. Wick & K. Carl (Hrsg.), *Talent im Sport,* (pp. 243-250). Schorndorf: Hofmann.

Seidel, I. (in press). *Zur Entwicklung von Nachwuchsleistungssportlern an Eliteschulen des Sports. Ausgewählte psychologische Persönlichkeitsmerkmale und deren Eignung als Leistungsprädiktoren. [The development of young athletes at elite sport schools. Selected personality factors and their suitability as predictors of athletic achievement].* Doctoral dissertation, University of Potsdam, Germany.

Seidel, I. & Hohmann, A. (1999). Ein Forschungsprojekt zum sportlichen Talent [A research project about athletic talent]. In J. Wiemeyer (Ed.), *Forschungsmethodologie in der Trainings- und Bewegungsforschung,* (pp. 351-355). Hamburg: Edition Czwalina.

Stipek, D. J. (1998). *Motivation to Learn: From Theory to Practice*. Boston: Allyn & Bacon.

Sturzbecher, D. & Lenz, H.-J. (1997). Wir woll'n Spaß, wir woll'n Spaß. Freizeitangebote in Brandenburg und ihre Nutzung. [We want to have fun, we want to have fun. Leisure activities in Brandenburg and their utilization]. In D. Sturzbecher (Ed.), *Jugend und Gewalt in Ostdeutschland. Lebenserfahrungen in Schule Freizeit und Familie* (pp. 82-110). Göttingen: Verlag für Angewandte Psychologie.

Urdan, T. (1999). *The Role of Context: Advances in Motivation and Achievement* (Vol. 11). Stamford, CT: JAI Press.

Wessling-Lünnemann, G. (1985). *Motivationsförderung im Unterricht [Enhancing motivation in the classroom]*. Göttingen: Hogrefe.

Williams, L. R. T., & Parkin, W. A. (1980). Personality profiles of three hockey groups. *International Journal of Sport Psychology, 11,* 113-120.

Williams, A. M. & Reilly, T. (2000). Talent identification and development in soccer. *Journal of Sports Science, 18,* 657-667.

Developing Peak Performers in Sport: Optimization versus Creativity

Michael Bar-Eli, Oded Lowengart, Michal Master-Barak, Shaul Oreg, Jacob Goldenberg, Shmuel Epstein, and Richard Douglas Fosbury

Contents

Summary

In the process of developing talented athletes into peak sport performers, coaches often attempt to be rational in the sense of applying various means (i.e., training models) believed to be effective or instrumental. This practice assumes that the ultimate goal of athletes in elite sport is the maximization of their performance. For example, athletes are mentally trained in order to enable and facilitate performance enhancement, bearing in mind the goal of performance maximization. The existing sport psychology literature provides many examples for such mental training methods (e.g., Williams, 2001).

Performance is defined as "goal-directed behavior" (e.g., by action theory; see Frese & Zapf, 1994; Nitsch & Hackfort, 1981). In order to maximize performance, athletes usually try to optimize something - be it, for example, their movement, as described by biomechanics (e.g., Zatsiorsky, 2000), or their arousal state, as proposed by sport psychology (Zaichkowsky & Baltzell, 2001). Thus, the pursuit of excellence in sport requires athletes to achieve performance "maximization through optimization" - a principle that is central among the major aspects of human rationality (Bar-Eli, Lurie, & Breivik, 1999). Moreover, sport psychology has been provided with rational models such as the Bayesian approach (see, for a review, Tenenbaum & Bar-Eli, 1993), which can be used to aid in optimizing the decision-makers' thought processes required for performance maximization.

Such models reflect rationality in its instrumental sense, which has to do with the effectiveness of one's application of means towards the accomplishment of a certain goal (Weber, 1919/1946). Instrumental rationality and/or reasoning are reflected, for example, in the current literature on expert sport performance (see, for review, Starkes & Ericsson, 2003), and on the professionalization processes of organized elite sport (Coakley, 2001). However, philosophers such as Descartes (1641/1987) maintained that being rational also has to do with a critical assessment of one's thoughts and actions. According to this concept, a rational athlete would be one who breaks with tradition, and through the logic of his or her non-dogmatic, critical thinking, invents new ways of meeting old, unresolved challenges. He or she would then be considered creative.

There is often controversy among researchers over the extent of the distinctive nature of creative processes (Boden, 1996). The major dispute is between the "total freedom" approach to creativity (e.g., Csikszentinihali, 1996), and various other approaches suggesting that creativity be conceived in a more systematic, structured way. Among these we can find the "creative cognition approach" (e.g., Finke, Ward, & Smith, 1992; Goldenberg & Mazursky, 2001) and the "confluence approach" (Sternberg, 1988; Sternbert & Lubart, 1999).

A well-known example of rationality as "critical thinking" in sport is the case of the elite high jumper Dick Fosbury, who - in the Mexico Olympics of 1968 - instead of trying to excel in the high jump by utilizing established means (as all the other high jumpers were doing), broke with tradition and invented a radically new approach to the high jump, later dubbed the "Fosbury Flop". A theoretical analysis of this case - using an extensively detailed introspective report provided recently by Fosbury himself - demonstrated that this radical innovation was not an outcome of "total freedom" of thought, but rather the outcome of a continuous development process, and a combination of converging abilities.

Several lessons may be drawn from a close examination of the Fosbury case (Goldenberg, Lowengart, Oreg, Bar-Eli, Epstein, Fosbury, submitted). For example, Fosbury reported that the incremental development of the new style was a spontaneous reaction during competition. In other words, the fact that he was highly intense and focused during competition did not make him stick to a well-learned behavior or habit (as would be predicted, for example, from classical learning theories such as the Hull-Spence model; e.g., Spence & Spence, 1966), but rather led him to seek changes and innovations!

Moreover, it is evident from Fosbury's case that experts' optimal (i.e., normative) solutions to various problems investigated in the expert sport performance literature (Starkes & Ericsson, 2003), can frequently be a matter of a transient consensus and/or or sheer ignorance. Two recent studies on "commission bias" among soccer goalkeepers with penalty kicks further strengthen this conclusion (Bar-Eli & Ritov, 1997; Keidar-Levin, 2003).

It is recommended that methods such as the paradoxical approach (Bar-Eli, 1991) be used to promote "irrationality" in sport. However, taking a closer look into creativity in sport - from both scientific and applied perspectives - should by no means lead to abandoning the "maximization through optimization" principle. It can be concluded that in order to develop peak performers, the principles of optimization and creativity-enhancement should not be considered controversial; they should rather be integrated through the complementary implementation of "creative optimization" and "optimized creativity".

INTRODUCTION

For several years the first author of this chapter closely observed the work of elite youth basketball coaches in Israel, mainly due to his intensive consultation activity in the Israel Basketball Association. Among other things, he noticed that coaches of these ages consistently insist on teaching the kids "the right way of throwing the ball to the basket", which of course assumes the existence of some optimal model for the respective movement. Being very familiar with Israeli basketball, however, he recalled that three of the greatest scorers in its history, namely Gershon Dekel, Louis Silver, and Guy Goodes - who also represent three different generations - threw in completely different ways: Dekel would put his throwing hand directly in front of his own eyes, practically hiding the basket from his view; Silver used to throw from behind his head (and even from behind his shoulder); Goodes - who just retired from active playing - threw from the height of his chest (and even sometimes his stomach). Needless to say, none of these "strange" movements would be considered "correct" (i.e., optimal) in the eyes of current elite youth coaches.

The observations raise a difficult question related to talent development in sport, namely - whether coaches erroneously insist on routine training according to models, whose optimality can be put in serious doubt. Moreover, at least since Smith, Smoll, and Hunt's (1977) classic study on (in)effective coaching, the practice of suppressing the creativity (e.g., using "incorrect" movements) of young athletes has been repeatedly criticized as being both "inhuman" and ineffective (for review, see Horn, 2002). The monotony of repeated practice may have detrimental effects (e.g., burnout) on the motivation of young athletes (Gould, 1996), and their creative and skill development endeavors.

In practice coaches attempt to be rational in the sense of applying some means believed to be instrumental for the attainment of a particular goal. However, the philosophical literature distinguishes between various meanings of the term "rationality" (Harman, 1995). For example, beside the common conception of instrumental rationality (Weber, 1919/1946), rationality has also been associated with critical thinking (Descartes, 1641/1987). In other words, to rationally enhance performance, one may sometimes actually apply creativity.

Indeed, creativity is considered an important psychological characteristic required for the development of a successful sport performer (Morris, 2000). At face value, promoting creativity may be associated with increased "total freedom" (Csikszentmihali, 1996), and would therefore contradict routine training. However, the training of optimal routines for talent development is rooted not only in top coaches' "Trainingslehre" (Weineck, 2003), and/or their "intuitive" professional experience, but also in sound scientific principles derived, for example, from the intensive research on "deliberate practice" (Ericsson, 1996, 2003). Moreover, it has recently been argued that even creative expertise can be systematically reproduced (Ericsson, 1999), and that creative "sparks" can be regularly produced by computerized idea-generating routines (Goldenberg, Mazursky, & Solomon, 1999d).

In general, the (quite rare) research conducted thus far on different aspects of sport creativity has primarily been descriptive, without being closely linked - theoretically and/or empirically - to the large body of (sport-) psychology. In this chapter, we discuss some intriguing issues related to the role creativity may play in developing peak performers in sport. However, we thereby argue that "optimization" and "creativity" do not necessarily contradict each other, if appropriately conceived. To do this, we present some interesting facets related to the invention of the "Fosbury Flop" in the high jump, which may be relevant to talent development.

MAXIMIZATION THROUGH OPTIMIZATION

The ultimate goal of athletes in elite sport is the maximization of their performance. The existing sport psychology literature provides many examples of psychological methods for mental training that are intended to enable and facilitate performance enhancement (see Williams, 2001, for review). Accordingly, mental training operates under the idea of performance maximization, to achieve peak performance, i.e., "superior functioning exceeding an individual's probable performance quality, or full use of potential in any activity... in athletics, this refers to the release of latent powers to perform optimally within a specific sport competition" (Kimiecik & Jackson, 2002, p. 503).

Performance, as distinguished from the term "behavior," is intentionally organized, and thus was defined as "goal-directed behavior" (e.g., by action theory; see Frese & Zapf, 1994; Nitsch & Hackfort, 1981). In essence, the pursuit of excellence in sport requires athletes to repeatedly train their capacity to acquire and apply knowledge (i.e., intelligence) in order to maximize performance through effectively dealing with old and/or new demands posed by the environment (Tenenbaum & Bar-Eli, 1995). In doing so, athletes usually try to optimize something - be it a movement (e.g., Zatsiorsky, 2000), an arousal state (e.g., Zaichkowsky & Baltzell, 2001), or a decision to be made (e.g.,

Tenenbaum & Bar-Eli, 1993). To achieve this goal, they may use cognitive intellectual capabilities such as attention, concentration, visual search for cues, and anticipation of upcoming events, as well as stress management and modulation of emotions (Hackfort, 1999). These are operated during physical effort until, hopefully, the most appropriate decision is made and the best motor response or action is executed (e.g., Wrisberg, 2001).

INSTRUMENTAL RATIONALITY

Essentially, "maximization through optimization" reflects instrumental rationality, which has to do with the effectiveness of one's application of means towards the accomplishment of a certain goal (i.e., choosing the course of action that most effectively brings about the realization of a particular goal; see Weber, 1919/1946). According to this conception, an attempt is made to achieve performance "maximization through optimization" - a principle that is quite central among the major aspects of human rationality in elite sport (Bar-Eli, Lurie, & Breivik, 1999). Moreover, it is often assumed (e.g., in the current literature on expert sport performance; see, for review, Starkes & Ericsson, 2003) that there is "a" solution for a particular athletic problem; in other words, one's expertise is examined in comparison to a normative, supposedly optimal solution.

For example, Tenenbaum and his associates (Tenenbaum, Levy-Kolker, Bar-Eli, & Weinberg, 1994; Tenenbaum, Levy-Kolker, Sade, Liebermann, & Lidor, 1996; Tenenbaum, Yuval, Elbaz, & Bar-Eli, 1993) asked top coaches from team-handball, what players should optimally do in various game situations on court (i.e., what is the correct solution for each given problem?). Then, they compared the players' solutions to those of the experts, to categorize the players according to various criteria. In such a procedure, it is actually assumed that when a performer has completed the perceptual processing of environmental information, he or she must decide on an appropriate response or action. However, as indicated by the above example, to determine what "appropriate" actually is, many studies on decision processes in skill acquisition (for review, see Wrisberg, 2001) use experts, whereas according to Starkes, Helsen, and Jack (2001), the question of who is actually an expert is still highly controversial (i.e., a "moot point"; p. 183) - not to mention their "optimal solutions...."

This view of human rationality conveys a quite technical meaning to this concept, which is primarily predicated on a notion of consistency. That is to say, what is important for a person's opinions, beliefs, or preferences, is first and foremost, to cohere in a normatively defensible manner (Shafir & LeBoeuf, 2002). It has been assumed that normative theories of rationality (e.g., Edwards, 1961; Glymour, 1992, Ross, 1997) may serve as paradigmatic approximations for modeling and/or predicting actual human rational behavior. In the past three decades, it has often been demonstrated how people systematically violate fundamental principles of normative reasoning, judgment, and decision-making (for review, see Hastie, 2001; Kahneman & Tversky, 2000). Despite this fact, instrumental rationality continues to be quite central in elite sport, as evident from the ongoing application of the "maximization through optimization" principle.

It seems that the dominance of this view of rationality in current elite sport is closely related to its continuous organized professionalization (Coakley, 2001). It was only about 100 years ago that people became interested in studying human performance (productivity) in (industrial) organizations, with ideas stemming from this field gaining widespread acceptance mainly in the second half of the previous century (Warner, 1994). In fact, the first studies of organizational behavior were derived from attempts made by engineers not only to construct more efficient machines, but also - as an almost natural expansion - to make workers more productive (Crainer, 2000). Along these lines, for example, it is said that Henry Ford was a great supporter of Weber's (1921/1947) ideas on how to make organizations operate more rationally (i.e., efficiently) by applying the major principles of the so-called "bureaucracy", such as the division of labor into specialized tasks (Greenberg & Baron, 2003). To increase performance, Ford even endorsed "the reduction of the necessity for thought on the part of the worker" (Colvin, 2000, p. 9) - an idea to which we will refer again later on in this chapter.

INSTRUMENTAL REASONING IN SPORT

Similar processes can be observed in current organized elite sport. For example, Weinberg and Gould (2003) maintained that children are frequently specializing too early in a single sport: "This 'professionalization' of children's sport is often driven by the assumption that one must start and specialize in single sports at a young age to become an elite athlete" (p. 505). However, this "modern-times"-like practice often has damaging effects with regard to talent development. After reviewing the existing studies on talent development in sport, Weinberg and Gould (2003, p. 505) concluded: "This research, then, emphasizes the importance of children's not specializing in sports too early, of taking a fun and development focus early, and of children's having highly supportive but not overbearing parents," who would drive them too early into such "professionalization."

One of the first psychologists who used the idea of "maximizing (the performance of the U.S. Army) through optimizing (the selection and placement procedures of new mass-recruits)", was none other than Robert Yerkes (Riggio, 2003). The wide acceptance of instrumental reasoning by contemporary elite sport can most probably be attributed to its accelerated, ongoing organized professionalization (Coakley, 2001). The engineering-like "industrialization" of sport was substantially affected by the "Cold War," during which the significance of sporting competitions between rival nations contributed substantially to growing achievement striving in, and social significance of, top-level sport (Dunning, 1986).

Along these lines, several methods have been proposed to aid the optimization of people's thought processes in elite sport, such as the Bayesian approach (see, for a review, Tenenbaum & Bar-Eli, 1993). Moreover, recent studies in management science, particularly in operations research, demonstrated that sport psychology can indeed be provided with rational models that have the potential of being used as effective optimization aids for performance maximization (Friedman, Mehrez, Sinuany-Stern, Bar-Eli, & Epstein, in press; Sinuany-Stern, Bar-Eli, & Israeli, in press).

CRITICAL THINKING

The philosophical literature distinguishes between various meanings of the term "rationality" (Harman, 1995). For example, the philosopher and mathematician Descartes (1641/1987) proposed that being rational also has to do with a critical assessment of one's thoughts and actions. According to this approach, a rational athlete would be one who breaks with tradition and by the logic of his or her non-dogmatic, critical thinking, invents new ways of meeting an old, unresolved challenge. In other words, the athlete would then be creative in the sense of being engaged in the process of reframing familiar problems in innovative ways, thereby making use of divergent (as opposed to convergent) thought processes (Runco, 1991, 2001).

Novel and useful ideas are produced by individuals and/or teams in the process of creativity (Amabile, 1988). Organizations often encourage employees' participation in training programs designed to promote their creative skills; according to Hesselbein and Johnston (2002), many companies reported creativity-boosts following such programs. It is thereby assumed that innovation, i.e., the effective implementation of creative ideas within an organization, is often a requirement for achievement, with many of the world's most successful companies (e.g., General Electric, IBM, and Westinghouse) also being the most innovative ones (Greenberg & Baron, 2003). Although in sport, the key to success is quite often working hard, with high levels of motivation and concentration, creativity is also considered a prerequisite for enhanced performance (Bar-Eli, et al., 1999; Morris, 2000).

CREATIVITY

THE CONTROVERSY

Creativity is usually considered an intrinsic human activity - a highly complex process, which is difficult to formalize and control. Although there is a general agreement regarding the distinctive nature of the creative product (e.g., idea, painting, poem, etc.), there is often controversy among researchers over the extent of the distinctive nature of the creative process, which is considered to be vague and even mysterious (Boden, 1996).

Some researchers hold that the creative thinking process is qualitatively different from ordinary day-to-day thinking, and involves a leap - a "creative spark" - which can not be sufficiently formulated, analyzed, or reconstructed (e.g., Guilford, 1950; Koestler, 1964; MacKinnon, 1970). In contrast, it was maintained more recently that creative products are the outcome of ordinary thinking, only quantitatively different from everyday thinking (e.g., Perkins, 1981, 1988; Weisberg, 1992). In fact, this approach conceives creative problem solving as a relatively structured thought process (e.g., "constrained stochastic behavior"; see Simonton, 2003), which is quite systematically reproducible, and therefore also learnable (Dasgupta, 1994; Maymon & Horowitz, 1999). Altschuller (1985) even viewed creativity as an "exact science".

"Total Freedom"

The first abovementioned approach to creativity maintained that one has to overcome mental obstacles and/or barriers in order to reach creative ideas, which led to the belief that one has to ensure "total freedom" by eliminating directional guidance, constraints, criticism, and thinking within a bounded scope (Csikszentmihali, 1996). The elimination of such barriers is expected to increase the accessibility of ideas that can be drawn and contemplated from a typically infinite space of ideas, during the creativity process (e.g., Grossman, Rodgers, & Moore, 1988; Parnes, 1992).

The "total freedom" view prompted the emergence of various methods such as focus groups, free associations, brainstorming, synectics, lateral thinking, random stimulation, and other projective techniques (see, for a review, O'Guinn, Allen, & Semenik, 1998), that all share the instructions of withholding judgment and relying on analogies from other members in a group (i.e., "synergetic effect"), or on randomly selected forced analogies. This family of methods relies on the assumption that enhancing randomness, breaking rules and paradigms, and generating "anarchy of thought," will increase the probability of creative idea emergence.

However, the postulated association between creativity and "total freedom" has recently been challenged from several directions. We turn now to discuss two current approaches to creativity that suggest different perceptions of this concept.

The Creative Cognition Approach

As opposed to the "total freedom" approach, which relies solely on general cognitive descriptions, the creative cognition approach seeks to understand and specify the basic components of mental processes underlying creative thought, such as retrieval, combination, analogy, and transformation. It emphasizes a wide range of perceptual abilities, as well as problem definition, insight and induction skills (Boden, 1992, 1999; Finke, Ward, & Smith, 1992; Lubart, 1994, Sternberg & Lubart, 1999, Ward, 2001).

For example, Finke et al. (1992) suggested the Geneplore model as a general framework for the Creative Cognition approach. According to this model, there are two main processing phases - generative and exploratory - in creative thought. In the generative phase, an individual constructs mental representations referred to as preinventive structures, which have properties promoting creative discoveries, with creative people being described as having knowledge of heuristics for generating novel ideas. In the exploratory phase, these properties are used to come up with creative ideas.

A different, related framework is the Creativity Templates approach, which suggests that a systematic and structured way of thinking is the key for creative thought. The first step in this direction was made by Altschuller (1986), who postulated that there must be identifiable and repeatable patterns or formulas underlying successful creative ideas and products. By backward analysis of problem-solution patterns underlying creative ideas (patents and technological inventions), he succeeded in identifying more than 40 patterns, which he labeled "standards". A further development of Altschuller's work (see

Goldenberg & Mazursky, 2001), suggests a taxonomy of templates in different domains, such as engineering problem solving (Maimon & Horowitz, 1999), new product development (Goldenberg & Mazursky, 1999; Goldenberg et al., 1999d), and advertising (Goldenberg, Mazursky, & Soloman, 1999b).

For example, in a series of investigations, Goldenberg, Mazursky, and Solomon (1999a, b, c) discovered that certain regularities underlie successful ads, and those that match some of these regularities, stand out as more creative than ads that don't fit these structures. Goldenberg et al. termed these regularities "creativity templates" and reported that 89% of the award-winning ads match as few as six major templates, about 25% of which could be schematically depicted as a simple template termed "Replacement". In a later work, Goldenberg et al. (1999d) used this approach to identify templates in "creative sparks", questioning whether creativity requires functions exclusive to the human mind or rather that it can be obtained by the performance of merely well-defined prescribed operations. Through structural analyses of a large mass of past advertising ideas, they isolated a set of conceptual structures that characterized generically creative ideas. To validate these findings, Goldenberg et al. (1999d) constructed idea-generating routines - implemented by a computer - that led to these conceptual structures. It was found that the computer-generated ideas ranked significantly higher on a creativity scale than the ideas produced by the human participants.

THE CONFLUENCE APPROACH

The Confluence approach assumes that multiple components must converge for creativity to occur (Amabile, 1983; Perkins, 1981; Sternberg, 1985, 1988; Sternberg & Lubart, 1991, 1999, Weisberg, 1993). This approach suggests that the discussion of creativity as solely a cognitive process is lacking some important aspects of this phenomenon. For example, Amabile (1983) described creativity as the confluence of intrinsic motivation, domain relevant knowledge and abilities, as well as creativity-relevant skills such as a cognitive style that involves coping with complexities and braking one's mental set during problem solving. Creativity-relevant skills also include knowledge of heuristics for generating novel ideas, and a work style characterized by concentrated effort, an ability to set aside problems, and high energy. Preliminary research conducted within this framework by Sternberg and Lubart (1991, 1999) showed that creative performance can be predicted by a combination of six distinct but interrelated resources: intellectual abilities, knowledge, styles of thinking, personality, motivation, and environment. With regard to personality, numerous investigations have supported the importance of certain personality attributes for creative functioning (Feist, 1999; Lubart, 1994; Sternberg & Lubart, 1991). These attributes include, among others, self-efficacy, as well as the will to overcome obstacles, take sensible risks, and tolerate ambiguity (See also Sternberg, 1988).

In the case of talent development in sport, this approach to creativity may help us understand that being able to achieve creativity in sport is not only a product of cognitive ability. Often, pursuing creative ideas may involve disagreeing with and/or challenging coaches who demand to "do things the right way", or spending valuable practice time on risky new moves. Therefore, being able to overcome the obstacles to implementing innovative ideas requires a combination of motivational power, personality structure, and supportive environment, as suggested by the confluence approach.

THE CASE OF DICK FOSBURY

SIGNIFICANCE

A well-known example of rationality as "critical thinking" is the case of the elite high jumper Dick Fosbury, who in the 1968 Mexico Olympics excelled in the high jump utilizing untraditional means, broke with tradition, and invented a radically new approach to the high jump, which utterly changed its face, later dubbed the "Fosbury Flop".

Without advance notice, Fosbury, at that time a relatively unknown high jumper, literally jumped backwards when compared to the style of all other jumpers; instead of approaching the bar face first, he approached the bar with his back to it. The significance of Fosbury's unusual innovation, which was adopted in less than 10 years by virtually every high jumper, is best described in the publications of the Olympic Movement and the Encyclopedia Britannica:

> Dick Fosbury ... owed this fame not only to his victory, which was also an Olympic record (2.24m), but specifically to the way in which he achieved it: the style - the "Fosbury flop". A real revolution ... an athlete will never again invent such a revolutionary style. Since this high jump approach, all specialists have adopted the "Fosbury flop" and the world record of the time, held by Soviet Valery Brumel (2.29m), was quickly broken. (Official Web Site of the Olympic Movement, 2002).

> Richard Douglas Fosbury. American high jumper who revolutionized the sport by replacing the traditional approach to jumping with an innovative backward style that became known as the "Fosbury flop". (Encyclopedia Britannica, 2002).

Historians of science frequently use significant discoveries as benchmarks of progress, whereas psychologists interested in creativity often investigate the process of discovery itself. Strangely enough, Fosbury's innovation has never been analyzed within such a framework. This lack of interest is even more amazing when the current scarcity of creativity research in sport is taken into account. As mentioned bef sport psychologists (e.g., Morris, 2000) believe that creativity is one of the important psychological characteristics required for the development of a successful sport performer. Whereas early researchers (e.g., Loy, 1981) investigated the personality characteristics of sport innovators, others have proposed various techniques for enhancing athletes' creativity (e.g., Bar-Eli, 1991; Mirvis, 1998; Piirto, 1998; Ringrose, 1993; Schmole, 2000), or have examined the effects of such techniques on athletes' performance (e.g., Everhart, Kernodle, Turner, Harshaw, & Arnold, 1999; Hanin, Korjus, Jouste, & Baxter, 2002).

In general, however, research in this area has been primarily descriptive, without being closely linked theoretically or empirically to the large body of the (sport-) psychological literature. A common practice among creativity researchers (see, for review, Simonton, 2003) is to conduct biographical studies of great innovators and discoverers, such as Galileo or Newton (Schaffer, 1996), Bell, Curie, Darwin, or Einstein (Runco & Pritzker, 1999). However, this practice was not applied with regard to Fosbury's invention, despite its recognized importance.

THEORETICAL ANALYSIS

In this section, we elaborate on the case of the Fosbery Flop, in an attempt to demonstrate that radical innovation is not necessarily an outcome of "total freedom" of thought, but rather the outcome of a more complex occurrence of a continuous development process, and a combination of converging abilities. For this purpose, we use an extensive detailed introspective report provided by Fosbury in February 2002.

Fosbury's technique in the high jump began as a result of first having learned, at the age of 10, an antiquated, inefficient technique called the Scissors. At the age of 11, Fosbury's physical education teacher and coach taught all the children trying out for track to jump using the classic style, the Straddle or "western roll." He also allowed the children to use the Scissors if they preferred, which Fosbury did. Fosbury used that old style until he reached high school, mainly because he did not do very well with the more advanced straddle.

After switching styles to the straddle and beginning all over, Fosbury fell behind the other jumpers, competitively. Fosbury was very frustrated and asked his coach if he could revert to the old scissors style to get a better result and maybe boost his confidence a bit. The coach did not encourage Fosbury to quit trying the straddle technique, but was sympathetic to his frustrations and agreed to let him try it.

An examination of the case thus far leads us to our first two observations, namely, that (a) Fosbury was not a super athlete at the beginning of his career, but he was highly motivated and willing to overcome obstacles on his way to success; (b) His coach was sympathetic to his frustration and gave him some degree of freedom to experience different methods. The second stage of the story reveals that the inventor faced a personal problem - lack of fit with the current technique. Feeling awkward yet persistent, Fosbury managed to clear his previous best jump to 1.63 meters, and then, facing a new height, he knew he had to adjust something. With the scissors style, the jumper typically hits the bar off with his/her behind, and sometimes with the movement of the legs. To compensate, Fosbury began to try to lift his hips up higher, which also dropped his shoulders simultaneously. Fosbury cleared the height. He continued with this raising of his hips until he eventually cleared 15 cm higher for a new personal record, and even placed fourth to score points for his team. Thus, one can conclude that (a) The development process followed two processing phases: a generative phase (the idea of lifting up the hips) and an exploratory phase of the new idea; (b) The development process resembled one of the inventive thinking patterns described, for example, by Goldenberg et al. (1999b). At this stage, no one knew what Fosbury was doing as he transformed this old technique into something new, as each attempt was a little different. Exploration, imagination, and persistence were essential components of this process.

Fosbury's coach, Dean Benson, was pleased with his success and asked to see him at practice in one of the following days. At that practice, he explained that he was not sure exactly what Fosbury was doing, but he thought that they could study some films he had of high jump techniques - perhaps there was some similar successful model that Fosbury could adopt. While they did not see anything similar, they had a session or two practicing these other techniques, which was a fun break for the high jumpers from the routine. At this stage there was no new style or development, but rather attempts to develop a hybrid technique.

Both Fosbury and his coach tolerated ambiguity and willingness to take risks in the exploration process of the new technique. The next two years were a continual, slow evolution of the technique. Using his curved approach to the bar, Fosbury intuitively began to turn his inside shoulder away from the bar, to get his head over it sooner. By the second year Fosbury had fully evolved to clearing the bar with his back to it, arching his hips over, then un-arching to kick his heels over, and land on his back in the pit. In other words, two years of small incremental changes were required for Fosbury to come up with the final, apparently radical, version of his jump. Thus, the new innovative high jump technique was in fact the result of a lengthy sequence of steps, and a systematic development process.

LESSONS

In a recent study (Goldenberg, Lowengart, Oreg, Bar-Eli, Epstein, & Fosbury, submitted), the case of Dick Fosbury was closely examined in order to determine whether a revolutionary invention is necessarily an extraordinary, discontinuous event, or if it can also be a continuous, day-to-day process. Among other things, this study used the extensive and detailed introspective report provided by Fosbury in February 2002, concerning various aspects of his invention. Although it was beyond the scope of that study's original intention, Fosbury's introspective report revealed some very interesting anomalies, as far as some accepted beliefs in sport psychology are concerned. Consider, for example, the following quotation:

> An interesting point was that the entire evolutionary process took place during competition; I never did practice to develop my style. This was mostly due to not having a model to follow. What was I supposed to look like? And internally, for me, I was much more intense during the competition, more focused on getting over the bar (the objective). So, my body was searching for the best way to clear the bar, being driven by my desire, my mind, to not lose against the others. It was a spontaneous reaction in a competitive environment (Fosbury, 2002 interview).

Thus, Fosbury actually argued that incremental development of the new style - rather than a giant leap - was a spontaneous reaction during competition! In other words, the fact that he was highly intense and focused during competition did not cause him to stick to a well-learned behavior or habit (as would be predicted, for example, from classical learning theories, such as the Hull-Spence model; e.g., Spence & Spence, 1966), but rather, to seek changes and innovations! At face value, this seems to be a serious violation of a major basic learning and/or training principle, namely, "in competition, stick to a well-learned behavior/habit."

Fosbury's report also puts the entire idea of experts being able to provide normative optimal solutions in question. As evident from the above citation, Fosbury attributed a significant part of this progress to the fact that he had no model to follow. Furthermore, consider the next quotation:

> Following my success at the 1968 Olympic Games, where I was the only jumper with this new technique, the revolution began with the kids. They had seen this radical new style and saw that it looked fun to try. The other elite level jumpers were not so fast to change over. They had too many hours invested in practicing their technique to simply give it up. So it seemed that most of the new floppers came from the secondary level jumpers who could risk learning a new style. Female jumpers also seemed to pick it up faster, I believe partially due to their better flexibility, mostly due to the lack of coaching in those days (Fosbury, 2002 interview).

It is evident from this quotation that the accepted consensus at that time concerning the normative, "optimal" style of the high jump - namely, straddle, perfectly conducted by Valerie Brumel of the USSR (including the supposedly "correct" coaching methods) - could actually inhibit, not facilitate, the progress of this sport discipline (Goldenberg, et al., submitted)! However, such a consensus concerning "optimal solutions" is frequently not only transient, but also quite often reflects sheer ignorance.

Another important lesson rising from the Fosbury case concerns the relationship between Fosbury and his coach. It is evident that the innovative athlete should possess all converging qualities. However, we argue that the coach working with that athlete should have qualities such as the ability to tolerate ambiguity, willingness to overcome obstacles and take risks, as well as posses a work style characterized by concentrated effort, an ability to set aside problems, and high energy. In the story of the Fosbury flop it is easy to imagine how an un-creative coach could have discouraged Fosbury's exploration efforts in different stages of the process. Therefore, a coaching approach that wishes to inspire creativity should enable some degrees of freedom to deviate from the normative acceptable practices, at the risk of "wasting time" and "damaging optimization efforts."

PENALTY KICKS IN SOCCER

The advocated approach becomes even clearer when one considers the results of two recent studies on penalty kick in soccer (Bar-Eli & Ritov, 1997; Keidar-Levin, 2003). In their study a multistage research project was carried out to detect "commission bias" among goalkeepers with penalty kicks, i.e., a state where they would feel better when a positive outcome (e.g., stopping a penalty) results from an action (e.g., jumping) rather than from an inaction (e.g., not jumping).

Among other things, these studies revealed that elite soccer coaches and players strongly believe that the optimal place to kick a penalty (that is, the place with the highest chances to score a goal) is on the ground, as close as possible to the goalpost. However, when the probabilities of stopping a penalty in actual elite soccer games were calculated for various areas of the goal, it was found that the real optimum would be one of the upper goal corners, in which the goalkeepers' chances of stopping the ball are literally tend to zero. Moreover, it was found that contrary to practitioners' beliefs, the actual chances of stopping a penalty kick are not different when the horizontal dimension of the kick is considered, but are substantially different when its vertical dimension is considered. In other words, regardless of the path of the ball and the type of shot, it is the height of the kick that is crucial!

As far as we know, soccer practitioners are mostly ignorant as to this simple statistical information. Moreover, having observed quite a few elite soccer training sessions, we have failed to identify any systematic penalty-kicks training strategy along the lines of any model whatsoever - be it optimal or not! It is not astonishing, then, that highly paid top soccer players repeatedly fail to score penalty kicks under pressure: it is often simply an untrained task. Although it is also possible that even if penalty kicks were appropriately trained, such failures may result from players reverting to older behavioral strategies under stress conditions.

PROMOTING "IRRATIONALITY" IN SPORT

The lesson from this discussion is by no means to discard all the theoretical and methodological conventions held by leading experts on athletes' training (e.g., Bompa, 1994). Instead, what is required would be to take a closer look into creativity in sport, from both scientific and applied perspectives. As was noted many years ago (e.g., Bar-Eli, 1984), elite sport participants tend towards being conservative (i.e., resist attitudinal revisions), due to human cognitive limitations as well as the socio-cultural pressures placed upon them.

To cope with this problem, the use of creative, "illogical" psychological interventions was proposed to sport-practitioners, recommending that they be integrated into the athletes' mental training processes. For example, Bar-Eli (1991) discussed the paradoxical techniques of symptom prescription (i.e., client is directed to carry out a problematic behavior intentionally), assenting joining a stand (i.e., consultant assents to client's pessimistic viewpoint), and confusion (i.e., consultant creates confusion in order to cause client's cognitive reorganization), as an effective means of boosting creativity through changing the meaning attributed to a problematic situation (i.e., reframing) by the client. More recently, other creativity-enhancement methods were discussed in the sport psychology literature (e.g., Everhart et al., 1999; Hanin et al., 2002; Schmole, 2000).

We should, however, not abandon the "maximization through optimization" principle, as the penalty kicks example demonstrates; on the contrary, we should rather encourage the use of this principle - as a reflection of "instrumental rationality" - when it is necessary and appropriate. We are even prepared to admit that the application of the abovementioned idea endorsed by Henry Ford (see Colvin, 2000, p. 9) may sometimes be functional for achieving peak performance. Lidor (1999, p. 77), for example, in reference to Boris Becker's Wimbledon championship, maintains that athletes often report "no thinking," or "a head empty of thoughts," during peak performance; at the same time, however, we strongly believe that in order to increase the probability of fantastic achievements such as

Fosbury's, we should actually encourage the other face of the athletic mind - namely, the critical, supposedly "irrational" one, which has thus far been relatively neglected in both sport psychology and practice.

OPTIMIZED CREATIVITY, CREATIVE OPTIMIZATION

In essence, the systematic reproductions approach to creativity reflects a quite instrumental view, which will be herewith labeled "optimized creativity;" it attempts to identify an optimal course of action that will most probably bring about the best solution to a given problem, thereby actually applying the "maximization through optimization" principle. In contrast, Fosbury's case reflects a successful attempt to "creatively optimize" the task of the high jump, thereby substantially improving the athletes' performances in this sport discipline. The penalty kicks example similarly demonstrates a "creative optimization" attempt, intended to maximize the chances to score a goal. As evident from the entire present discussion, both approaches actually stem from the world of work, industry, and business, where the ultimate goal is to achieve maximal productivity. No wonder, then, that one of the most celebrated professional basketball players of all time, Larry Bird, was quoted during his term as head coach of the Indiana Pacers of the NBA, as having said that: "I don't like players who don't do what I say, and I don't like players who do exactly what I say" in order to maximize athletes' performance (see Bar-Eli, et al., 1999, p. 35).

This is not to say, of course, that while practicing their throws, young, talented athletes like the basketball players mentioned in the introduction to this chapter, shouldn't use routines - on the contrary. Routine training is rooted not only in top coaches' "Trainingslehre" (Weineck, 2003) and their "intuitive" professional experience, but also in sound scientific principles intensively documented, for example, by the research conducted within the framework of the "deliberate practice" paradigm (Ericsson, 1996; 2003). The crucial question is, exactly which routines should be deliberately practiced? In other words, it is the content and quality of practice which counts (Singer & Janelle, 1999), or as Starkes et al. (2001, p. 176) put it: "Crucial is what is practiced, how it is practiced, and, from a developmental perspective, when" - not necessarily the amount of deliberate practice per se. Hence, on the one hand, athletes' creative solutions (e.g., as to the nature of such routines) should not necessarily be dismissed, but rather (selectively) adopted and systematically trained, as both Fosbury's case and the examples from basketball demonstrate. On the other hand, however, creativity itself can also be systematically trained, as demonstrated previously in detail. Thus, Larry Bird seems to be right; it can be concluded that in order to develop peak performers, we should by no means consider the principles of optimization and creativity-enhancement as being controversial, but rather try to integrate them through the complementary implementation of both ideas endorsed here, namely, "creative optimization" and "optimized creativity."

REFERENCES

Altschuller, G. S. (1985). *Creativity as an exact science.* New York: Gordon & Breach.

Altschuller, G. S. (1986). *To find an idea: Introduction to the theory of solving problems of inventions.* Novosibirsk, USSR: Nauka.

Amabile, T. M. (1983). *The social psychology of creativity.* New York: Springer-Verlag.

Amabile, T. M. (1988). A model of creativity and innovation in organizations. In B. M. Staw & L. L. Cummings (Eds.), *Research in organizational behavior* (Vol. 10, pp. 123-167). Greenwich, CT: JAI Press.

Bar-Eli, M. (1984). *Zur Diagnostik individueller psychischer Krisen im sportlichen Wettkampf - Eine wahrscheinlichkeitsorientierte, theoretische und empirische Studie unter besonderer Berücksichtigung des Basketball spiels [Diagnosis of individual psychological crisis in sports competition - a probabilistically oriented, theoretical and empirical study giving special attention to the game of basketball.]* Unpublished doctoral dissertation, Deutsche Sporthochschule, Cologne.

Bar-Eli, M. (1991). On the use of paradoxical interventions in counseling and coaching in sport. *The Sport Psychologist, 5,* 61-72.

Bar-Eli, M., Lurie, Y. & Breivik, G. (1999). Rationality in sport: A psychophilosophical approach. In R. Lidor & M. Bar-Eli (Eds.), *Sport psychology: Linking theory and practice* (pp. 35-58). Morgantown, WV: Fitness Information Technology.

Bar-Eli, M. & Ritov, I. (1997). Judgmental heuristics and biases in sport: Theory and preliminary research. In S. Tiryaki (Ed.), *Proceedings of the Mersin's 1ˢᵗ International Symposium of Sport Psychology* (pp. 14-19). Mersin, Turkey: Mersin University.

Boden, M. A. (1992). *The creative mind: Myths and mechanisms.* New York: Basic Books.

Boden, M. A. (1996). (Ed.). Dimensions of creativity. London, UK: MIT Press.

Boden, M. A. (1999). Computer models of creativity. In R. J. Sternberg (Ed.), *Handbook of Creativity* (pp. 351-372). New York: Cambridge University Press.

Bompa, T. (1994). *Theory and methodology of training: The key to athletic performance* (3ʳᵈ ed.). Dubuque, IA: Kendal/Hunt.

Coakley, J. J. (2001). *Sport in society: Issues and controversies* (7ᵗʰ ed.). Boston: McGraw-Hill.

Colvin, G. (2000, March 6). Managing in the info era. *Fortune,* pp. F6-9.

Crainer, S. (2000). *The management century.* San Francisco: Jossey-Bass.

Crews, D. J., Lochbaum, M. R. & Karoly, P. (2001). Self-regulation: Concepts, methods and strategies in sport and exercise. In R. N. Singer, H. A. Hausenblas, & C. M. Janelle (Eds.), *Handbook of sport psychology* (pp. 566-581). New York: Wiley.

Csikszentmihalyi, M. (1996). *Creativity, flow and the psychology of discovery and invention.* New York: Harper Perennial.

Dasgupta, S. (1994). *Creativity in invention and design: Computational and cognitive explorations of technical originality.* New York: Cambridge University Press.

Descartes, R. (1987). *Meditations on first philosophy* (E. S. Haldane & G. R. T. Ross, Trans.). New York: Cambridge University Press. (Original work published 1641)

Dunning, E. (1986). The sociology of sport in Europe and the United States: Critical observations from an "Eliasian" perspective. In R. Rees & W. Miracle (Eds.), *Sport and social theory* (pp. 29-65). Champaign, IL: Human Kinetics.

Edwards, W. (1961). Behavioral decision theory. *Annual Review of Psychology, 12,* 473-498.

Encyclopedia Britannica (2002), available online at: http://www. britannica.com.

Ericsson, K. A. (Ed.) (1996). *The road to excellence: The acquisition of expert performance in the arts and sciences, sports and games.* Mahwah, NJ: Erlbaum.

Ericsson, K. A. (1999). Creative expertise as a superior reproducible performance: Innovative and flexible aspects of expert performance. *Psychological Inquiry, 10,* 329-333.

Ericsson, K. A. (2003). Development of elite performance and deliberate practice: An update from the perspective of the expert performance approach. In J. L. Starkes & K. A. Ericsson (Eds.), *Expert performance in sports: Advances in research on sport expertise* (pp. 49-84). Champaign, IL: Human Kinetics.

Everhart, B., Kernodle, M., Turner, E., Harshaw, C. & Arnold, D. (1999). Gameplay decisions of university badminton students. *Journal of Creative Behavi, 33,* 138-149.

Feist, G. J. (1999). The influence of personality on artistic and scientific creativity. In R. J. Sternberg (Ed.), *Handbook of creativity* (pp. 273-296). New York: Cambridge University Press.

Finke, R. A., Ward, T. B. & Smith, S. M. (1992). *Creative cognition: Theory, research, and applications.* Cambridge, MA: MIT Press.

Frese, M. & Zapf, D. (1994). Action as the core of work psychology: A German approach. In H. C. Triandis, M. D. Dunnette, & L. M. Haugh (Eds.), *Handbook of industrial and organizational psychology* (Vol. 4, pp. 271-340). Palo Alto, CA: Consulting Psychologist.

Friedman, L., Mehrez, A., Sinuany-Stern, A., Bar-Eli, M. & Epstein, S. (in press). *Optimal threshold in multistage sport games. International Journal of Services and Technology Management.*

Glymour, C. N. (1992). *Thinking things through: An introduction to philosophical issues and achievements.* Cambridge, MA: MIT Press.

Goldenberg, J., Lowengart, O., Oreg, S., Bar-Eli, M., Epstein, S. & Fosbury, R. D. *Fly high: Is a revolution an extraordinary event or a day-to-day process?* Manuscript submitted for publication.

Goldenberg, J. & Mazursky, D. (1999). The voice of the product: Templates of new product emergence. *Innovation and Creativity Management, 8,* 157-164.

Goldenberg, J. & Mazursky, D. (2001). *Creativity in product innovation.* New York: Cambridge University Press.

Goldenberg, J., Mazursky, D. & Solomon, S. (1999a). Toward identifying the inventive templates of new products: A channeled ideation approach. *Journal of Marketing Research, 36,* 200-210.

Goldenberg, J., Mazursky, D. & Solomon, S. (1999b). The fundamental templates of quality ads. *Marketing Science, 18,* 333-351.

Goldenberg, J., Mazursky, D. & Solomon, S. (1999c). Templates of original innovation: Projecting original incremental innovations from intrinsic information. *Technical Forecasting and Social Change, 61,* 1-12.

Goldenberg, J., Mazursky, D. & Solomon, S. (1999d). Creative sparks. *Science, 285,* 1495-1496.

Gould, D. (1996). Personal motivation gone awry: Burnout in competitive athletes. *Quest, 48,* 275-289.

Gould, D., Greenleaf, C. & Krane, V. (2002). Arousal-anxiety and sport behavior. In T. Horn (Ed.), *Advances in sport psychology* (2nd ed., pp. 207-241). Champaign, IL: Human Kinetics.

Greenberg, J. & Baron, R. A. (2003). *Behavior in organizations* (8th ed.). Upper Saddle River, NJ: Prentice Hall.

Grossman, R. S., Rodgers, B. E & Moore, B. R. (1988). *Innovation Inc.: Unblocking creativity in the workplace.* Plano, TX: Wordware.

Guilford, J. P. (1950). Creativity. *American Psychologist, 5,* 10-18.

Hackfort, D. (1999). The presentation and modulation of emotions. In R. Lidor & M. Bar-Eli (Eds.), *Sport psychology: Linking theory and practice* (pp. 231-244). Morgantown, WV: Fitness Information Technology.

Hanin, Y., Korjus, T., Jouste, P & Baxter, P. (2002). Rapid technique correction using old way/new way: Two case studies with Olympic athletes. *The Sport Psychologist, 16,* 79-99.

Harman, G. (1995). Rationality. In E. E. Smith & D. N. Osherson, D. N. (Eds.), *Thinking: An invitation to cognitive science* (2nd ed., Vol. 3). Cambridge, MA: MIT Press.

Hastie, R. (2001). Problems for judgment and decision making. *Annual Review of Psychology, 52,* 653-683.

Hebb, D. O. (1955). Drives in the C.N.S. (conceptual nervous system). *Psychological Review, 62,* 243-254.

Hesselbein, F. & Johnston, R. (2002). *On creativity, innovation, and renewal: A leader-to-leader guide.* New York: Wiley.

Horn, T. S. (2002). Coaching effectiveness in the sport domain. In T. S. Horn (Ed.), *Advances in sport psychology* (2nd ed., pp. 309-354). Champaign, IL: Human Kinetics.

Kahneman, D. & Tversky, A. (Eds.). (2000). *Choices, values, and frames.* New York: Cambridge University Press/Russell Sage Foundation.

Keidar-Levin, Y. (2003). *Commission bias amongst expert soccer goalkeepers: The case of penalty kicks. Thesis submitted in partial fulfillment of the requirements for the degree of Master of Arts.* Ben-Gurion University of the Negev, Beer-Sheva, Israel.

Kimiecik, J. & Jackson, S. A. (2002). Optimal experience in sport: A flow perspective. In T. S. Horn (Ed.), *Advances in sport psychology* (2nd ed., pp. 501-527). Champaign, IL: Human Kinetics.

Koestler, A. (1964). *The age of creation.* London, UK: Penguin.

Lidor, R. (1999). *Thought processes and decision making in sport.* Tel-Aviv: Ministry of Defense. (Hebrew)

Loy, J. W. (1981). Social psychological characteristics of innovators. *American Sociological Review, 34,* 73-82.

Lubart, T. I. (1994). Creativity. In R. J. Sternberg (Ed.), *Creative thinking and problem solving* (pp. 289-332). San Diego, CA: Academic.

MacKinnon, D.W. (1970). Creativity: A multi-faceted phenomenon. In J. Roslansky (Ed.), *Creativity* (pp. 19-32). Amsterdam: Elsevier.

Maymon, O. & Horowitz, R. (1999). Sufficient condition for inventive ideas in engineering. *IEEE Transactions, Man and Cyberbetics, 29,* 349-361.

Mirvis, P. H. (1998). Practice improvisation. *Organization Science, 9,* 586-592.

Morris, T. (2000). Psychological characteristics and talent identification in soccer. *Journal of Sports Sciences, 18,* 715-726.

Nitsch, J. R. & Hackfort, D. (1981). Stress und Schule [Stress and school]. In J. R. Nitsch (Ed.), *Stress* (pp. 263-311). Bern: Huber.

O'Guinn, T. C., Allen, C. T. & Semenik, R. J. (1998). *Advertising.* Cincinnati, OH: South-Western.

Official Web Site of the Olympic Movement (2002), available on line at: http://www.olympic.org.

Parnes, S. (1992). *Sourcebook for creative problem solving.* New York: Creative Education Foundation.

Perkins, D. N. (1981). *The mind's best work.* Cambridge, MA: Harvard University Press.

Perkins, D. N. (1988). The possibility of invention. In R. J. Sternberg (Ed.), *The nature of creativity* (pp. 362-385). New York: Cambridge University Press.

Piirto, J. (1998). *Understanding those who create* (2nd ed.). Schottsdale, AZ: Great Potential.

Riggio, R. E. (2003). *Introduction to industrial/organizational psychology* (4th ed.). Upper Saddle River, NJ: Prentice Hall.

Ringrose, C. A. D. (1993). Enhancing creativity in athletes. In S. Serpa, J. Alves, & V. Pataco (Eds.), *Proceedings of the 8th World Congress of Sport Psychology* (pp. 282-285). Lisbon: Technical University of Lisbon.

Ross, S. M. (1997). *A first course in probability* (5th ed.). Upper Saddle River, NJ: Prentice Hall.

Runco, M. A. (1991). *Divergent thinking.* Norwood, NJ: Ablex.

Runco, M. A. (Ed.). (2001). *Critical creative processes.* New York: Hampton.

Runco, M. A. & Pritzker, S. R. (Eds.). (1999). *Encyclopedia of creativity.* San Diego, CA: Academic Press.

Schaffer, S. (1996). Making up discovery. In M. A. Boden (Ed.), *Dimensions of creativity* (pp. 13-51). London, UK: MIT Press.

Schmole, M. (2000). Synergetische Sportspielmethodik [Synergetical method of teaching sport games]. *Sportonomics, 6,* 41-47.

Schwartz, G. E. (1979). Disregulation and systems theory: A biobehavioral framework for biofeedback and behavioral medicine. In N. Birbaumer & H. D. Kimmel (Eds.), *Biofeedback and self-regulation* (pp. 19-48). New York: Erlbaum.

Shafir, E. & LeBoeuf, R. A. (2002). Rationality. *Annual Review of Psychology, 53,* 491-517.

Simonton, D. K. (2003). Scientific creativity as constrained stochastic behavior: The integration of product, person and process perspectives. *Psychological Bulletin, 129,* 475-494.

Singer, R. N. & Janelle, C. M. (1999). Determining sport expertise: From genes to supremes. *International Journal of Sport Psychology, 30,* 117-150.

Sinuany-Stern, Z., Bar-Eli, M., Israeli, Y. (in press). Application of the analytic hierarchy process for evaluation of basketball teams. *International Journal of Services and Technology Management.*

Smith, R. E., Smoll, F. L. & Hunt, E. (1977). A system for the behavioral assessment of athletic coaches. *Research Quarterly, 48,* 401-407.

Spence, J. & Spence, K. (1966). The motivational components of manifest anxiety: Drive and drive stimuli. In C. D. Spielberger (Ed.), *Anxiety and behavior* (pp. 291-326). New York: Academic Press.

Starkes, J. L. & Ericsson, K. A. (Eds.) (2003). *Expert performance in sports: Advances in research on sport expertise.* Champaign, IL: Human Kinetics.

Starkes, J. L., Helsen, W. & Jack, R. (2001). Expert performance in sport and dance. In R. N. Singer, H. A. Hausenblas & C. M. Janelle (Eds.), *Handbook of sport psychology* (pp. 174-201). New York: Wiley.

Sternberg, R. J. (1985). Implicit theories of intelligence, creativity, and wisdom. *Journal of Personality and Social Psychology, 49,* 607-627.

Sternberg, R. J. (1988). A three facet model of creativity. In R. J. Sternberg (Ed.), *The nature of creativity* (pp. 125-147). New York: Cambridge University Press.

Sternberg, R. J. & Lubart, T. I. (1991). An investment theory of creativity and its development. *Human Development, 34,1-32.*

Sternberg, R. J. & Lubart, T. I. (1999). The concept of creativity: Prospects and paradigms. In R. J. Sternberg (Ed.), *Handbook of creativity* (pp. 3-15). New York: Cambridge University Press.

Tenenbaum, G. & Bar-Eli, M. (1993). Decision making in sport: A cognitive perspective. In R. N. Singer, M. Murphey, & L. K. Tennant (Eds.), *Handbook of research on sport psychology* (pp. 171-192). New York: Macmillan.

Tenenbaum, G. & Bar-Eli, M. (1995). Personality and intellectual capabilities in sport psychology. In D. Saklofske & M. Zeidner (Eds.), *International handbook of personality and intelligence* (pp. 687-710). New York: Plenum.

Tenenbaum, G., Levy-Kolker, N., Bar-Eli, M. & Weinberg, R. (1994). Information recall of younger and older skilled athletes: The role of display complexity, attentional resources, and visual exposure duration. *Journal of Sports Sciences, 12,* 529-534.

Tenenbaum, G., Levy-Kolker, N., Sade, S., Liebermann, D. & Lidor, R. (1996). Anticipation and confidence of decisions related to skilled performance. *International Journal of Sport Psychology, 27,* 293-307.

Tenenbaum, G., Yuval, R., Elbaz, G. & Bar-Eli, M. (1993). The relationship between cognitive characteristics and decision making. *Canadian Journal of Applied Physiology, 18,* 48-62.

Wallas, G. (1926). *The art of thought.* New York: Harcourt Brace.

Ward, T. B. (2001). Creative cognition, conceptual combination, and the creative writing of Stephen R. Donaldson. *American Psychologist, 56,* 350-354.

Warner, M. (1994). Organizational behavior revisited. *Human Relations, 47,* 1151-1166.

Weber, M. (1946). Politics as a vocation. In H. H. Gerth, & C. W. Mills (Eds.), *From Max Weber: Essays in sociology* (pp77-156). New York: Oxford University Press. (Original work published 1919)

Weber, M. (1947). *Theory of social and economic organiation* (A. M. Henderson & T. Parsons, Trans.). London: Oxford University Press. (Original work published 1921)

Weinberg, R. S. & Gould, D. (2003). *Foundations of sport and exercise psychology* (3rd ed.). Champaign, IL: Human Kinetics.

Weineck, J. (2003). Optimales Training [Optimal training] (13th ed.). Balingen: Spitta.

Weisberg, R. W. (1992). Creativity beyond the myth of genius. New York: Freeman.

Williams, J. M. (Ed.) (2001). *Applied sport psychology: Personal growth to peak performance* (4th ed.). Mountain View, CA: Mayfield.

Wrisberg, C. A. (2001). Levels of performance skill: From beginners to experts. In R. N. Singer, H. A. Hausenblas, & C. M. Janelle (Eds.), *Handbook of sport psychology* (2nd ed., pp. 3-19). New York: Wiley.

Yerkes, R. M. & Dodson, J. D. (1908). The relation of strength of stimulus to rapidity of habit formation. *Journal of Comparative Neurology and Psychology, 18,* 459-482.

Zaichkowsky, L. D. & Baltzell, A. (2001). Arousal and performance. In R. N. Singer, H. A. Hausenblas, & C. M. Janelle (Eds.), *Handbook of sport psychology* (pp. 319-339). New York: Wiley.

Zatsiorsky, V. M. (Ed.). (2000). *Biomechanics in sport: Performance enhancement and injury prevention.* London: Blackwell.

Perfectionism: A Hallmark Quality of World Class Performers, or a Psychological Impediment to Athletic Development?

Howard K. Hall

Contents

Summary

In the last fifteen years, empirical research into perfectionism has developed rapidly in the areas of social, counseling, educational and clinical psychology (see Flett & Hewitt, 2002 for a review). During the same period, sport psychology research that has attempted to understand how perfectionism influences athletes has progressed more slowly. While both sport psychology practitioners and coaches have observed that elite athletes often appear to demonstrate qualities of perfectionism in their achievement striving, many questions currently remain unanswered regarding the specific meaning of the term perfectionism, and the influence that the disposition has on achievement related cognition, affect and behaviour in athletes. This chapter will provide a review of current empirical research on perfectionism in sport and exercise. It will demonstrate that while perfectionism can energise motivation and lead to a number of positive achievement outcomes, it can also underpin dysfunctional cognition and negative affect. Moreover, it can underpin patterns of achievement behaviour that not only impair athletic development, but may lead to psychological debilitation, health problems and interpersonal difficulties. The chapter will draw upon a broad range of psychological literature in order to define the term perfectionism and identify how it has been operationalised. The empirical evidence presented from sport and exercise contexts will confirm the assertions of Flett and Hewitt (2002), that perfectionism is essentially a debilitating personality characteristic, which can lead to maladaptive cognitions, negative affective responses and dysfunctional achievement behaviours. As a consequence, sport psychologists should be cautious about considering perfectionism as a hallmark quality of elite performance and attempt to understand the psychological processes that are taking place when perfectionistic athletes strive to achieve. Only then will it be possible to intervene effectively, and help athletes to manage the potentially debilitating consequences of this disposition.

INTRODUCTION

A recent observation made by both sport psychology researchers and practitioners is that the achievement striving of many elite athletes appears to be characterised by perfectionism (Anshel & Eom, 2002, Dunn, Causgrove Dunn, & Syrotuik, 2002; Hardy, Jones & Gould, 1996; Henschen, 2000). While there is a belief that this personality disposition has contributed to the athletic development and competitive accomplishments of a number of elite athletes, it is not possible to draw any firm conclusions to support such contentions at this time. This is because the term perfectionism currently has multiple interpretations and is associated with a wide variety of outcomes reflecting both functional and dysfunctional achievement striving. It is therefore, unclear whether the athletic success of these elite athletes has been achieved as a consequence of perfectionism or in spite of it.

In their recent book, Flett and Hewitt (2002) list more than 20 different terms that reflect various forms of perfectionistic behaviour. These terms imply that perfectionism incorporates a range of both adaptive and maladaptive motivational qualities. It seems that because there has never been agreement on a common definition of perfectionism, contradictory views have surfaced in the sport psychology literature about whether this disposition aids or undermines athletic development. One consequence of this definitional ambiguity is uncertainty among practitioners about whether perfectionism is a quality that should be systematically developed in athletes in order to help maximise performance potential, or whether it should be carefully managed to enable athletes to cope with its negative consequences. This apparent controversy has been further fuelled by inconsistent findings from sport psychology research. Some investigators have noted that while there is evidence of perfectionism being associated with negative affective responses and potentially debilitating cognitions in sub-elite and recreational sport performers (Frost & Henderson, 1991; Gould, 1996; Hall, Matthews & Kerr, 1998; Dunn, Gotwals, Cosgrove-Dunn & Syrotiuk, in press), others have reported that in elite athletes, perfectionism can be a powerful motivational force underpinning successful achievement (Gould Dieffenbach & Moffatt, 2002; Hardy et al., 1996; Henschen, 2000).

The identification of perfectionism as a characteristic of high achieving athletes appears consistent with a widely held view that perfectionism can have motivationally adaptive qualities (Frost, Marten, Lahart & Rosenblate, 1990; Hamachek, 1978; Slaney, Ashby & Trippi, 1995; Terry-Short, Owens, Slade & Dewey, 1995). In its adaptive form it is characterised by the relentless pursuit of excessively high performance standards that leads to a sense of self-satisfaction and heightened self-esteem (Hamachek, 1978). Perfectionism of this kind was reported to characterise the motivation of a sample of US Olympic Gold medallists who were asked by Gould et al. (2002) to describe the personal qualities that underpinned competitive success. Gould et al. (2002) classified these Olympians as perfectionists due to their pursuit of challenging personal goals and their highly organised approach to preparation and performance. Although reporting no evidence to support a causal relationship, it was implied that these qualities contributed to the athletes' sporting development and the attainment of peak performance.

Others working with elite athletes have noted similar relationships. For example, in a study of motivation in Australian Olympic and World Championship track and field athletes, Mallett and Hanrahan (2003) reported that successful achievements were thought to be a direct consequence of a form of perfectionistic achievement striving. However, in contrast to the athletes in Gould's et al. (2002) sample, Mallett and Hanrahan (2003) stated that many of the Australian athletes reported being driven by an intense need to demonstrate their competence in order to prove their self-worth to their peers and others. An important point that this research did not address, however, was that while a desire for self-validation may have been a crucial energising force underpinning the motivation and achievement of this group of athletes, such a focus may not always have positive psychological outcomes (Dykman, 1998).

Although many benefits may accrue from this form of perfectionism, it is not usually considered to be an asset that will aid achievement, but rather a burden that can lead to both impairment and distress (Flett & Hewitt, 2002). Clearly, if it is not to become an impediment to their development, athletes must learn how to cope with its debilitating consequences. Hardy et al. (1996) recognised this fact, and based on evidence from their consultancy experiences, concluded that one critical psychological skill that can be attributed to world class athletes is their ability to manage their perfectionistic striving in a positive manner so that it facilitates rather than inhibits both athletic development and performance.

Despite the fact that there have been few attempts to examine the effects of perfectionism on athletes' cognition, affect, and behaviour, one consistent factor that has emerged from research on the subject is that the disposition appears to be a crucial energising force underpinning achievement striving in some individuals. This finding may have been sufficient to convince both sport practitioners and researchers that the disposition is a positive characteristic, as most people involved in sport would rarely consider that achievement striving can be inherently debilitating. It is also possible that the implied association between perfectionism and athletic success in some elite athletes reflects a recognition by those in the coaching and sport science community that if athletes are to reach the pinnacle of their sport, they must strive to reach standards that lie well beyond their current capabilities, and they must demonstrate an extraordinary degree of commitment that, to some, appears to border on obsession (Mallett & Hanrahan, 2003; Hardy et al., 1996).

Such views do have a credible scientific basis, as they are consistent with the findings from many empirical studies on goal setting in sport (Burton, Naylor & Holliday, 2001; Hall & Kerr, 2001) and a body of research that has investigated the development of expert performance in a number of different domains. Research on the development of expertise has established that approximately 10,000 hours of deliberate practice are necessary if an athlete is to reach international excellence (Ericsson, 1996; Starkes, 2000). Moreover, to achieve elite status in sport requires intense commitment, that extends beyond time spent playing the sport. Ericsson (1996) has suggested that deliberate practice differs from the playing of sport because it is explicitly structured to improve performance, requires both effort and persistence, is not considered to be inherently enjoyable, and therefore has little intrinsic value to the athlete other than its role in improving performance. However, while there is a large body of scientific evidence to support the contention that commitment to challenging goals may be a characteristic of elite athletes (Burton, Weinberg, Yukelson & Weigand 1998; Weinberg, Burton, Yukelson & Weigand, 2000), there is currently no research evidence to suggest that when the definition of perfectionism is broadened beyond the pursuit of high personal standards, it is a quality that can energise motivation and adaptive functioning for a sufficient duration to acquire expertise and elite status, or facilitate a sense of enduring achievement.

On the contrary, there is a burgeoning literature, which suggests that while perfectionism can energise investment, it is a critical antecedent of dysfunctional achievement behaviour that can become manifest at all developmental stages of an athlete's career. It may therefore be premature to suggest that perfectionism is a hallmark feature of world-class athletes, and a characteristic that should be developed, without first considering what is meant by the term perfectionism, and the findings from the extant literature which provide evidence of the influence of the construct on athletes' sporting experiences. This chapter will provide the reader with an overview of a developing body of research on perfectionism in sport. The chapter begins by describing a number of documented examples of athletic perfectionism in order to demonstrate that perfectionism in elite athletes is associated with a broad range of psychological and behavioural consequences. It will then explore various definitions of perfectionism, present commonly used approaches to measurement, and describe some of the psychological mechanisms which are considered to underpin the relationship between perfectionism and achievement behaviour. This information is critical to understanding the arguments behind an ongoing debate about whether perfectionism can be considered to be an adaptive disposition, or whether it is fundamentally, a psychologically debilitating characteristic. This debate has contributed to differing views about whether perfectionism should be considered as a hallmark quality of elite athletes. Finally, empirical evidence is presented that demonstrates a clear link between perfectionism and potentially maladaptive achievement related cognition, affect and behaviour in sport. The findings, which will be limited to sport related research, will suggest that perfectionism is far from being an adaptive disposition. Consequently, sport psychologists ought to be looking to manage its debilitating consequences if the disposition is not going to inhibit long-term athletic development or undermine the psychological well-being of athletes.

SOME DOCUMENTED CASES OF PERFECTIONISM IN ELITE ATHLETES

Despite views to the contrary (Gould et al., 2002), most reports that describe elite athletes who display characteristics of perfectionism, suggest that the long-term consequences of their achievement behaviour may be problematic. However, because it is recognised that intense achievement striving is a critical factor underpinning sporting excellence, there are few in the sporting world who have registered concern about any detrimental impact that perfectionism may have on the psychological or physical health of athletes. This is not only because of the benefits and rewards that striving for excellence can bring, but because the motivational attributes being demonstrated by perfectionistic athletes reflect qualities that are highly valued in western societies.

One only has to consider how the British news media reported on the preparation of the England rugby player, Johnny Wilkinson prior to the 2003 rugby World Cup competition to see how the motivational qualities of this self-confessed perfectionist were presented as revered qualities to be modelled by all aspiring athletes who sought a career as an international sportsman. Alison Kervin in the Times newspaper reported that the perfectionism demonstrated by England's star player throughout his developmental years had been the critical factor enabling him to become a professional athlete and perform with consistency at a world-class level. The article identified that Wilkinson displayed relentless work practices, was obsessive about on field practices, and was introspective and analytical about his practice and match performances. While these were the qualities that were reported to have taken Wilkinson to a level of performance achieved by few others in the game, the article also identified some of the less desirable psychological consequences of his achievement striving. These included relaxation difficulties, worry, and the experience of stress when he perceived that his performances did not reach his own high standards. It is important to note however, that these effects were portrayed as minor inconveniences to be endured, as a consequence of pursuing such lofty standards, rather than outcomes which may signal psychological dysfunction and lead to future debilitation.

Highly driven perfectionistic athletes may not only experience cognitive and emotional difficulties as a result of their achievement striving, but their intense behaviour may also create a hostile atmosphere with team mates and colleagues. Ultimately, this may have an undermining influence on important inter-personal relationships. An illustrative example that received considerable media attention in the UK was that involving Roy Keane, the Manchester United and Republic of Ireland footballer. He was an international athlete whose outstanding achievements throughout a long career were considered by many to have been a result of his perfectionistic achievement striving. While the pursuit of exceptionally high standards enabled Keane to develop and maintain a career as a world class athlete it was also reported to have undermined team cohesion and inter-personal relationships in the Irish international soccer camp prior to the 2002 World Cup in Japan and Korea (The Observer, June, 2002). The high expectations Keane had of his team mates, coupled with dissatisfaction with progress, and complaints about unprofessional training standards, poor training facilities, and poor preparation for the World Cup, not only led to team disunity and arguments with the manager, but eventually to Roy Keane's ejection from the Ireland squad for the 2002 World Cup competition as the Irish management attempted to avoid further disruption to their preparation for the tournament. While these two well publicized examples reflect some common consequences of athlete perfectionism, more disturbing effects have been noted in some athletes who show the same relentless motivational qualities exhibited by Johnny Wilkinson and Roy Keane. Krane, Greenleaf and Snow (1997) described the case of a former elite gymnast whose intense desire to excel was exacerbated because she internalised into her own goals the high expectations and demands placed upon her by parents and coaches. While reaching an elite level in her career, success for this athlete became so narrowly conceived, that it made the perception of failure inevitable. Success could only be achieved by winning in competition, and working intensely to perfect skills only served as a strategy to achieve that goal. Unfortunately the feelings of anxiety and self-doubt that preceded performance, and the feelings of anger, despair and complete ineptitude that resulted from her perceived failures became instrumental in the development of dysfunctional behaviours, that included emotional outbursts, an unhealthy approach to nutrition, over-training, and an inability to heed medical advice during rehabilitation from injury. After retiring from the sport, the former gymnast was able to recognise that her perfectionism was a contributory factor in the dysfunctional behaviour that had threatened her physical health. However, it is somewhat paradoxical that when asked to reflect on her career the athlete reported "she'd do it all again". One can only infer that, on reflection, the athlete considered that the benefits she had gained from investment, outweighed the debilitating consequences that her perfectionism had brought about.

Regrettably, some perfectionistic athletes do not have the opportunity to reflect back on the benefits gained from a career spent striving to achieve. For example, the tragic circumstances surrounding the death of Christy Heinrich were described by Joan Ryan (1995) in her critique of the training and development of US gymnasts in the 1980s and 1990s. An American gymnast, Heinrich began her career at 12 years of age, which was significantly later than most female athletes entering the sport. She felt that success was within her reach, but only if she monitored her diet carefully and worked to the highest standards of excellence. The consequence of this mindset was an important factor leading to her premature death. Her obsession with losing weight to allow her to compete with her rivals, led to unhealthy eating practices that eventually undermined her ability to perform. This forced Heinrich to retire from the sport in 1991. She recognised that she was suffering from an eating disorder in 1993, and died in 1994 weighing less than 70lbs.

Christy Heinrich is not the only athlete whose apparent perfectionism has resulted in tragic consequences. Jonathon Macari was an apprentice professional footballer with Nottingham Forest. He was the son of a Scottish international footballer, and signed his first professional contract with the club in 1996. After striving for two years in the club's youth training scheme, Macari was released with a year of his contract still remaining. The humiliation associated with the public failure was thought to have been a contributory factor in Macari's depression that led to him taking his own life. At the time of his death, his father suggested that a considerable amount of stress is experienced by young professional footballers as they attempt to succeed in the game, and because so few progress to establish a career in the game, it puts additional pressure on these young men, who may be ill equipped to cope.

Similar feelings of depression associated with public rejection were thought to have contributed to the suicide of another former professional footballer. Ashley Herapath had been an apprentice professional footballer with Swansea City, but when the club experienced financial difficulties Herapath was cut. Described as an extraordinary sportsman who had dreams of becoming a top class professional footballer, Herapath had committed suicide by throwing himself in front of a train because, in his depressed state, he couldn't face the prospect of further rejection.

Thankfully, while cases of suicide are not common in sport, the examples described highlight the possible dangers associated with perfectionistic achievement striving. It is clear that perfectionism can have beneficial consequences when athletes experience positive outcomes or receive tangible rewards as a result of their striving, but the psychological processes underpinning this disposition make it unlikely that athletes will avoid its many negative consequences. These may range from mild disaffection (Frost & Henderson, 1991), to shame (Tangney, 2002), performance anxiety (Hall, Kerr & Matthews, 1998), inter-personal difficulties (Hill, Zrull & Turlington, 1997), self-handicapping (Hobden & Pliner, 1995) helplessness (Flett, Hewitt, Blankstein & Pickering, 1998), burnout (Lemyre, Roberts & Hall, 2004) depression (Hewitt & Flett, 1991), eating disorders (Haase, Prapavessis & Owens, 2002) and suicide ideation (Hewitt, Flett & Turnbull-Donovan, 1992)). This is far from an exhaustive list, but in order to fully understand these and other consequences of perfectionism it is first necessary to consider how the construct has been defined, and how it may give rise to the psychological processes underpinning both positive and debilitating outcomes.

PERFECTIONISM DEFINED

Early conceptualisations of perfectionism loosely defined the construct as the setting of excessively high personal standards for performance (Burns, 1980; Hamachek, 1978; Hollander, 1965; Pacht, 1984). Leading researchers still maintain the view that the pursuit of high standards is central to a definition of perfectionism. For example, Hewitt and Flett (1993) specify that it is an achievement based construct that involves the tenacious pursuit of personally important goals. However, while the predilection towards intense achievement striving may be a necessary quality of perfectionism, this alone is not sufficient to adequately define it. Hamacheck (1978) and Burns (1980) suggested that perfectionism did not simply involve the pursuit of important goals, but it reflected the tendency to engage in over critical evaluation of achievement when striving to reach personally challenging standards.

Although it is acknowledged that perfectionism may have significant motivational effects that help to energise action, it is also recognized that this form of achievement striving has the potential to be psychologically debilitating, especially when self-worth is tied to achievement and accomplishment (Burns, 1980). Under these circumstances, the pursuit of excessively high performance standards tends to be accompanied by a preoccupation with failure. As a result, concerted effort is not viewed exclusively as a means to achievement, but rather it is a necessary quality that must be exhibited in order to avoid the possibility of criticism or the appearance of personal inadequacy resulting from failure. It is when effort is considered to be insufficient to prevent these outcomes that maladaptive cognition, affect, and achievement strategies occur. Thus, debilitation is not a direct outcome of achievement striving, but it appears to be a consequence of an individual's intense self-scrutiny and harsh self-criticism. Regardless of performance on the part of the athlete, any perceived failure to live up to internalised high standards precipitates feelings of self-doubt and further vulnerability to the criticism of others (Flett & Hewitt, 2002).

Burns (1980) and others (Garner, Olmstead & Polivy, 1983) considered that perfectionism was a unidimensional, cognitively based construct that was grounded in the irrational beliefs (Ellis, 1962; Jones, 1968) and the dysfunctional attitudes (Burns, 1980; Weissman & Beck 1978) held by individuals. Perfectionism was considered to be irrational because those exhibiting the disposition appeared to be pre-occupied with the pursuit of unrealistically high standards where the probability of success was negligible. Perfectionism became dysfunctional however, when the inevitable perceived failures were met with both excessive and unreasonable self-criticism. The dysfunctional pattern of cognition was further compounded if individuals sought to establish their self-worth on the basis of accomplishments resulting from achievement striving (Flett & Hewitt, 2002).

Contemporary researchers have largely rejected the notion that perfectionism is a unidimensional construct, which is characterised solely by self-directed cognitions. Instead, they have argued that perfectionism exhibits a more complex multidimensional structure where both personal and interpersonal elements contribute to different forms of achievement striving and underpin various adaptive and maladaptive outcomes (Frost, Marten, Lahart & Rosenblate, 1990; Hewitt & Flett, 1991; Flett & Hewitt, 2002). One multidimensional conceptualisation of perfectionism was advanced by Frost et al., (1990). Based upon the extant literature, which had identified the characteristic features of perfectionism, they developed an instrument that reflected six important qualities that were considered to be central to a definition of the construct (Multidimensional Perfectionism Scale-Frost). The instrument comprised four sub-scales that reflected personal qualities of perfectionism. These included: (i) the pursuit of exceptionally high personal standards, (ii) an over concern about making mistakes, (iii) a generalised sense of self-doubt about whether performance is ever satisfactory, and (iv), a concern about precision and order. Two further sub-scales reflected inter-personal qualities: (i) a perception of high parental expectation, and (ii) a perception that one's parents are overly critical.

Frost and DiBartolo (2002) consider that it is advantageous to conceptualise perfectionism in this manner, because the endorsement of different dimensions makes it is possible to distinguish between adaptive achievement striving in pursuit of high standards and the failure avoidant striving which is characterised by concern about mistakes and doubts that ones actions are of sufficient quality. It is generally accepted that the dimensions measuring high personal standards and organisation reflect more adaptive aspects of perfectionism, while the dimensions measuring concern about mistakes, doubts about action, parental expectations and parental criticism reflect more debilitating qualities (Frost et al, 1990). However, it remains questionable whether the term "perfectionist" can adequately describe an individual who exhibits both of the adaptive qualities but shows little evidence of any of the other characteristics thought to define the construct.

Although they have a measure of overall perfectionism that reflects an individual's score on all six sub-scale dimensions, Frost et al. (1990) did not stipulate that to be labelled a perfectionist one had to score high on all of the subscales. They did, however report that the setting of high standards was not the most important component of perfectionism. Rather, they argued that concern about mistakes was more central to a definition of the concept. Furthermore, they suggested that individuals may demonstrate varying amounts of overall perfectionism and varying amounts of each of the qualities measured by the different sub-scales, speculating that different combinations of personal standards and concern about mistakes would lead to different psychological outcomes. One drawback of adopting this measurement approach is that it is based upon a definition of the construct that is rather vague. As a result, it remains possible for athletes who pursue high personal standards and appear well organised to be mistakenly labelled as perfectionists, when they ought to be more accurately described as demonstrating adaptive patterns of motivation. This is because they lack the central defining quality of perfectionism, an over-concern with making mistakes.

The ambiguity in the definition of the construct can be traced to the writing of Hamacheck (1978). He noted a distinction between individuals exhibiting patterns of adaptive and maladaptive striving, and suggested that perfectionism may take one of two forms. The first was labelled normal perfectionism, where individuals strive to achieve high personal standards, but exercise a degree of flexibility when monitoring and evaluating performance. This form of perfectionism is associated with positive outcomes in many achievement contexts, and appears to be underpinned by the anticipation of positive emotions, rather like those experienced when individuals are high in motivation to approach success and low in failure avoidance (Atkinson, 1957), or when individuals are truly task oriented and the meaning of success is self-referenced (Duda, 2001; Nicholls, 1989; Roberts, 2001). The second form of perfectionism was labelled neurotic perfectionism, and it is considered to be a considerably more destructive disposition. It is characterized by inflexible evaluation criteria and is associated with a variety of maladaptive cognitions and affective responses to achievement outcomes.

Individuals who are considered to be neurotic perfectionists not only set excessively high standards, but they do not allow themselves the flexibility to make mistakes while performing (Hamachek, 1978). They adopt an overly self-critical perspective on performance, and this means that they are rarely satisfied with their level of achievement. They further, appear motivated by fears over the implications of failure rather than by a desire to seek excellence (Burns, 1980; Frost et al., 1990; Hamacheck, 1978; Pacht, 1984). Consequently, mistakes are not considered to be valuable aspects of the achievement process which facilitate learning, mastery, and personal growth, but instead, they pose significant threats to an individual's self-esteem. It is when they are in this chronic state of self-focused attention that neurotic perfectionists consider it a responsibility rather than a challenge to perform at some ideal-self imposed standard (Frost & Marten, 1990). Because of their preoccupation with maintaining a specific self-image these individuals often consider minor flaws in performance to constitute failure (Frost et al., 1990). This leads to the unfortunate tendency to overgeneralize their perceived failures in a manner that undermines their overall sense of self-worth (Hewitt & Flett, 1991). Because this predisposition toward being overly self-critical is frequently accompanied by an overall sense of doubt regarding the quality of performance, it tends to lead to an almost obsessive belief that any task is never satisfactorily completed (Hewitt & Flett, 1991), and can fuel further achievement striving as a compensatory strategy.

When defined in this manner it becomes possible to understand why neurotic perfectionism can lead to positive outcomes that result from achievement striving, as well as psychologically debilitating consequences. This is because the psychological processes, which underpin achievement striving, are transparent. What is less than clear is how the psychological processes underpinning normal perfectionism differ from those of highly motivated individuals who are striving to reach challenging goals, and are exhibiting patterns of adaptive motivation. Among other characteristics, individuals demonstrating adaptive motivation view effort as an end in itself, rather than as a means to an end. They are also considered to show an intrinsic desire to excel, experience pleasure from the process of striving, monitor and attribute performance outcomes rationally, consider mistakes to be a part of learning and have the ability to disassociate a sense of self from performance outcomes. If it is not possible to differentiate between the achievement characteristics of individuals showing adaptive motivation and normal perfectionists, it might be argued that it does little more than generate conceptual confusion to refer to adaptive forms of achievement striving by using the term perfectionism.

A second multidimensional conceptualisation of perfectionism was put forward by Hewitt and Flett (1991). This approach attempted to avoid the conceptual ambiguity evident in the work of others described earlier, because perfectionism was not considered to be an adaptive disposition. Rather, it was thought to underpin various forms of behavioural impairment and psychological distress. The approach taken by Hewitt and Flett (1991) in the conceptualisation and measurement of the construct was distinct from that adopted by Frost et al. (1990). They argued that rather than examining specific behaviour patterns to differentiate between various forms of perfectionism, it was necessary to examine the individual to whom the perfectionism was directed.

Three distinct forms of perfectionism were identified. The first was labelled self-oriented perfectionism because of its inward focus. It was characterised not only by the pursuit of exceedingly high personal standards but by harsh self-criticism. These characteristics were considered to be underpinned by both motivational approach and failure avoidance tendencies that reflect a pattern of behaviour similar to a construct described by Covington (1992) as overstriving. Moreover, the psychological processes underpinning the achievement behaviour of self-oriented perfectionists seem congruent with those of the overstriver. Covington (1992) stated that overstrivers are both attracted to and repelled by thoughts about achievement, and are thus motivated to avoid failure by intensively seeking out success. Consistent with Covington's approach, self-oriented perfectionism appears to be a significant motivational energiser that leads to considerable achievements, but as with overstriving, the resulting achievement related cognition, affect and behaviour tend to be defensive and often self-defeating. For example, even a single instance of failure can be debilitating to a self-oriented perfectionist, because it acts to confirm fears that, despite the expenditure of effort, the achievement of self-set high standards may be beyond them. Flett and Hewitt (2002) have noted that anxiety, depression, anger and guilt are often observed in these individuals as a consequence of their achievement striving. These emotions are thought to be a function of self-oriented perfectionists developing an internal locus of control which influences their achievement related cognition. It is because these individuals have a tendency to take personal responsibility for achievement outcomes that the psychological consequences of failure are reflected in strong negative emotions. Unfortunately, because these individuals will often fall short of their own high standards, it means that the experience of strong negative emotions may be frequent.

The second dimension of perfectionism outlined by Hewitt and Flett (1991) was similar in its characteristics to self-oriented perfectionism, but the pattern of behaviour was interpersonal in nature. That is, other oriented perfectionists are considered to direct their unreasonable expectations and harsh criticism toward other people. Whereas self-oriented perfectionism is described as being self-defeating, other oriented perfectionism is similarly destructive, but it tends to undermine interpersonal interactions. The psychological processes are similar to those governing the cognition, affect and behaviour of self-oriented perfectionists, but they engender blaming others for undesirable outcomes, reduce interpersonal trust and precipitate hostile interpersonal feelings because other oriented perfectionists are rarely satisfied with the standards achieved or the qualities of striving displayed by others (Flett & Hewitt, 2002).

Socially prescribed perfectionism was the third dimension of perfectionism described by Hewitt and Flett (1991). This pattern of perfectionism is directed inwards, but unlike self-oriented perfectionists who pursue their own high standards, socially prescribed perfectionists pursue standards that they perceive significant others would expect them to achieve. Furthermore, these individuals perceive that their achievement striving may be subjected to exceedingly critical evaluation by significant others. Like self-oriented perfectionism this dimension has been shown to be related to a number of maladaptive emotional consequences such as anger, anxiety and depression. However, the psychological processes underpinning these emotions differ from those regulating the achievement behaviour of self-oriented perfectionists. Hewitt and Flett explained that this is because the focus of socially prescribed perfectionists is predominantly on gaining approval or avoiding the disapproval of others, and it is the perceived recognition of others which socially prescribed perfectionists seek in order to validate a sense of self. Unlike self-oriented perfectionists, whose striving reflects an intrinsic desire for self-improvement and perfection, the motivational regulation underpinning the achievement striving of socially prescribed perfectionists tends to be low in self-determination (Hewitt and Flett, (1991), demonstrating characteristics of introjection such as anxiety, pressure and guilt (Deci & Ryan, 1995). That is, individuals feel obliged to strive to meet high standards rather than being motivated by any intrinsic desire to achieve. Further, because the standards being pursued by socially prescribed perfectionists are the perceived expectations of others, the perception of control over outcomes is largely external (Periasamy & Ashby, 2002). This focus has led to the construct being associated with a range of motivationally dysfunctional behaviours such as helplessness, poor coping, procrastination and hopelessness (Hewitt & Flett, 1991). Because socially prescribed perfectionists do not consider that they have full responsibility for achievement outcomes, they can mistakenly conclude that their efforts have been futile when the outcome of their striving is perceived to be discrepant from the standards they are trying to achieve. They may also be more prone than self-oriented perfectionists to consider that future discrepancies will exist between standards and performance because of a tendency to perceive that achievement is largely under external control.

Cambell and Di Paula (2002) have provided evidence that the dysfunctional pattern of behaviour demonstrated by socially prescribed perfectionists is primarily a function of believing that self-worth and acceptance are contingent on achievement, rather than a perception that others expect high performance standards from them. In contrast, Campbell and Di Paula report that the less extreme forms of debilitation seen in self-oriented perfectionists are due to endorsing a belief that it is important to be perfect. While this belief underpins both conscientious striving and effortful pursuit of challenging goals, it is also associated with depressed self-esteem and an unwillingness to change ones pattern of achievement striving when failures are experienced. Campbell and Di Paula's findings point to socially prescribed perfectionism being regulated by failure avoidance whereas self-oriented perfection is largely reflective of a primary motive to achieve success. It is because it is underpinned by failure avoidance and the protection of self worth that, over a protracted time period socially prescribed perfectionism is considered to have a destructive influence on both achievement striving and psychological well being. Conversely, because self-oriented perfectionism appears to be regulated by a more adaptive focus, it has been suggested that over time, the construct will be associated with positive psychological and behavioural outcomes. However, such a conclusion would not necessarily be warranted, because there is evidence that self-oriented perfectionism has been found to render individuals vulnerable to anxiety and depression (Flett, Hewitt, Endler & Tassone, 1994; Hewitt & Flett, 1993) under conditions when achievement stressors or negative life events are experienced (Hewitt, Flett & Eidiger, 1996). It remains distinctly possible, that under these conditions, the psychological processes reflective of overstriving become activated. That is, the self-oriented perfectionists experience existential threat, and intensively strive for success in order to avoid failure and its consequences for self-definition.

CAN PERFECTIONISM BE HEALTHY OR ADAPTIVE?

While the development of valid and reliable measures has advanced empirical research on perfectionism, a lack of clarity concerning both the definition and measurement of perfectionism has contributed to an ongoing dispute about whether perfectionism can reflect adaptive and healthy achievement striving, or whether it reflects a wholly debilitating construct. Attempts to demonstrate that the measurement of the construct matched with Hamachek's definitions of normal and neurotic perfectionism have led to further debate (Greenspon, 2000; Parker 2000), but no resolution of the controversy. For example, after conducting an exploratory factor analysis, Frost, Heimberg, Holt Mattaia and Neubauer (1993) combined related dimensions from both the Frost et al (1990) Multidimensional Perfectionism Scale (MPS-F) and the Hewitt and Flett (1991) Multidimensional Perfectionism Scale (MPS-H). Those dimensions measuring high personal standards, order and

H. K. Hall

organisation, self-oriented perfectionism and other oriented perfectionism were combined to produce a construct called positive achievement striving. In contrast, those dimensions measuring concern about mistakes, doubts about action, parental expectation, parental criticism and socially prescribed perfectionism were combined to form a construct which was called maladaptive evaluative concerns. Because the two constructs demonstrated conceptually consistent associations with measures of positive and negative affect experienced by college students, Frost et al (1993) concluded that Hamachek's (1978) initial contentions could be confirmed, and that perfectionism was associated with both normal adaptive functioning as well as with more pathological forms of striving. Others, have concurred with this, (Parker (1995; 1997; 2000; Rice Slaney & Ashby, 1998) and have suggested that perfectionism may be considered healthy when individuals derive pleasure from maximising their potential and experience a sense of self-actualisation from their accomplishments. A further perspective supporting the idea that perfectionism can be both adaptive and dysfunctional has adopted a more behavioural approach. Terry-Short, Owens, Slade and Dewey (1995) have suggested that perfectionism may be positive when its reinforcement leads to approach behaviours and negative when avoidance of aversive outcomes is the goal.

Despite the fact that there is a belief among some scholars that perfectionism can be healthy, Flett and Hewitt (2002) are among a handful of researchers to have raised doubts about the use of the term adaptive or healthy when referring to perfectionism. Their principle concern is that researchers have demonstrated too little in the way of scepticism, and too much uncritical acceptance of the adaptive perfectionism construct, and because of this, they consider that the issue is far from being resolved. They argue that while measures such as their self-oriented perfectionism scale may be associated with adaptive qualities such as conscientiousness, perfectionism is much more than adaptive, conscientious, self-disciplined achievement striving (Flett & Hewitt, 2002). That is, despite the fact that their achievement striving may lead to positive outcomes, the self-critical qualities demonstrated by self-oriented perfectionists will render them vulnerable under stressful conditions.

Flett and Hewitt (2002) further suggest that it is unknown whether those individuals categorised as adaptive perfectionists are different from maladaptive perfectionists because they simply report lower scores on various scales assessing key elements of perfectionism, or whether adaptive and maladaptive perfectionists are qualitatively different from each other as a result of different psychological processes underpinning their achievement striving. They speculate that if the difference is quantitative rather than qualitative, then it is probable that when levels of perfectionism become elevated this will also render individuals vulnerable.

Despite arguments to suggest that perfectionism can be adaptive, the position of Flett and Hewitt (2002) seems clear. They consider perfectionism to be a debilitating personality characteristic rather than an adaptive one. They note that while it may be true that self-oriented perfectionists tend to deal effectively with most daily events, they also experience dysfunctional affective responses when placed in environments that they appraise as threatening (Flett, Hewitt, Blankstein & Mosher (1995); Hewitt & Flett, 1993; Hewitt, Flett &

190

Ediger, 1996), and it is under these conditions where debilitating cognition, affect and behaviour are observed. They suggest that without further testing of this issue, it might be premature to conclude that specific dimensions of perfectionism are adaptive.

While the views of Flett and Hewitt (2002) urge caution about the use of the term adaptive perfectionism, Greenspon (2000) has expressed a more sceptical opinion, stating that the term "healthy perfectionism" is an oxymoron. He suggested that Hamachek's (1978) original use of the term normal perfectionist was inappropriate because it contradicted the basic definition of the construct. That is, the term was being used to describe behaviours of individuals who were not striving for perfection, but were engaged in healthy achievement striving. Greenspon (2000) pointed out that because perfection is such a rarely observed quality, it is illogical to consider it normal, healthy or adaptive to engage in its pursuit. In contrast, when individuals are striving to achieve high standards and are interpreting success and failure in a self-referent manner, the behaviour may be both healthy and adaptive. However, this form of achievement striving does not warrant the label perfectionism because it lacks some of the fundamental defining qualities of the characteristic.

When Greenspon (2000) examined the empirical evidence in support of healthy perfectionism, he noted that individuals were frequently characterised as healthy perfectionists as a function of their scores on the two dimensions of the Frost MPS, reflecting the pursuit of high standards and a tendency toward order and organisation. He argued that to classify individuals as perfectionists based on high scores on only two dimensions ignored the crucial defining qualities of perfectionism such as harsh self-criticism, concern about mistakes, fear of failure and conditional self-worth that were characteristics of the other dimensions. Moreover, he stated that it was a dangerous strategy that flouted sound scientific methods to have the measures defining the construct. It seems that those claiming the existence of a construct labelled healthy or adaptive perfectionism have missed an important point raised by Frost at al. (1990) in the validation of the multidimensional perfectionism scale. They stated that: "Although the definitions of perfectionism have emphasized the setting of excessively high standards of performance, the present series of studies suggests that Concern about Mistakes is more central to the concept, and is the major component in other measures of perfectionism as well." (p465). Therefore, in the absence of a heightened concern about making mistakes, one cannot be classified as a perfectionist

The thrust of Greenspon's (2000) argument is that there is no logical or psychological reason to support the existence of a construct named healthy perfectionism, and congruent with the views of Flett and Hewitt (2002) he believes that the emergence of such a construct was based largely on uncritical acceptance rather than strong empirical evidence. These arguments raise questions about whether the elite athletes identified by Gould et al., (2002) could really be classified as perfectionists, or whether they might have more accurately been described as high achievers. These arguments also suggest that sport psychology researchers should consider striving to achieve difficult goals as a necessary, but not necessarily a sufficient condition, to define perfectionism. Only when the critical dimensions that reflect the construct are considered, does it become possible to understand the broad range of psychological consequences associated with perfectionism.

WHAT IS THE EVIDENCE FROM SPORT AND EXERCISE?

Despite the fact that sport would appear to be an ideal context to examine the influence of perfectionism, research on sport participants has been slow to develop. Evidence is now beginning to accrue however, which suggests that perfectionism is largely associated with a pattern of achievement cognition, affect, and behaviour that is considered by motivational researchers to be maladaptive, and which has the potential to undermine an individual's psychological well being. There may be those who would argue that much of the research undertaken with sport participants has used sub-elite performers, and that the findings are not generalisable to those with elite status, but one only has to consider the evidence from educational research on perfectionism to see that the findings for gifted students are consistent with those of other students representing a wide range of learners (Adderholt-Elliott, 1989; 1991; Beilling, Israeli, Smith & Antony, 2003; Grzegorek, Slaney, Franze & Rice, 2004; Schuler, 2000). This research suggests that over time, the cognitive and emotional responses to perfectionistic achievement striving, and the achievement strategies adopted by these individuals lead to distress, a chronic negative emotionality, an enduring sense of failure and the possibility of performance impairment (Bieling, et al., 2003). Athletes who exhibit similar achievement patterns may not only risk undermining their chances of fulfilling their sporting potential, but may risk damaging their psychological health.

PERFECTIONISM EVALUATIVE THREAT AND NEGATIVE AFFECT

One of the first empirical studies to examine the effects of perfectionism in sport was conducted by Frost and Henderson (1991). They asserted that perfectionism in athletes is debilitating because an underlying fear of failure, concern about making mistakes and living up to social expectations interferes with both athletic enjoyment and performance. Although the various psychological processes underpinning athletes' debilitation were not specified by Frost and Henderson (1991), they inferred that different processes became prominent at different stages of the performance sequence. For example, in the time period immediately preceding competition, debilitation was thought to result from athletes ruminating about potential consequences of negative outcomes. After making errors during performance, debilitation was considered to result from cognitive interference brought about by intrusive and distracting thoughts, and after poor performance it was thought to result from enduring negative emotions such as shame, anger and anxiety.

Frost and Henderson (1991) examined some of the psychological processes underpinning debilitation, by testing two hypotheses. First, whether perfectionism, and especially concern about mistakes, was related to the nature of athletes' thoughts in the 24 hours leading up to competition, and second, whether perfectionism was related to negative reactions to mistakes during competition. Data were collected from a small sample of female university athletes who were participating in various sports. The results indicated that perfectionists who were high in concern about mistakes not only considered performance as an opportunity for failure but they perceived the competitive environment to be high in evaluative threat. Moreover the perfectionism dimensions reflecting concern about mistakes, doubts about action and high personal standards showed moderate to strong positive associations with a failure orientation where a predominant concern was with what others were thinking. Consistent with recent literature on the conceptualisation and measurement of perfectionism (Blatt, 1995; Campbell & DiPaula, 2002), it could be argued that the heightened sense of threat experienced by these athletes was not simply a function of sport being an important context to test skills and strive to achieve, but because sport is the context in which identity, self-definition, and self-worth are established. For these individuals, self-worth is often contingent on achievement, and a perception that achievement is recognised by others. Therefore, sporting contexts that are perceived as a threat to self will invariably induce negative affect at different stages of the performance process.

Frost and Henderson found support for this contention, identifying that perfectionism was associated with both trait anxiety and trait sport-confidence. In their sample of female athletes they reported a moderate positive association between overall perfectionism and trait anxiety and a moderate negative relationship between overall perfectionism and trait sport confidence. An examination of the perfectionism subscales revealed that it was concern about mistakes that contributed most to the relationship between perfectionism and trait anxiety, while concern about mistakes and doubts about action contributed to the negative relationship with trait sport confidence. These findings suggest that when faced with important sporting contexts, those high in concern about mistakes and doubts about action appear predisposed to experience heightened negative affect because they perceive the context to be high in evaluative threat

In the time leading up to competition, Frost and Henderson found that perfectionistic athletes' cognitions tended to be largely negative, drift towards errors, failure, and the evaluative judgement of others rather than focusing on more positive aspects of the upcoming task. They reported that in the 24 hours prior to competing, those high in concern about mistakes indicated greater fears about mistakes and recurring images of mistakes. This led to lower confidence, concentration difficulties and increased worry about the reaction of others. For these athletes, the maladaptive cognition did not abate when performing, for when mistakes occurred during competition, those high in concern about mistakes seemed fixated with their errors. Frost and Henderson reported that these athletes worried about others' reactions and felt that they had let themselves down as a result of their poor play. Their attention became drawn to their mistakes, resulting in negative self-talk, perceived pressure to compensate for an error, recurring images of the mistake and attentional distractions that resulted from their efforts to forget about the mistake.

Anger is also an emotional consequence of perfectionistic athletes underperforming, and this may further contribute to performance debilitation. A recent study by Dunn, Gotwals, Causgrove Dunn and Syrotuik (under review) provides evidence that this destructive emotion is experienced by perfectionistic athletes following failure. As a result of examining the association between dimensions of an adapted version of Frost's MPS and various anger measures, Dunn et al. reported that a combination of moderate to high personal standards, a high concern about mistakes and high perceived coach pressure was positively associated with two dimensions of trait anger and three dimensions of anger in response to mistakes. One might infer from these findings that some athletes appear more likely to be angered by failure when they have expended effort in the pursuit of challenging goals. This is because they consider achievement to be a central source of self-definition, and because they are concerned that performance errors and failure to live up to the expectations of the coach will undermine the self. The central point that is highlighted by this research is that perfectionism appears to predispose athletes to a way of thinking about achievement, and while it can encourage individuals to put forth effort in the pursuit of important goals, it leads to a particular ruminative pattern, which can occur at various times in the performance process. This can be psychologically and behaviourally destructive and indirectly undermine athletic performance.

Building upon the initial work of Frost and Henderson (1991), that provided evidence for relationships between perfectionism, trait anxiety and debilitating cognitions resulting from performance error, Hall, Kerr and Matthews (1998) examined whether perfectionism influenced the state anxiety and confidence levels reported by athletes in the week leading up to an important athletic competition. As Frost and Henderson's study had relied exclusively on bivariate correlational analysis, Hall et al. (1998) sought to determine the motivational variables that would best predict both negative affect and confidence in athletes as competition approached. Hall et al. utilised a sample of schoolchildren who had been selected to take part in an important cross-country meet. Measures of achievement goals, perceived ability and multidimensional perfectionism (F-MPS) were taken one week prior to the event. In addition, the children's cognitive and somatic anxiety and state confidence were assessed at intervals of one week, two days and one day prior to the meet. Finally, the affective measures were assessed on a further occasion approximately 30 minutes prior to performance.

Similar to the findings of Frost and Henderson (1991), concern about mistakes was a critical factor underpinning the performance anxiety of the athletes in the sample. This construct emerged as a significant predictor of cognitive anxiety at three of the four time points. In addition, doubts about action was found to be the sole predictor of cognitive anxiety 30 minutes prior to performance, while perceived ability combined with concern about mistakes was found to predict cognitive anxiety two days before the event. Overall, the dimensions of perfectionism accounted for between 5% and 18% behavioural variance in the athletes cognitive anxiety. Furthermore, those high in overall perfectionism were significantly higher in cognitive anxiety at every time point in the lead up to competition. Moreover, while the anxiety scores of those low in perfectionism remained relatively stable, the scores of those high in perfectionism became gradually elevated as the time to the event approached. These findings are consistent with those of Frost and Marten (1990) and Flett, Hewitt, Endler and Tassone (1994) who found that when either evaluative threat or ego involvement were emphasised during performance of an important achievement task, perfectionists would respond with elevated levels of state anxiety.

When Hall et al. examined which variables underpinned somatic anxiety in their sample of runners, they found that on two occasions high personal standards emerged as a significant predictor, while on three occasions doubts about action was significantly related. Those with high standards were considered to experience lower levels of somatic anxiety because they were either confident of achieving success or they were pursuing standards over which they had a strong sense of personal control. Both of these explanations were validated by further analyses that revealed personal standards to be a significant predictor of confidence on three of the four occasions leading up to competition.

Overall, the findings of Hall et al. (1998) indicate that characteristics of neurotic perfectionism such as a concern about mistakes may predispose athletes to experience negative affect in the lead up to an important event. However, to suggest that athletes will suffer psychological or performance debilitation as a direct result of their perfectionism ignores the possible moderating effects of other variables, which contribute to an overall appraisal of the sporting environment. Using Lazarus's (1999) model of emotion as a framework to guide conceptual thought on athletes' performance related anxiety, it can be argued that while dispositional variables such as perfectionism provide a set of propositions to guide the interpretation of goal directed information, secondary appraisal characteristics reflective of the coping process may moderate any emotional outcomes resulting from an athlete's appraisal of the sporting context.

The research of Mor, Day, Flett and Hewitt (1995) provides some support for using Lazarus's model as a framework for understanding the process by which perfectionism may influence performance related emotion. They set out to test whether perceptions of personal control would moderate the influence of self-oriented and socially prescribed perfectionism on debilitating and facilitating forms of anxiety in professional performers, including musicians, actors and dancers. Mor et al. (1995) found that debilitating performance anxiety was predicted by high socially prescribed perfectionism and low personal control. It was also reported that low levels of control resulted in elevated levels of debilitating anxiety, but only in performers who were high in socially prescribed perfectionism. This same group also experienced lower goal satisfaction. Further analysis revealed that while perceived control directly predicted increased facilitative anxiety, lower levels of facilitative anxiety were associated with high levels of self-oriented perfectionism and low levels of personal control. That is, when self oriented perfectionists who are characterised as extremely self-critical perceive that they have little control, they tend to consider that their emotional state cannot assist their performance.

The findings from this research are particularly relevant to sporting contexts, as they suggest that in sport, where the pursuit of excellence is socially valued, the management of debilitating anxiety that is underpinned by socially prescribed perfectionism might be achieved by establishing a sense of perceived control in athletes. In sum, the findings from a limited number of studies exploring the relationship between perfectionism and performance related affect point to the fact that negative affect can occur at any time as a result of particular forms of dispositional perfectionism. Furthermore, it is evident that the intensity of the negative affect or the debilitative nature of associated cognitions can be moderated by other constructs that enable an individual to cope, by ensuring that an athlete's appraisal of both situational demands and personal resources minimise existential threats to self.

PERFECTIONISM AND PHYSIQUE ANXIETY

In most sporting contexts evaluative threat will be experienced when athletes begin to express self-doubt about their ability. However, in some sporting contexts where evaluation is based upon the aesthetic qualities of performance, athletes may experience a form of evaluative threat that is associated with self-presentation, a condition where individuals are attempting to control impressions that others' hold about them. This form of evaluative threat has also been noted in exercise contexts where the outcome is described as social physique anxiety. Individuals who are physique anxious appear to have a chronic concern about what others think about their bodies. This may have the effect of deterring some individuals from exercising in public places, reduce the sense of positive affect that can be gained from exercise involvement, or more worryingly, encourage unsafe weight control practices in athletes who might have to maintain a particular type of physique in order to perform in their sport.

Noting that exercise classes seemed to induce anxiety in some individuals Hall, Wigmore and Kerr (1999) set out to test whether dispositional perfectionism in exercise participants could be identified as an antecedent of social physique anxiety. In a sample of female participants who were enrolled in public exercise classes offered at commercial leisure facilities, it was found that 14% variance in social physique anxiety was accounted for by physical competence and socially prescribed perfectionism. That is, individuals who were high in socially prescribed perfectionism and low in physical competence experienced higher levels of social physique anxiety, whereas those who were high in self-oriented perfectionism did not suffer from physique anxiety.

Similar findings were reported by Haase et al. (2002) in a sample of 316 elite athletes from Australia and New Zealand. They found moderate positive correlations between a construct labelled negative perfectionism and social physique anxiety, but low correlations between positive perfectionism (goal directed achievement striving) and social physique anxiety. Regardless of whether it is with athletes or exercisers, it is clear that a concern that one should meet the perceived standards of others, and a sense of self-doubt about achieving those standards plays a significant role in inducing anxiety about one's body. Haase et al (2002) suggested that this is a result of a desire on the part of the athletes to have others recognise them and validate a particular impression of self. However, because there is always the possibility that significant others will fail to reinforce an athlete's self-presentational image, social physique anxiety may result.

PERFECTIONISM AND MALADAPTIVE BEHAVIOUR

While research is beginning to demonstrate that perfectionism is associated with negative affective responses in athletes, those who would advocate that elite athletes are not ill-served by this disposition would fail to be convinced of its debilitative nature if the research evidence was limited to demonstrating its emotional effects. However, research is beginning to emerge which clearly demonstrates that neurotic perfectionism may not only be destructive to athletic performance, but may undermine the physical health of athletes because they deliberately or unwittingly employ various maladaptive behaviours in their quest for achievement.

NUTRITIONAL BEHAVIOUR

One body of evidence has been gleaned from examining athletes' disturbed eating attitudes and disordered eating behaviours. For example, in their study of Australian and New Zealand athletes, Haase et al. (2002) found that perfectionism and social physique anxiety had both an independent and a combined influence on athletes' disordered eating scores. They found that 19% variance in disturbed eating attitudes was predicted by athletes' scores on a negative perfectionism scale. A further 12% variance was predicted by social physique anxiety, and an additional 10% variance was accounted for by the interaction of the two predictors. The interaction revealed that females who had high negative perfectionism scores and high scores in social physique anxiety suffered greater levels of disturbance in eating attitudes.

Haase at al. (2002) put forth three explanations for their findings. First, they considered that the disturbed eating attitudes demonstrated by these athletes may have been representative of a coping strategy aimed at managing anxiety, which resulted from the negative perfectionism. Second, they considered that the disturbed eating attitudes may have been an attempt to compensate for the failure to meet some self-presentation ideal and the anxiety surrounding this failure. Third, they proposed that the athletes' perfectionistic standards were predominantly associated with weight control, meaning that while perfectionism directly influenced social physique anxiety, its effects on the disturbed attitudes to eating were moderated by the level of social physique anxiety experienced by the athletes. The weight control hypothesis received some support in a second study by Haase, Prappevasis & Owen (1999). Specifically, they found that disturbed eating attitudes in elite rowers were a result of negative perfectionism, but that greater disturbance scores were more prevalent in female lightweight rowers who had higher scores on the Body Mass Index and were higher in negative perfectionism. It could be said that the contextual pressures to maintain weight in the female lightweight rowing crews had a greater influence on the eating attitudes of negative perfectionists who had recorded higher scores on the Body Mass Index.

The studies of Haase and her colleagues indicate that perfectionism plays a significant role in the disturbed eating attitudes of athletes. Further evidence of disturbance has been reported by McLaren, Gauvin and White (2001), who demonstrated that perfectionism influences the adoption of both poor nutritional strategies and engagement with pathological forms of exercise behaviour. Their research with female students showed that while there was a direct relationship between various forms of perfectionism and dietary restraint, the relationship was partially mediated by a commitment to excessive exercise. McLaren et al. (2001) suggested that in their pursuit of unrealistic standards for both appearance and body weight, individuals who are high in self-oriented and socially prescribed perfectionism, as well as those showing elevated levels of perfectionistic self-presentation, engage in obligatory and pathological exercise behaviours in order to restrain their dietary intake.

DYSFUNCTIONAL EXERCISE BEHAVIOURS

While the research of McLaren et al. (2001) utilised a student sample, a number of studies have demonstrated links between perfectionism and forms of self-destructive exercise behaviour in athletes. The first was by Coen and Ogles (1993) who were attempting to determine if there were personality differences between athletes who displayed healthy forms of exercise behaviour and those whose exercise was defined as obligatory and considered to be both physically and psychologically debilitating. In a sample of distance runners Coen and Ogles (1993) found that obligatory exercisers reported significantly higher levels of perfectionism when compared to non-obligatory exercisers, and that the greatest differences were in those dimensions reflecting neurotic perfectionism on the Frost MPS. While reporting higher scores on the personal standards dimension, indicating that they set higher goals, obligatory exercisers also scored higher in concern about mistakes, doubts about action and organisation than did the non-obligatory exercisers. What Coen and Ogles (1993) research did not reveal, however, was the degree to which the various dimensions of perfectionism predict obligatory exercise behaviour.

In order to address this limitation, Hall, Kerr, Kozub and Finnie (under review) recently conducted a follow up study using a sample of British middle distance runners that ranged in standard from recreational to elite. Using hierarchical regression analyses they found that 34% of obligatory exercise behaviour was accounted for by a combination of athletes' achievement goal orientations, perceived ability, and concern about mistakes. Further analyses implicated neurotic perfectionism as the critical antecedent of obligatory exercise behavior in females, with 63% variance in obligatory exercise behaviour being accounted for by a combination of perceived ability, concern about mistakes, and doubts about action.

Hall et al. (under review) concluded that while dispositional forms of motivation that direct athletes to consider achievement to be reflective of self-worth may energise action, they also underpin a range of dysfunctional cognitions and affective responses that contribute to unhealthy forms of exercise behaviour. It has been argued that the compulsive exercise behaviour of some perfectionistic athletes is a result of attempting to establish an identity, which is based largely on athletic accomplishment. The unfortunate consequence of adopting this strategy is that when this goal is not being achieved, or when individuals are prevented from exercising, the esteem of athletes may suffer and this leads them to engage in further dysfunctional behaviours which undermine physical and /or psychological health, in the belief that they must continue to exercise in order to maintain a desired sense of self.

ATHLETE BURNOUT

A similar psychological process may underpin the observed relationship between perfectionism and athlete burnout when athletes tie their sense of self to their athletic accomplishments. The possibility for perfectionistic athletes to experience psychological debilitation and burnout can be seen in recent qualitative research conducted with elite athletes that has sought to examine their motivation and its consequences. Conroy, Poczwardowski and Henschen (2001) found that when elite athletes and performing artists were asked about the criteria they use to evaluate failure, they not only identified competence issues such as unfulfilled goals and insufficient control, but the generation of negative feelings in others. When asked about the consequences of experiencing failure, these athletes identified seven general consequences. One of these was to engage in an adaptive motivational strategy involving the alteration of investment patterns. The other six appeared largely dysfunctional and could be interpreted as being reflective of the cognitive and emotional debilitation seen in perfectionists. These included, feelings of tangible loss, a perceived loss of control, changes in interpersonal interactions, increased negative emotions, self-criticism that undermines the self, and public humiliation and shame. It is likely that if this debilitating pattern was to persist for any length of time, burnout would be a probable outcome.

Research by Gould et al. (1996) has found evidence to support such a contention. Using elite junior tennis players Gould et al. (1996) compared those experiencing burnout with a comparison group of tennis players who remained positively motivated toward their sport. They found that the group experiencing burnout was more amotivated (unsure about why they were participating) and that these athletes were higher on the dimensions reflecting neurotic perfectionism (concern about mistakes, perceived parental criticism, high parental expectations). They also found that the burnout group was lower in their use of adaptive coping strategies. It is possible that poor coping resulting from perfectionism would further contribute to feelings of both emotional and physical exhaustion in these athletes because research by Magnasson, Nias and White (1996) has confirmed that neurotic perfectionism often leads to the adoption of maladaptive coping strategies, which predispose individuals to experience fatigue.

The quantitative analyses presented by Gould et al. (1996) were supported by a further qualitative analysis of the three athletes who reported the highest burnout scores. The findings revealed that each of the athletes showed perfectionistic characteristics, although Gould et al. (1996) suggested that the underlying reasons for burnout appeared to differ for each athlete. Characteristics of perfectionism could be observed in one athlete whose goal to become a professional player, while high, was also inflexible. This athlete described himself as highly motivated but intensely self-critical, and this seems to reflect what Hewitt and Flett (1991) described as self-oriented perfectionism. A second athlete described feeling intense pressure to succeed from both her mother and her coach. She also described being both self-critical, but filled with self-doubts especially when compared to an older sibling and other better players. This pattern, in conjunction with worry when she was being observed by her mother and coach, high athletic identity and a negative self-concept appears to be reflective of debilitating neurotic perfectionism described by Frost and Henderson (1991). A third athlete described a broader range of personal characteristics that were reflective of both neurotic and socially prescribed forms of perfectionism. This athlete described her own goals as unrealistic and her training schedule as physically intense, to the point of feeling that it was necessary to increase quantity to make up for deficiencies in quality. For this athlete, self-esteem was reportedly based upon winning, and the defeats that she suffered, simply undermined her sense of self. The difficulties that she experienced as a result of being unable to validate a sense of self through her achievements were further exacerbated by the fact that the athlete felt extreme pressure to excel and to win from both her father and her coach. Riddled with persistent doubts and a perceived lack of control over the standards defining achievement, the athlete repeatedly felt that her performances were never sufficient for her father to feel any sense of pride in her.

Gould (1996) has suggested that burnout is "motivation gone awry". He implies that it is a process by which athletes adaptive motivational patterns somehow become maladaptive as a result of chronic stress. A contrasting social cognitive motivational perspective on burnout suggests that while the initial cognitive, affective and behavioural patterns of future burnouts might appear adaptive, the true maladaptive nature of the underlying motivational framework will only be observable under conditions of difficulty, extreme challenge, and perceived sporting failure. The basis of this argument lies in the work of Dweck (1986) who suggested that the maladaptive patterns of learning of those endorsing an ego orientation would best be observed under aversive conditions. As most athletes experiencing burnout tend to be high achievers, and frequently highly able, the conditions which foster the development of the burnout syndrome in this group are rarely seen at the initial stages of sporting investment. However, the way a potential burnout gives meaning to achievement provides the basis for impending problems. If athletes are socialized into viewing achievement in a comparative manner which provides little recourse to protect the self against the impact of prolonged difficulty or perceived failure, it is simply a matter of time before the potential for psychological, emotional, and behavioural disengagement from sport becomes realized. This can certainly be seen in the athletes described by Gould et al. (1996; 1997). Their perfectionism initially acts as an energiser, but over time, it becomes a psychological impediment as the strategies the athletes adopt in the pursuit of high achievement standards are predominantly dysfunctional.

The work of Gould et al. (1996; 1997) suggests that many of the perfectionistic athletes who report high levels of burnout perceive that their parents and coaches impose pressure on them to perform through the imposition of high expectations and critical evaluations of performance. This has been confirmed in recent empirical work by Dunn et al. (2002) who argued that both parental and coach pressure are important dimensions of sport related perfectionism. Whether considered to be dimensions of perfectionism or antecedent factors that underpin the development of perfectionism, elite athletes often experience external pressures from coaches and parents in their development. This creates a performance environment that is high in evaluative threat and can render perfectionists vulnerable to experiencing the debilitating cognitions, affective responses and behaviours that are reflective of burnout. Unfortunately, for some athletes, the contexts in which they are asked to develop may contribute to or exacerbate motivational problems.

For example, many English soccer academies and centres of excellence have the potential to be high in evaluative threat. They select, develop and train young athletes who aspire to play professional soccer, and throughout their developmental years the coaching staff at the club are required to make decisions about whether the club will continue to invest in a player. Because so few young players are selected to join the professional ranks, the learning environment can often be perceived as being highly pressured. Hill and Hall (2004) chose this context to build upon the work of Gould et al. (1996; 1997), and examine whether self-oriented and socially prescribed perfectionism were related to dimensions of burnout in elite young soccer players. They further sought to examine whether the potentially debilitating influence of perfectionism was moderated by unconditional self acceptance (a measure of contingent self worth) in a sample of 10-16 year old athletes. Correlational analysis revealed that self-oriented perfectionism was negatively related to the three dimensions of Raedeke and Smith's (2002) measure of burnout including a reduced sense of accomplishment, physical and emotional exhaustion and devaluation of the activity. In contrast, socially prescribed perfectionism was positively related to all three burnout dimensions. While the relationship between socially prescribed perfectionism and burnout dimensions was predicted, the finding that low levels of self-oriented perfectionism were related to burnout can not be easily explained. It is feasible however, that those athletes who were low in self-oriented perfectionism reported elevated burnout scores because their achievement behaviour was not congruent with the environmental norms and contextual requirements of the soccer academies and centres of excellence where coaches value intense goal directed striving. If these athletes perceived that their motivational investment was incongruent with that desired by the coaches, and that the clubs were unlikely to retain their services at the end of the season, it is possible that higher burnout scores would be recorded.

Further regression analyses of perfectionism and unconditional self-acceptance on the burnout dimensions revealed that thirty percent of variance in emotional and physical exhaustion was predicted by the direct effects of socially prescribed perfectionism and unconditional self acceptance. Similarly, 30% variance in reduced sense of accomplishment was predicted by socially prescribed perfectionism and unconditional self acceptance, while 25% variance in devaluation of the activity was predicted by self-oriented perfectionism. The finding that socially prescribed perfectionism predicted physical and emotional exhaustion and reduced sense of accomplishment, but did not predict devaluation of the activity should not be surprising, because when the activity is instrumental in defining oneself as an athlete, any claim that the activity has less value may be perceived as undermining one's sense of self.

While this research implicates both socially prescribed perfectionism and unconditional self acceptance as direct antecedents of burnout in young soccer players, a predicted interaction between these variables was not observed. However, given the strong negative relationship that was found to exist between socially prescribed perfectionism and unconditional self-acceptance, it points to the fact that rather than moderating the influence of socially prescribed perfectionism, contingent self-worth may be a defining characteristic of this disposition. Other variables that may moderate the relationship between perfectionism and burnout dimensions need to be examined if the burnout process is to be better understood in this context.

The research by Gould et al. (1996;1997) and by Hill and Hall (2004) suggest that as athletes are developing towards the elite echelons of their sport, those who are neurotic or socially prescribed perfectionists may be vulnerable to experiencing debilitating patterns of cognition affect and behaviour that may be reflective of burnout. Rather than viewing the burnout process as one where adaptive motivation becomes dysfunctional, Hall, Kerr and Cawthra (1997) have questioned Gould's (1996) contention that the onset of burnout is because motivation goes awry. Instead, they argue that development of dispositions such as socially prescribed or neurotic perfectionism will energise the motivational patterns displayed by these athletes as their careers begin to take shape, but suggest that they are ultimately responsible for the debilitating patterns that are observed when elite athletes begin to burn out. At first, the effort expended in striving to reach high personal standards results in success and enhanced perceptions of competence for perfectionistic young performers. However, as these athletes begin to progress toward elite status, experience more difficult challenges and experience the performance difficulties that result from competing at an advanced level, their self-worth often becomes undermined because self-validation is contingent on achievement. While initial perceptions of failure may precipitate increased achievement striving, such a strategy will increasingly undermine self worth if performance difficulties and increased perceptions of failure are regularly experienced. Athletes will then begin to experience the kind of debilitating patterns of cognition and affect that may develop into burnout because their perceptions of high ability are no longer sufficient to moderate the effects of perfectionism. It is at this point that athletes will begin to engage in self-protective behaviours, but whereas dropping out of sport may be an option to protect the self-worth of low ability participants who have invested little into an activity; it is not likely to be an immediate option for athletes whose identity may have been formed through their sporting commitments. This obvious dilemma means that athletes become entrapped (Schmidt & Stein, 1991) and the symptoms of burnout intensify progressively. What is clear from the arguments put forward by Hall et al. (1997) is that the same motivational dispositions that may have led to investment under conditions of perceived success do not facilitate adaptive investment when challenges and difficulties that are characteristic of performing at an elite level are perceived. When athletes begin to perceive failure in these contexts, and are unable to validate self-worth, disaffection becomes chronic and achievement strategies become maladaptive because perfectionism and other related dispositions such as an ego orientation guide how achievement information is processed.

Lemyre, Roberts and Hall (2004) set out to test the model proposed by Hall et al. (1997). They measured a number of motivational variables early in a season for athletes participating in five winter sports. These included the athletes' achievement goals, the perceived achievement climate, and dimensions of the Frost multi-dimensional perfectionism scale. The same athletes completed the Raedeke and Smith (2002) burnout inventory toward the end of the competitive season. The sample of athletes included Olympians and junior elite athletes studying at national sporting academies in Norway. A cluster analysis was undertaken on the motivational variables, and two clusters emerged that were labelled adaptive and maladaptive patterns of motivation. The cluster of athletes showing an adaptive motivational pattern reported higher task orientation, higher perceptions of a mastery climate and higher perceived ability. Those identified as having a maladaptive pattern of motivation were higher in ego orientation, were of the opinion that the achievement climate was performance oriented, and were higher on all dimensions of the Frost MPS. When the two clusters were compared using multivariate analysis of variance, it was revealed that the scores on all three dimensions of burnout were significantly higher for those endorsing the maladaptive pattern of motivation. While few of the athletes in this study showed extreme burnout scores on any of the three dimensions, the adoption of a motivational pattern reflective of neurotic perfectionism and the perception that the learning environment is high in evaluative threat demonstrates that elite and Olympic standard athletes can demonstrate vulnerability to burnout.

ACHIEVEMENT RELATED COGNITIONS

While the research by Lemyre et al. (2004) has identified a potentially debilitating pattern of motivational variables that underpin athlete burnout, their research did not examine how negative outcomes might be moderated by constructs that reduce the perception of evaluative threat. Some have argued (Hall et al., 1998; Dunn et al., 2002) that endorsing a task orientation might moderate the potentially debilitating influence of perfectionism, and enable athletes to demonstrate an adaptive motivational profile. To date, research has found no evidence to support the moderating effects of task goals on the relationship between perfectionism and variables such as state anxiety. What has emerged is evidence from canonical correlation analysis that a moderate task orientation in combination with a high ego orientation is related to all dimensions of Frost's MPS. This finding has emerged in two studies (Hall et al. 1998; under review), while a third study (Dunn et al., 2002) has reported that a strong ego orientation is associated with all aspects of Dunn's modified MPS. The fact that perfectionistic athletes seem to endorse both ego and task orientations supports the overstriving phenomenon described earlier, where individuals are driven to put forth effort and achieve success largely by their need to avoid failure and maintain self-worth. McArdle, Duda and Hall (2004) report some initial evidence to support this view, and have shown that when athletes endorse high ego and moderate task goals, in conjunction with high personal standards, a concern about mistakes and doubts about action, a debilitating pattern of cognition and affect results.

McArdle et al. (2004) employed a hierarchical cluster analysis with elite athletes from a number of individual sports to reveal four clusters of athletes, each demonstrating a unique pattern of motivational attributes. In conjunction with the qualities listed above, a group labelled achievement driven negative perfectionists indicated that their investment was regulated by high levels of intrinsic, identified, introjected and extrinsic motivation. In addition this cluster reported high levels of amotivation. While the level of disaffection is easily explained by its association with the dimensions of neurotic perfectionism, the high levels of intrinsic motivation reported by these athletes are more difficult to explain. One might speculate that because the self-worth of this cluster of athletes is contingent on achievement, previous success would have not only brought about enjoyment and the appearance of intrinsic motivation, but would have contributed to the identity of the athlete. Although failure to achieve would impact negatively on self-worth, these athletes may find it difficult to admit that their investment was not regulated by intrinsic reasons because to do so may have the effect of undermining their identity. That is, to admit to not having an intrinsic love of the sport through which one defines oneself could be interpreted as an indirect act of self-deprecation

When compared to the three other clusters, McArdle et al. found that the achievement driven negative perfectionists were not only lower in self-esteem but they also reported higher labile self-esteem, indicating their self-esteem fluctuated from moment to moment. This finding clearly indicates that while these individuals feel good about themselves when successfully accomplishing their goals, their self-worth is diminished when they perceive they are failing. This leads to further pressure to achieve, and while these individuals may give the appearance of being highly motivated, it is the pressure to validate self-worth that is the key regulatory factor, and this energises further dysfunctional cognition, affective responses and achievement behaviour.

The fact that some individuals feel pressured to achieve and validate their self-worth has been confirmed in two further studies, which reported findings that are consistent with those of McArdle et al. (2004). First, research on elite athletes by Koivula, Hasmann and Fallby (2002) found that those demonstrating high levels of neurotic perfectionism reported low levels of self-acceptance, and high levels of contingent self-worth. These athletes also expressed low levels of confidence, and high levels of state anxiety prior to performing in competition. Second, Gotwals, Dunn and Wayment (2002) found that in a sample of University athletes the dimensions of concern over mistakes and doubts about action were associated with low levels of self-esteem, low performance satisfaction and low levels of perceived athletic competence. Clearly, neurotic perfectionism not only has the potential to undermine self-esteem but it can lead to heightened levels of labile self-esteem in athletes who perceive their worth to be contingent on achievement.

CONCLUDING THOUGHTS

Research on perfectionism is still in its infancy and although advances have been made in clinical, social and educational psychology, little is known about the construct in sport and exercise contexts. Early work is encouraging, but if the construct is to play a meaningful role in understanding the psychological processes associated with achievement striving in sport and exercise, a clear definition of perfectionism is required. Flett and Hewitt (2002) have noted the lack of agreement among various researchers who have attempted to define the term perfectionism, and they have urged caution when interpreting the findings from research studies that may have adopted different measures.

To date, the research evidence accrued from sport and exercise contexts, while limited, presents a relatively consistent picture. That is, neurotic perfectionism, negative perfectionism and socially prescribed perfectionism appear to be associated with a number of psychological and behavioural outcomes that are potentially debilitating to the long term motivation, performance and psychological well being of athletes performing at all levels. What is less clear at this point, is whether self-oriented perfectionism is also associated with dysfunctional patterns of achievement related cognition, affect and behaviour. This is because few studies have used Hewitt and Flett's (1991) measure in sport and exercise contexts. Furthermore, it has yet to be determined whether the maladaptive nature of self-oriented perfectionism will be manifest under aversive conditions such as heightened evaluative threat or elevated life stress as Flett and Hewitt (2002) predict.

While neurotic and socially prescribed perfectionism are associated with numerous negative outcomes, it is interesting to note that dispositional perfectionism has little association with positive cognitions and affective responses such as satisfaction and enjoyment, even following successful outcomes. Perfectionistic athletes often perceive that success is fleeting, and it therefore becomes difficult for them to experience any lasting pleasure beyond the event in which success occurred (McArdle et al., 2004). For example, in a recent interview with Johnny Wilkinson, the England rugby player, Alison Kervin (2004) asked the player about his plans for the future after England's successful World Cup win in November 2003. He responded that he was determined to enjoy playing rugby more, and was reported to have said: "Once I get back from this injury, I'm going to have fun. But the trouble is, for me to have fun, I have to be winning, which means working hard. So I don't know how much will change" (p17). It is hard to see how much fun Wilkinson will allow himself to have when one considers some of the other statements he made in the newspaper interview with Kervin, that confirmed his perfectionistic thinking. In the interview he says that he cannot bear the thought of letting down his family or anyone who has helped him to develop his rugby skills. Not only does he appear to be concerned with the views of important others, he also indicates that he is terrified at the thought of defeat, and fears letting himself down. The coping strategy he adopts in order to manage this constant worry is to immerse himself into his rugby training, over which he perceives control. But although he indicates that his intense training reduces persistent doubts about whether he'll do OK, there's a part of him that never thinks he's done enough, either on the practice field or in competition, suggesting that the strategy to invest in training doesn't always provide the desired level of control. Unfortunately, because these achievement related cognitions appear to have been a constant throughout Wilkinson's development as a rugby player, one wonders just how much enjoyment the player will ever be able to experience from rugby in the future, without drastically altering his perfectionistic cognitions or developing further coping strategies that can moderate the potentially debilitating influence of the disposition.

When one considers the achievement behaviour of individuals like Johnny Wilkinson it is clear that dispositional perfectionism is an important factor that can energise motivation. This was noted by Roedell (1984) in the context of education some twenty years ago. Roedell stated that: "In its positive form, perfectionism can provide the driving energy which leads to great achievement. The meticulous attention to detail necessary for scientific investigation, the commitment which pushes composers to keep working until the music realizes the glorious sounds playing in the imagination, and the persistence which keeps great artists at easels until their creation matches their conception all result from perfectionism. Setting high standards is not itself a bad thing. However, perfectionism coupled with a punishing attitude towards one's own efforts can cripple the imagination, kill the spirit, and so handicap performance that an individual may never fulfil the promise of early talent." (p127)

It appears that in the case of Johnny Wilkinson, certain qualities of perfectionism enable him to achieve at a high level, but his achievements in rugby have not prevented him from experiencing numerous psychological difficulties that may be associated with other aspects of perfectionism (Kervin, 2004). Without the development of adaptive coping strategies, perfectionism that is characterised by self-criticism and contingent self-worth will almost certainly stifle rather than facilitate the development of athletic talent, because it leads to psychological impairment (Flett & Hewitt, 2002). In contrast, athletic talent will flourish when athletes feel able to pursue high standards without being overly critical of their performance, see effort as an end in itself rather than as a means to an end, recognise that mistakes are part of learning, and accept that they have worth regardless of their athletic accomplishments. This is because this form of achievement striving is associated with patterns of psychologically adaptive cognition, affect and behaviour (Duda & Hall, 2001). A number of researchers advocate using the label positive perfectionism to describe this form of achievement behaviour (Haase & Prapavessis, 2004; Terry-Short, Owens, Slade & Dewey, 1995). However, it is questionable whether perfectionism is an appropriate term because the achievement behaviour in question lacks any of the central defining characteristics of perfectionism, such as excessive self-criticism, concern about making mistakes, worry about disappointing others, and a fear of failure. In the absence of these defining qualities it is difficult to justify that this form of achievement behaviour is reflective of perfectionism. The research evidence from sport points to the fact that perfectionism is not a positive disposition, although it may be a powerful energiser underpinning achievement striving. While this may result in positive outcomes, they are often short lived and they are rarely perceived to be satisfactory. Thus, based on the available evidence, the long term consequences of perfectionism are likely to be debilitating to the fulfilment of athletic potential, and unless managed, may become psychologically dysfunctional, or in the most extreme cases lead to disturbing pathological consequences.

REFERENCES

Adderholt-Elliott, M. (1989). Perfectionism and underachievement. *Gifted Child Today, 12,* 19-21.

Adderholt-Elliott, M. R. (1991). Perfectionism and the gifted adolescent. In M. Bireley & J. Genshaft (Eds.), *Understanding the gifted adolescent: Educational, developmental, and multicultural issues* (pp. 65-75). New York, NY: New York Teachers College Press.

Anshel, M. H. & Eom, H. (2002). Exploring the dimensions of perfectionism in sport. *International Journal of Sport Psychology, 34,* 255-271.

Atkinson, J. (1957). Motivational determinants of risk taking behavior. *Psychological Review, 64,* 359-372.

Bieling, P. J., Israeli, A., Smith, J. & Antony, M. M. (2003). Making the grade: The behavioural consequences of perfectionism in the classroom. *Personality and Individual Differences, 35,* 163-178.

Blatt, S. J. (1995). The destructiveness of perfectionism: Implications for the treatment of depression. *American Psychologist, 50,* 1003-1020.

Burns, D. D. (1980). The perfectionists script for self-defeat. *Psychology Today(November),* 34-51.

Burton, D., Naylor, S. & Holliday, B. (2001). Goal setting in sport: Investigating the goal effectiveness paradox. In R. N. Singer & H. A. Hausenblas & C. M. Janelle (Eds.), *Handbook of Sport Psychology* (Second ed., pp. 497-528). New York, NY: Wiley.

Burton, D., Weinberg, R. S., Yukelson, D. & Weigand, D. A. (1998). The goal effectiveness paradox in sport. *The Sport Psychologist, 12,* 404-418.

Coen, S. P & Ogles, B. M. (1993). Psychological characteristics of the obligatory runner: A critical examination of the anorexia analogue hypothesis. *Journal of Sport & Exercise Psychology, 15,* 338-354.

Conroy, D. E., Poczwardowski, A. & Henschen, K. P. (2001). Evaluative criteria and consequences associated with failure and success for elite athletes and performing artists. *Journal of Applied Sport Psychology, 13,* 300-322.

Covington, M. V. (1992). *Making the grade: A self-worth perspective on motivation and school reform.* Cambridge University Press.

Deci, E. L. & Ryan, R. M. (1995). Human autonomy: The basis for true self-esteem. In M. H. Kernis (Ed.), *Efficacy, Agency and Self-Esteem.* New York, NY: Plenum Press.

Duda, J. L. (2001). Achievement goal research in sport: Pushing the boundaries and clarifying some misunderstandings. In G. C. Roberts (Ed.), *Advances in Motivation in Sport and Exercise* (pp. 129-182). Champaign, IL: Human Kinetics Publishers.

Duda, J. L. & Hall, H. K. (2001). Achievement goal theory in sport: Recent extensions and future directions. In R. N. Singer & C. M. Janelle & H. A. Hausenblas (Eds.), *Handbook of Sport Psychology* (Second ed., pp. 417-443). New York, NY: Wiley.

Dunn, J. G. H., Causgrove Dunn, J., & Syrotuik, D. G. (2002). Relationship between multidimensional perfectionism and goal orientations in sport. *Journal of Sport and Exercise Psychology, 24,* 376-395.

Dunn, J. G. H., Gotwals, J. K., Causgrove Dunn, J. & Syrotuik, D. G. (in press). Examining the relationship between perfectionism and trait anger in competitive sport. *International Journal of Sport and Exercise Psychology.*

Dweck, C. S. (1986). Motivational processes affecting learning. *American Psychologist, 41,* 1040-1048.

Dyckman, B. M. (1998). Integrating cognitive and motivational factors in depression: Initial tests of a goal oreintation approach. *Journal of Personality and Social Psychology, 74,* 139-158.

Ellis, A. (1962). *Reason and emotion in psychotherapy.* New York: Lyle Stuart.

Ericsson, K. A. (1996). The acquisition of expert performance: An introduction to some issues. In K. A. Ericsson (Ed.), *The road to excellence: The acquisition of expert performance in the arts and sciences, sports and games.* (pp. 1-50). Hillsdale, NJ: Lawrence Erlbaum.

Flett, G. L. & Hewitt, P., L. (2002). Perfectionism and maladjustment: An overview of theoretical, definitional, and treatment issues. In G. L. Flett & P. Hewitt, L. (Eds.), *Perfectionism: Theory, research, and treatment.* (pp. 5-31). Washington, DC: American Psychological Association.

Flett, G. L., Hewitt, P., L., Blankstein, K. R. & Mosher, S. W. (1995). Perfectionism, life events and depressive symptoms: A test of diathesis-stress model. *Current Psychology, 14,* 112-137.

Flett, G. L., Hewitt, P., L., Endler, N. S. & Tassone, C. (1994). Perfectionism and components of state and trait anxiety. *Current Psychology, 13,* 326-350.

Flett, G. L., Hewitt, P. L., Blankstein, K. R., & Pickering, D. (1998). Perfectionism in relation to attributions for success and failure. *Current Psychology, 17,* 249-262.

Frost, R. O., & DiBartolo, P. (2002). Perfectionism, anxiety, and obsessive-compulsive disorder. In G. L. Flett & P. Hewitt, L. (Eds.), *Perfectionism: Theory, research, and treatment.* (pp. 341-372). Washington, DC: American Psychological Association.

Frost, R. O., Heimberg, R. G., Holt, C. S., Mattia, J. I. & Neubauer, A. L. (1993). A comparison of two measures of perfection. *Personality and Individual Differences, 14,* 119-126.

Frost, R. O. & Henderson, K. J. (1991). Perfectionism and reactions to athletic competition. *Journal of Sport & Exercise Psychology, 13,* 323-335.

Frost, R. O. & Marten, P. A. (1990). Perfectionism and evaluative threat. *Cognitive Therapy & Research, 14,* 559-572.

Frost, R. O., Marten, P. A., Lahart, C. & Rosenblate, R. (1990). The dimensions of perfectionism. *Cognitive Therapy and Research, 14,* 449-468.

Garner, D. M., Olmstead, M. P. & Polivy, J. (1983). Development and validation of a multidimensional eating disorder inventory for anorexia nervosa and bulimia. *International Journal of Eating Disorders, 2,* 15-34.

Gotwals, J. K., Dunn, J. G. H. & Wayment, H. A. (2002). An examination of perfectionism and self-esteem in intercollegiate athletes. *Journal of Sport Behavior, 26,* 17-38.

Gould, D. (1996). Personal motivation gone awry: Burnout in competitive athletes. *Quest, 48,* 275-289.

Gould, D., Tuffey, S., Udry, E. & Loehr, J. (1996). Burnout in competitive junior tennis players: I. A quantitative psychological assessment. *The Sport Psychologist, 10,* 332-340.

Gould, D. R., Dieffenbach, K., & Moffett, A. (2002). Psychological characteristics and their development in Olympic champions. *Journal of Applied Sport Psychology, 14,* 172-204.

Gould, D. R., Tuffey, S., Udrey, E., & Loehr, J. (1997). Burnout in competitive junior tennis players III: Individual differences in the burnout experience. *The Sport Psychologist, 11,* 257-276.

Greenspon, T. S. (2000). "Healthy perfectionism" is an oxymoron!: Reflections on the psychology of perfectionism and the sociology of science. *The Journal of Secondary Gifted Education, 11,* 197-208.

Grzegorek, J. L., Slaney, R. B., Franze, S. & Rice, K. G. (2004). Self-criticism, dependency, self-esteem, and grade point average satisfaction among clusters of perfectionists and nonperfectionists. *Journal of Counseling Psychology, 51,* 192-200.

Haase, A. M. & Prapavessis, H. (2004). Assessing the factor structure and composition of the positive and negative perfectionism scale in sport. *Personality and Individual Differences, 36,* 1725-1740.

Haase, A. M., Prapavessis, H. & Owens, R. G. (1999). Perfectionism and eating attitudes in competitive rowers: Moderating effects of body mass, weight classification and gender. *Psychology and Health, 14,* 643-657.

Haase, A. M., Prapavessis, H. & Owens, R. G. (2002). Perfectionism, social physique anxiety and disordered eating: A comparison of male and female elite athletes. *Psychology of Sport and Exercise, 3,* 209-222.

Hall, H. K., Cawthra, I. W. & Kerr, A. W. (1997). Burnout: Motivation gone awry or a disaster waiting to happen? In R. Lidor & M. Bar-Eli (Eds.), *Innovations in sport psychology: Linking theory and practice. Proceedings of the IX ISSP World Congress in Sport Psychology* (Vol. 1, pp. 306-308). Netanya, Israel: Ministry of Education, Culture and Sport.

Hall, H. K., & Kerr, A. W. (2001). Goal-setting in sport and physical activity: Tracing empirical developments and establishing conceptual direction. In G. C. Roberts (Ed.), *Advances in Motivation in Sport and Exercise* (pp. 183-234). Champaign, IL: Human Kinetics.

Hall, H. K., Kerr, A. W., Kozub, S. A. & Finnie, S. B. (2004). *The motivational antecedents of obligatory exercise: The influence of achievement goals and perfectionism.* Manuscript Under Review.

Hall, H. K., Kerr, A. W. & Matthews, J. (1998). Precompetitive anxiety in sport: The contribution of achievement goals and perfectionism. Journal of Sport and Exercise Psychology, 20, 194-217.

Hall, H. K., & Wigmore, A. (1999). Perfectionism and its influence on social physique anxiety. *Journal of Sport and Exercise Psychology, 21,* S53.

Hamacheck. (1978). Psychodynamics of normal and neurotic perfectionism. *Psychology, 15,* 27-33.

Hardy, L., Jones, J. G. & Gould, D. W. (1996). *Understanding psychological preparation for sport: Theory and practice of of elite performers.* Chichester: Wiley.

Henschen, K. (2000). Maladaptive fatigue syndrome and emotions in sport. In Y. L. Hanin (Ed.), *Emotions in sport* (pp. 231-242). Champaign, Illinois: Human Kinetics.

Hewitt, P., L. & Flett, G. L. (1993). Dimensions of perfectionism, daily stress and depression: A test of the specific vulnerability hypothesis. *Journal of Abnormal Psychology, 102,* 58-65.

Hewitt, P., L., Flett, G. L. & Ediger, E. (1996). Perfectionism and depression: Longitudinal assessment of a specific vulnerability hypothesis. *Journal of Abnormal Psychology, 105,* 276-280.

Hewitt, P. L. & Flett, G. L. (1991). Perfectionism in the self and social contexts: Conceptualization, assessment, and association with psychopathology. *Journal of Personality and Social Psychology, 60,* 456-470.

Hewitt, P. L., Flett, G. L. & Turnbull-Donovan, W. (1992). Perfectionism and suicide potential. *The British Journal of Clinical Psychology, 31*, 1-11.

Hill, A. & Hall, H. K. (2004). *Burnout and self-esteem in youth football: The impact of perfectionism, unconditional self-acceptance and negative rumination.* Unpublished BSc, De Montfort University, Bedford.

Hill, R. W., Zrull, M. C. & Turlington, S. (1997). Perfectionism and interpersonal problems. *Journal of Personality Assessment, 69*, 81-103.

Hobden, K., & Pliner, P. (1995). Self-handicapping and dimensions of perfectionism: Self-presentation vs self-protection. *Journal of Research in Personality, 29*, 461-474.

Hollander, M. H. (1965). Perfectionism. *Comprehensive Psychiatry, 6*, 94-103.

Jones, R. G. (1968). A factorial measure of Ellis's irrational belief system, with personality and maladjustment correlates. *Dissertation Abstracts International, 29*, 4379B-4380B.

Kervin, A. (2003, February 15th). Wilkinson driven to new peaks by fear of failure. *The Times*, pp. 31.

Kervin, A. (2004, October 24th). The importance of being Johnny. *The Sunday Times*, pp. 16-17.

Koivula, N., Hassmen, P & Fallby. (2002). Self-esteem and perfectionism in elite athletes: Effects on competitive anxiety and confidence. *Personality and Individual Differences, 32*, 865-875.

Krane, V., Greenleaf, C. A. & Snow, J. (1997). Reaching for gold and the price of glory: A motivational case study of an elite gymnast. *The Sport Psychologist, 11*, 53-71.

Lemyre, P. N., Roberts, G. C. & Hall, H. K. (2004). *Testing the tenets of a cognitive model of burnout in elite athletes.* Manuscript under review.

Magnusson, A. E., Nias, D. K. B. & White, P. D. (1996). Is perfectionism associated with fatigue. *Journal of Psychosomatic Research, 41*, 377-383.

Mallett, C. J. & Hanrahan, S. J. (2003). Elite athletes: Why does the fire burn so brightly? *Psychology of Sport and Exercise.*

McArdle, S., Duda, J. L. & Hall, H. K. (2004). *Motivational processes contributing to perfectionism profiles in talented athletes.* Manuscript under review.

McLaren, L., Gauvin, L. & White, D. (2001). The role of perfectionism and excessive commitment to exercise in explaining dietary restraint: Replication and extension. *International Journal of Eating Disorders, 29*, 307-313.

Mor, S., Day, H. I., Flett, G. L. & Hewitt, P., L. (1995). *Perfectionism, control and components of performance anxiety in professional artists,* Cognitive Therapy and Research, 19, 207-225.

Nicholls, J. G. (1989). *The competitive ethos and democratic education.* Cambridge, MA: Harvard University Press.

Pacht, A. J. (1984). Reflections on perfection. *American Psychologist, 39*, 386-390.

Parker, W. D. (1995). An examination of the multidimensional perfectionism scale with a sample of academically talented youth. *Journal of Psychoeducational Assessment, 13*, 372-383.

Parker, W. D. (1997). An empirical typology of perfectionism in academically talented children. *American Educational Research Journal, 34*, 545-562.

Parker, W. D. (2000). Healthy perfectionism in the gifted. *Journal of Secondary Gifted Education, 11*, 173-182.

Periasamy, S., & Ashby, J. S. (2002). Multidimensional perfectionism and locus of control: Adaptive vs. maladaptive perfectionism. *Journal of College Student Psychotherapy, 17*, 75-86.

Raedeke, T. D. & Smith, A. L. (2001). Development and preliminary validation of an athlete burnout measure. *Journal of Sport and Exercise Psychology, 23,* 281-306.

Rice, K. G., Ashby, J. S., & Slaney, R. B. (1998). Self-esteem as a mediator between perfectionism and depression: A structural equations analysis. *Journal of Counseling Psychology, 45,* 304-314.

Roberts, G. C. (2001). Understanding the dynamics of motivation in physical activity: The influence of achievement goals on motivational processes. In G. C. Roberts (Ed.), *Advances in Motivation in Sport and Exercise* (pp. 1-50). Champaign, IL: Human Kinetics Publishers.

Roedell, W. C. (1984). Vulnerabilities of highly gifted children. *Roeper Review, 5,* 21-26.

Ryan, J. (1995). *Little girls in pretty boxes: The making and breaking of elite gymnasts and figure skaters.* London: The Women's Press Ltd.

Schmidt, G. W. & Stein, G. L. (1991). Sport commitment: A model integrating enjoyment, dropout, and burnout. *Journal of Sport and Exercise Psychology, 13,* 254-265.

Schuler, P. A. (2000). Perfectionism and gifted adolescents. *The Journal of Secondary Gifted Education, 11,* 183-196.

Slaney, R. B., Ashby, J. S. & Trippi, J. (1995). Perfectionism: Its measurement and career relevance. *Journal of Career Assessment, 3,* 279-297.

Starkes, J. (2000). The road to expertise: Is practice the only determinant. *International Journal of Sport Psychology, 31,* 431-451.

Tangney, J. P. (2002). Perfectionism and the self-conscious emotions: Shame, guilt, embarrasment and pride. In G. L. Flett & P. L. Hewitt (Eds.), *Perfectionism: Theory, research and treatment.* (pp. 199-215). Washington, DC.: American Psychological Association.

Terry-Short, L. A., Owens, R. G., Slade, P. D. & Dewey, M. E. (1995). Positive and negative perfectionism. *Personality and Individual Differences, 18,* 663-668.

Weinberg, R. S., Burton, D., Yukelson, D. & Weigand, D. A. (2000). Perceived goal setting practices of Olympic athletes. *The Sport Psychologist, 14,* 279-295.

Weissman, A. N. & Beck, A. T. (1978). *Development and validation of the dysfunctional attitudes scale. Paper presented at the Paper presented at the Association for the Advancement of Behavior Therapy.* Chicago.

BIOGRAPHICAL SKETCHES – AUTHORS AND EDITORS

Joe Baker

Joe Baker, PhD, is an assistant professor with the School of Kinesiology and Health Science at York University in Toronto, Canada. His research examines the development and maintenance of expert sport performance. Dr. Baker has published numerous articles on the psychosocial and biological factors influencing expertise, particularly during early stages of development. Past research has examined the training and development of expert decision-makers in basketball, netball, and field hockey (with Bruce Abernethy and Jean Côté) and his PhD research examined the development of ultra-endurance triathletes. Currently, he is involved in several international projects examining elite performance in sports such as rugby (UK), golf (Canada), and middle-distance running (Kenya). Dr. Baker's research is funded by the Social Sciences and Humanities Research Council of Canada, Hockey Ontario, Hockey Canada, and the Ontario Neurotrauma Foundation.

Address: School of Kinesiology and Health Science
York University 4700 Keele St Toronto
ON M3J 1P3 Canada

Phone: 416 736 2100 ext. 22361
Internet: www.yorku.ca/bakerj

Michael Bar-Eli

Michael Bar-Eli is a Professor in the Department of Business Administration, Ben-Gurion University of the Negev, and senior researcher at the Wingate Institute. He studied psychology and sociology in Israel and Germany. Bar-Eli has published over 100 international refereed journal articles and book chapters, and numerous publications in Hebrew. He has been the associate- and section-editor of two leading sport psychology journals. He served in senior psychology positions of the Israel Defense Forces and has often acted as psychological consultant to elite athletes. Bar-Eli is current senior vice president of ASPASP (Asian South-Pacific Association of Sport Psychology).

Address: Prof. Dr. Michael Bar-Eli
Department of Business Administration
School of Management
Ben-Gurion University of the Negev
P.O. Box 653
Beer-Sheva 84105
Israel

Phone: +972-8-6472208
Fax: +972-8-6477691
E-mail: mbareli@som.bgu.ac.il

Dr. Jean Côté

Dr. Jean Côté is an associate professor in the School of Physical and Health Education at Queen's University in Kingston, Canada. His research interests focus on the developmental and psychosocial factors that affect sport performance and participation. He has published numerous articles on youth and elite sport including studies on athletes, parents, coaches, and referees. He is on the editorial boards of the Journal of Applied Sport Psychology, The Sport Psychologist, Revue International des Sciences du Sport et de l'Education Physique, and Physical Education and Sport Pedagogy. He is a section editor for the International Journal of Sport and Exercise Psychology. Dr. Côté was a visiting academic at the University of Queensland in Australia and has been invited to present his research in various countries including France, Brazil, Greece, Ireland, Malaysia and the United States.

Address: School of Physical and Health Education
Kingston, Ontario, Canada
K7L 3N6

Phone: (613) 533-3054
E-mail: jc46@post.queensu.ca

Rod K. Dishman

Rod K. Dishman is Director of the Exercise Psychology Laboratory and Professor of Exercise Science at the University of Georgia, USA. He advises graduate students studying behavioral neuroscience and interventions to increase physical activity. Dr. Dishman received his Ph.D. at the University of Wisconsin-Madison and has focused his research on neurobiological aspects of the mental health outcomes associated with physical activity and on behavioral determinants of physical activity. He is a fellow of the American College of Sports Medicine, the American Psychological Association, and the American Academy of Kinesiology and Physical Education. He has served as a consultant on exercise behavior to the National Institutes of Health, the Sports Medicine Council for the United States Olympic Committee, and the Olympic Prize sub-committee of the Medical Commission of the International Olympic Committee. He also is one of 22 founding members of the IOCs Olympic Academy of Sport Sciences.

Address: Prof. Dr. Rod K. Dishman
The University of Georgia
Ramsey Student Center
300 River Road
Athens, Georgia 30602-6554
USA

Phone: 1 706 542 9840
Fax: 1 706 542-3148
E-mail: rdishman@coe.uga.edu

Natalie Durand-Bush

Natalie Durand-Bush, Ph.D., is an assistant professor of sport psychology in the School of Human Kinetics at the University of Ottawa. Her areas of interest and specialization include (a) sport and life based counseling, (b) resonance, feel and their role in the development of optimal performance and well-being, and (c) the development and maintenance of expertise in sport. Dr. Durand-Bush is the co-author of the Ottawa Mental Skills Assessment Tool (OMSAT-3*(c)), an instrument developed to help athletes and coaches evaluate a variety of mental skills perceived to be important for consistent high-quality performance. She has presented her research and applied work at numerous international conferences and published several refereed articles and book chapters. Among other accomplishments, Dr. Durand-Bush received the Young Scientist Award from the Canadian Society for Psychomotor Learning and Sport Psychology in 1998.

Aside from teaching and conducting research, Dr. Durand-Bush has been working for the past 10 years as a performance psychology specialist with hundreds of athletes competing at different levels in various sports, including athletes on Canadian national teams and University varsity teams, and individual professional athletes. Dr. Durand-Bush is currently the Chair for the Canadian Mental Training Registry. She is also a member of the managing council of the ISSP.

Address: School of Human Kinetics
University of Ottawa
125 University St.
Ottawa, Ontario
Canada K1N 6N5

Phone: (613) 562-5800 ext. 4281
Fax: (613) 562-5149
E-mail: ndbush@uottawa.ca

Anne-Marie Elbe

Anne-Marie Elbe is a sport psychology researcher at the University of Potsdam, Germany. She received her PhD from the Free University in Berlin, Germany in 2001. She is currently working on a research project examining the personality and performance development of young elite athletes.

Her publications and research interests focus on motivational and self-regulatory aspects of athletic performance, recovery, and cross-cultural comparisons. Anne-Marie is vice-president of the Berliner Sport-Club, vice-chair of the Berlin board for women in sports, and member of the German Association for Sport Psychology. She is a licensed track and field coach and currently consulting the German track and field athletes preparing for the Athens Olympics in 2004.

Address: Dr. Anne-Marie Elbe
Universitaet Potsdam
Institut fuer Sportwissenschaft
AB Sportpsychologie
Am Neuen Palais 10
D-14469 Potsdam
Phone: 0049 331 977 1592
Fax: 0049 331 977 1263
E-mail: elbe@rz.uni-potsdam.de

Jürgen Beckmann

Jürgen Beckmann is a professor for sport psychology at the University of Potsdam, Germany. His research interests are motivation, volition and stress/recovery. He is the author of numerous German and international publications on these topics. Before becoming a professor he worked as a senior researcher at the Max-Planck-Institute of Psychological Research in Munich, was a visiting scholar at Florida Atlantic University and the University in Oslo, and a lecturer in organizational and personnel psychology at the University of Maryland.

From 1991 to 1994 he was a team psychologist of the German Alpine Ski Team (Men). He is a dedicated skier and holds a coaching and instructor licence for skiing. Currently he is a consultant to several top-level athletes and is a team psychologist of the German Boys National Golf Team. Additionally, he conducts management trainings, which employ sports as a medium to improve management skills.

Address: Prof. Dr. Jürgen Beckmann
Universitaet Potsdam
Institut fuer Sportwissenschaft
AB Sportpsychologie
Am Neuen Palais 10
D-14469 Potsdam

Phone: 0049 331 977 1040
Fax: 0049 331 977 1263
E-mail: jbeck@rz.uni-potsdam.de

Shmuel Epstein

Shmuel Epstein is an exercise physiologist at the Ribstein Center for Sport Medicine Sciences and Research at the Wingate Institute for Physical Education and Sport, Israel. He received his M.Sc. at the Sackler Medical School, Tel Aviv University. He is currently working with elite athletes - exercise testing and consultation on nutritional supplements. His research interests are children and exercise, and children with chronic disease (e.g., cystic fibrosis, hemophilia, diabetes) and exercise. He is the former Secretary of the Israel Anti-doping Committee of the Israel Olympic Committee. He was a member of the Israel Track and Field National Team (100 and 200 meters), and serves as a track and field commentator for the Israel television sports channel.

Dr. Dieter Hackfort

Dr. Dieter Hackfort is a professor for sport and exercise psychology, and is currently serving as Dean of the Department for Quality Management, Education, and Social Affairs (QESA) in ASPIRE the Academy for Sports Excellence in Doha, Qatar. He received his doctoral degree in 1983 from the German Sports University. In 1986 he was a visiting professor at the Center for Behavioral Medicine and Health Psychology at the University of South Florida in Tampa; and received tenure at the University of Heidelberg.

From 1991 to 2004 he was the Head of the Institute for Sport Science at the University AF of Munich. Since 1986 he has served as a counselor for professional performers and athletes of various sports at the Olympic Centers in Germany. Dr. Hackfort is the editor of several national (Germany) and international book series in sport science and sport and exercise psychology. Since 1996 to present he serves as the Editor of the International Journal of Sport and Exercise Psychology (IJSEP). His research has been published in 25 books and edited volumes, and in more than 150 contributions in national and international journals.

His main research interests are in (1) stress, emotions, anxiety with respect to its functional meaning for action regulation in sports with an emphasis on elite sports, (2) self presentation with a focus on emotion presentation, (3) career management in elite sports, and (4) the development of a mental test and training program. These special issues are connected with the development of an action theory approach in sport and exercise psychology and the development of psycho-diagnostic measurements based on this conceptual framework. In 1984 he received an award from the German Sports Federation for the best research in the social sciences 1983/84 (Carl-Diem-Plaque), 2001 he received the Honor Award of the International Society of Sport Psychology (ISSP) in recogniton of significant contributions to national and international sport psychology through leadership, research, and personal service. 1999 he was appointed Honor Professor of Wuhan Institute of Physical Education, China.

Address: ASPIRE Academy of Sports Excellence
           P. O. Box 22287
           Doha, Qatar

           Phone: +974 413 6222
           Fax: +974 413 6221
           E-mail: dieter.hackfort@aspire.qa

Michael Johnson

Michael Johnson is a PhD candidate at Florida State University (FSU) in the (a) Sport Psychology and (b) Combined Counseling and School Psychology programs. His studies and research have been directed by Dr. Gershon Tenenbaum since August 2000. Additionally, he has worked with FSU athletes from six sports. He has presented at the American Psychological Association's, North American Society for the Psychology of Sport and Physical Activity's, and the Association for the Advancement of Applied Sport Psychology's national conferences.

His field practicum experience in counseling psychology includes local, minority, low SES populations; FSU students and local residents in a career counseling setting; and inpatient/outpatient individuals at a local regional hospital. He is currently on a year long counseling psychology internship at the University of California, Riverside. Michael's areas of research interest include (a) the development of expertise in sport and (b) the affect-performance relationship in sport. Mr. Johnson received his bachelor's degree in economics from Brown University where he earned four varsity letters in swimming. He has also run eight marathons. His coaching experience includes local, regional, and national level swimmers while he lived in the Washington, DC area.

Address: 307 Stone Building
Department of Educational Psychology
and Learning Systems College of Education
Florida State University
Tallahassee, FL 32306 USA

Michal Master-Barak

Michal Master-Barak is a Ph.D. student at the school of business, the Hebrew University of Jerusalem. Her research focuses on innovation adoption, with a special interest on opinion leaders, and influence formation.

Address: Michal Master- Barak
School of Business Administration
The Hebrew University of Jerusalem

E-mail: msmaster@mscc.huji.ac.il

Shaul Oreg

Shaul Oreg is an assistant professor at the department of sociology and anthropology at the University of Haifa, Israel. He received his PhD in organizational behavior from Cornell University in 2003. His research focuses on individual differences in social and organizational contexts. In his dissertation he studied the dispositional and contextual sources of resistance to organizational change. Alongside continued work on resistance to change his current projects involve an investigation of persuasiveness and resistance to persuasion as well as the study of laggards and their dispositional characteristics. Dr. Oreg is a member of the Academy of Management, the Society of Industrial and Organizational Psychology, and the European Association of Personality Psychology.

Address: Shaul Oreg, Ph.D.
Department of Sociology and Anthropology
University of Haifa
Mount Carmel, 31905 Haifa
ISRAEL

Phone: 972-4-8249639
Fax: 972-4-8240819
E-mail: oreg@soc.haifa.ac.il

Dr. Pargman

Dr. Pargman is a Professor Emeritus in the Department of Educational Psychology and Learning Systems at Florida State University. He did his undergraduate work at the City College of New York, and completed his Masters degree at Teachers College, Columbia University, and Ph.D. at New York University. David Pargman has authored or co-authored more than 80 articles and book chapters, and has delivered approximately 200 regional, national and international lectures at various professional forums.

Dr. Pargman has served on the Executive Board of the Association for the Advancement of Applied Sport Psychology, was Chairman of its Health Psychology Section, and is a past Chairman of the Sport Psychology Academy of the American Alliance for Health, Physical Education, Recreation and Dance. He is a Fellow of the Association for the Advancement of Applied Sport Psychology, the Research Consortium of the American Alliance for Health, Physical Education, Recreation and Dance, and the American College of Sports Medicine. He is a member of the United States Olympic Committee Sport Psychology Registry and a Certified Consultant of the Association for the Advancement of Applied Sport Psychology.

David Sacks

David Sacks earned his Ph.D. in sport psychology at Florida State University (FSU). He also holds a Master's degree in Education and Bachelor's in English, both from Stanford University. Dr. Sacks is currently an Associate in Research for the Learning Systems Institute at FSU, as well as an adjunct professor at FSU and Flagler College. Prior to assuming his present positions, he worked with children, athletes, and families in a variety of capacities. He spent several years as a high school teacher and coach before serving as a counselor for ungovernable children and their families. He has also coached youth sport clubs at the local, national, and international level, both in the United States and New Zealand. For the past 11 years, he has also been a high school sports referee. As an athlete, Dr. Sacks was captain of the varsity wrestling team at Stanford, and he twice competed at the United States Olympic Festival in Greco-Roman wrestling, earning a silver medal in 1991.

Address: Psychological and Counseling Center
Vanderbilt University
Baker Building, Suite 1120
110 21st Avenue South
Nashville, TN 37203
USA

John Salmela

Address: Rua Capri 480
Bandeirantes, Belo Horizonte
Brazil

Gershon Tenenbaum

Professor Gershon Tenenbaum earned BA (1974) and MA (1977) at Tel-Aviv University, and a PhD (1982) at the University of Chicago in Measurement and Statistics in Social Sciences. Since February 2000, he is a Professor of sport and exercise psychology at Florida State University, USA. From 1982-1994, he worked and directed the Ribstein Center for Research and Sport Medicine at the Wingate Institute in Israel. From 1994-2000 Dr. Tenenbaum established and coordinated the Sport and Exercise Psychology Program at the University of Southern Queensland in Australia. He served as the President of the International Society of Sport Psychology (ISSP) between the years 1997-2001, and since 1996 to present, as the Editor of the International Journal of Sport and Exercise Psychology (IJSEP). He is a member of numerous scientific societies in the fields of sport and exercise psychology and statistics, and a member of the editorial boards, and reviewer for 16 journals. Dr. Tenenbaum published more than 150 articles in peer-refereed journals such as The Journal of Sport and Exercise Psychology, The Sport Psychologist, Applied Sport Psychology, Ergonomics, The Journal of Applied Social Psychology, The Journal of Applied Cognitive Psychology, as well as in several medical journals. He published 40 book chapters, and edited two English books (The Practice of Sport Psychology, and Brain and Body in Sport and Exercise-Biofeedback Applications in Performance Enhancement with Blumenstein and Bar-Eli), and 6 books in the Hebrew language. Dr. Tenenbaum received several scientific honorary and meritorious awards for contributions to science and practice, including the 1987 Award for Meritorious Contribution to Educational Practice through Research (Journal of Educational Research), the ISSP Honor Award (1997), and Award for Excellence in Research (University of Southern Queensland). He recently became a fellow of the American Academy of Kinesiology and Physical Education. His main research interests are: (a) emotions-cognitions-performance linkage, (b) information processing, decision-making and expertise, (c) measurement and methodology in sport and exercise sciences, and social-cognitive approach to coping with effort sensations; applied interests are: linking science and practice, supervision of practicum, and ethical considerations in providing psychological services to athletes.

Kim Thompson

Kim Thompson is a Ph.D. student in the Faculty of Education at the University of Ottawa. With an extensive background in sport, as a competitive athlete, varsity coach, professional consultant, and dedicated spectator, she has always been fascinated by the relationships that exist between parents and youth sport participation. Her current research interest focuses on the behaviors of parents in sport, and more specifically in hockey. Kim completed a baccalaureate in the School of Human Kinetics (2001) before completing her Masters degree in Sport Psychology (2003), which investigated the use and effectiveness of imagery in indoor group cycling.

Address: Faculty of Education
           University of Ottawa
           Ottawa, Ontario
           Canada K1N 6N5

           E-mail: kim_thompson@rogers.com

Reinhard Stelter/Kirsten Kaya Roessler

New Approaches to Sport and Exercise Psychology

The book is a collection of the keynote addresses of the 11th European Congress of Sport Psychology in Copenhagen, July 2003.

It includes three additional articles, one from the president of the congress, Reinhard Stelter, one from the winner of the Young Researchers award, and one from the new president of FEPSAC.

The book is an important contribution to the future development of sport.

192 pages
5 photos, 15 illustrations
Paperback, 6^1/2" x 9^1/4"
ISBN: 1-84126-149-1
£ 14.95 UK/$ 19.95 US
$ 29.95 CDN/€ 18.90

MEYER & MEYER Sport | sales@m-m-sports.com | www.m-m-sports.com

Gershon Tenenbaum/
Marcy Driscoll

**Methods of Research
in Sport Sciences –
Quantitative and
Qualitative Approaches**
A Handbook

776 pages
300 illustrations
Paperback, 6$\frac{1}{2}$" x 9$\frac{1}{4}$"
ISBN: 1-84126-133-5
£ 39.95 UK/$ 59.95 US
$ 89.95 CDN/€ 49.90

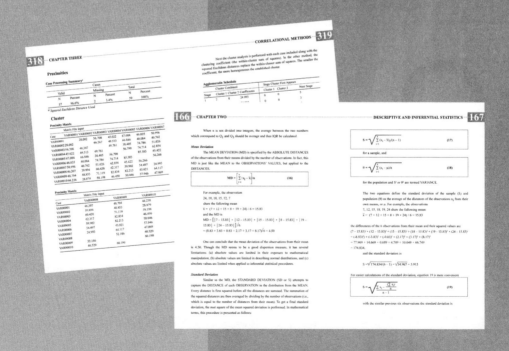

MEYER & MEYER Sport | sales@m-m-sports.com | www.m-m-sports.com

MEYER
& MEYER
SPORT

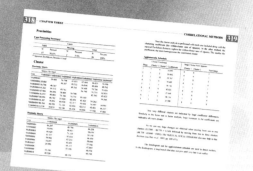

The Book

The handbook consists of a solid theoretical and scientific rationale that is presented in a simple language, which both the beginning and advanced students can understand. It also presents a balance between quantitative and qualitative methods of research and analysis, and advocates for problem-focused methodology and mixed design when the questions asked by the researcher or the scientists require doing so.

The most distinctive feature of the book is that the contents are presented in a hierarchy in terms of complexity. Therefore, the handbook can be used for teaching simple topics such as asking questions that deserve scientific methods of investigation, and simple statistical techniques, as well as complex multivariate methods of inquiry.

The mathematical terms are presented in symbols and graphs only when the concepts were clarified in a simple language and friendly manner. Each of the chapters develops in a clear and sequential order, so that students and researchers accumulate knowledge based on concept mapping rather than memorization. The didactics of the book enable the learner to carry over the learning contents to other courses and apply them to other domains of interest.

The Authors

Gershon Tenenbaum earned his BA (1974) and MA (1977) from Tel-Aviv University, and a PhD (1982) from the University of Chicago in Measurement and Statistics in Social Sciences. Since February 2000, he is a Professor of sport and exercise psychology at Florida State University, USA.

Marcy P. Driscoll is Professor and the Dean of the College of Education at Florida State University.

MEYER & MEYER Sport | sales@m-m-sports.com | www.m-m-sports.com

MEYER & MEYER SPORT